Charles Shadwell

The Fair Quaker of Deal

The Humours of the Navy - A Comedy

Charles Shadwell

The Fair Quaker of Deal
The Humours of the Navy - A Comedy

ISBN/EAN: 9783744673853

Printed in Europe, USA, Canada, Australia, Japan

Cover: Foto ©Thomas Meinert / pixelio.de

More available books at **www.hansebooks.com**

THE
FAIR QUAKER OF DEAL;

OR, THE

HUMOURS OF THE NAVY.

A

COMEDY.

By Mr. CHARLES SHADWELL.

ADAPTED FOR

THEATRICAL REPRESENTATION,

AS PERFORMED AT THE

THEATRE-ROYAL, IN DRURY-LANE.

REGULATED FROM THE PROMPT-BOOK,

By Permission of the Manager.

" The Lines distinguished by inverted Commas, are omitted in the Representation."

LONDON:

Printed for the Proprietors, under the Direction of
JOHN BELL, British Library, STRAND,
Bookseller to His Royal Highness the Prince of Wales.

MDCCXCI.

GENTLEMEN,

THIS Play was both designed and finished in your county, and therefore comes for protection to the place of its nativity. It drags not a sluggish and unwilling pace, as timorous of its reception, and the hardness of its fate; but pants for its native air, where it was brought forth with pleasure, and flies to the good treatment of your experienced hospitality.

To fix upon any particular patron from among you, would be a general offence, because so many of you have a special claim to my gratitude for your peculiar favours; and to incorporate you, by name, into one common body, would require a college of heralds to order the precedence, and a more difficult exactness to marshal my obligations. I rather choose to confess them by a general acknowledgment; and as each of you know what title you have to my thanks, I pay them in due proportion,

A ij

with the utmost cheerfulness, and with the profoundest respect.

There is a nicety, it seems, in love, and, some will have it, in friendships, which will not endure numbers in such a strictness of union. Did I presume to claim friendships as unbounded as my dedication, I would adventure to oppose that ungenerous notion; but as I only take to myself the less envied name of a client, and declare my good fortune in having met with so many singular patrons, gratitude, I hope, without cavil, may be as unlimited as favours, and favours will be as diffusive as good-nature and ability can make them.

The wonder will be, that under the happy influence of such a general kind treatment, I have not been able to produce a more strenuous and lively play. It may be, your indulgence to the parent has spoiled his offspring; for writers, they say, as well as breeders, must be under diet and prescription: mine, if it is a muse, has been under no such restraint; but has fed high, and lived well among you, and must plead her bounty in excuse of her irregularities.

Accept this Play, then, as an offering, gentlemen, and screen it as a composure. It should, indeed, have been more perfect, considering to whom, and for what reasons, it is addressed; but it is my first effort, and therefore the first public opportunity I could take of declaring how much I am,

> Gentlemen,
>> Your most obliged,
>>> Most thankful, and
>>>> Obedient servant,

Tʜɪꜱ Play was written about three years since, and put into the hands of a famous comedian belonging to the Haymarket Play-house, who took care to beat down the value of it so much, as to offer the author to alter it fit to appear on the stage, on condition he might have half the profits of the third day, and the dedication entire; that is as much as to say, that it may pass for one of his, according to custom. The author not agreeing to this reasonable proposal, it lay in his hands till the beginning of this winter, when Mr. Booth read it, and liked it, and persuaded the author, that, with a little alteration, it would please the town. Indeed the success of it has been wonderful; notwithstanding the trial in Westminster-Hall, and the rehearsal of the new opera, it has answered the ends of the poet, and, he hopes, that of the town too.

I cannot omit mentioning the extraordinary performances of Mrs. Bradshaw, Mrs. Santlow, Mr. Pack, and Mr. Leigh, who are the only people on the English stage that could have acted those parts so much to the life.

It may be expected I should give some reasons for my scribbling, and make excuses for the irregularities of the play; find fault with those things the town are good-natured enough to overlook; most arrogantly stand up for time and place; brag of the newness of the characters, &c. But I beg pardon for not shewing the conceited part of me. I am called in haste to my duty in Portugal; but, at my return, it is probable I may be as insolent as the rest of the scribblers of the town.

THE
FAIR QUAKER OF DEAL.

THIS Comedy is by no means remarkable for smartness of dialogue, or keenness of observation—yet I believe the Humours of the Navy are here better reflected than in any other nautical mirror.—Though, perhaps, the pleasure such characters afford, when broadly sketched, is to be felt by few beyond themselves—The characters of Commodore FLIP and MIZEN are certainly fine contrasts, and in expression, seem to warrant the remark, that they were drawn from individual nature.

Much of the roughness of the naval manner is, however, wearing off—All that remains to be wished is, that the high spirit of valour, exulting in peril unequalled through the various stations of life, may not, by the change, be lowered, and the British Navy in consequence cease to be deemed invincible.

PROLOGUE.

IN early times, when plays were first in fashion,
The bus'ness of the stage was reformation;
The well-wrought scene, for public good design'd,
With imitable virtue fill'd the mind,
And lash'd the growing follies of mankind.
That was its golden age, which, soon outworn,
Romantic love and honour took their turn.
Such windmill knights, such odd fantastic ladies,
Sprung from the brain of their poetic daddies;
Prince Prettyman and Amaryllis scarce
Could turn the lulling nonsense into farce.
Drove from those beds of dreaming indolence,
The Muse flew downwards, till she gave offence;
For as our sage inquisitors do tell us,
Her finest parts were jilts and rakish fellows;
And as corrupters of this harmless town,
We were presented, and almost put down.
How would your useless time, 'twixt five and eight,
Have dragg'd its wings, without this lov'd retreat?
What other nameless place would be so fit
For pit to ogle boxes, boxes pit?
At length, kind judges, merry be your hearts,
You're pleas'd to relish best our lowest parts;
Give you but humour, tickle but your spleen,
No matter how we furnish plot or scene.

Soon *pleas'd; but that, alas!* you're squeamish too;
Your light digestion must have something new,
Or else you'll drive away to puppet-shew.
Under these terms of grace young Bayes has writ,
With double title to be dubb'd a wit,
First, *'cause* poeta nascitur, non fit.
From a fam'd stock our tender scyon grows,
And may be laureat too himself, who knows?
But that his other plea may be admitted,
You're both with new and merry humour fitted.
Come, break him in, and when he writes again,
Perhaps he'll find a more diverting pen.

DRURY-LANE.

Men.

FLIP, *the Commodore, a most illiterate Wappineer-tar,* - - - } Mr. Moody.

MIZEN, *a finical sea fop,* - - - Mr. Dodd.

WORTHY, *a Captain of the Navy,* - - Mr. Brereton.

ROVEWELL, *a man of fortune,* - - Mr. Phillimore.

Sir CHARLES PLEASANT, *Worthy's Lieutenant, a man of quality,* - } Mr. R. Palmer.

CRIBBIDGE, Flip's *Lieutenant,* - - Mr. Williames.

EASY, *a Lieutenant of Marines,* - - Mr. Barrymore.

INDENT, Flip's *Purser,* - - - Mr. Burton.

COCKSWAIN, - - - - - Mr. Wrighten.

HATCHWAY, - - - - - Mr. Bannister.

BINNACLE, - - - - - Mr. Parsons.

Women.

ARABELLA ZEAL, *bred a churchwoman,* Mrs. Wilson.

DORCAS ZEAL, *her sister, bred a Quaker,* Miss Pope.

BELINDA, *a woman of fortune,* - - Mrs. Ward.

JENNY PRIVATE, - - - - Miss Hull.

JILTUP, - - - - - - Mrs. Granger.

ADVOCATE, Belinda's *maid,* - - ─────

Maid to Arabella, - - - - ─────

Bar-maid, - - - - - ─────

SCENE, Deal. Time, *five hours.*

THE

FAIR QUAKER OF DEAL;

OR, THE

HUMOURS OF THE NAVY.

ACT I. SCENE I.

Enter WORTHY *as from on board; Cockswain and Crew following.*

Worthy.

So, thank Heaven, I have at last reached my native land. Cockswain, take care the water be sent on board with expedition, and bid the purser hasten to Dover for fresh provisions, and let the sick men be sent on shore the next trip. There's something for the boat's crew; go and refresh yourselves.

Cock. All your orders shall be punctually complied with.

All Sailors. Thank your noble honour. Huzza, huzza!   [*Exeunt Cockswain and Crew,*

Enter ROVEWELL.

Wor. My dear Rovewell!

Rove. Welcome on shore, dear Worthy! How have you **fared** this voyage? Pr'ythee, relate me some of your adventures.

Wor. Why, faith, Rovewell, my voyage was attended with little pleasure, being generally confined to the barbarous conversation of Flip, my commodore, a most obstinate, positive, ignorant, Wappineer-tar: in short, he has been my eternal plague.

Rove. Why, was only you two the convoy?

Wor. Yes, to make me completely wretched, Beau Mizen was the third man; a sea-fop, of all creatures the most ridiculous.

Rove. I cann't say I am sorry for the usage you have met with; because I am in hopes the nauseous conversation of these coxcombs will make you relish **my** company the better.

Wor. The true sense I have of your wit and judgment will always make me covet your acquaintance; therefore I needed not the wretched preparative I have met with. But how does all our Deal angels?

Rove. Why, the few virtuous women are as proud and as insolent as **they** used to be, and the whores you left here about ten months since, are dead with rottenness, and young strums supply their rooms. This is a monstrous place for wickedness! Fornication flourishes more here than in any sea-port in Europe. You gentlemen of the navy are great encou-

ragers of sin, and traffic mightily in that sort of mer-
chandise; and for your money, receive as lasting
French diseases here, as any you can meet with in
Covent-Garden, or the Mediterranean.

Wor. Ay, as thou observest, Rovewell, the marine
race are a debauched generation. The poets will
tell us, that Venus herself was born of the sea; troth,
her fabulous divinity has too many real worshippers
bred up upon her own salt element.

Rove. 'Tis a strange thing, that people that face
death so near, and so often, should have no thoughts
of saving their souls.

Wor. Being constantly in danger of them, so that
they look death in the face with as much impudence
as a Deal whore does a poor tar after a long voyage.
But what news of my dear Quaker?

Rove. She's as proud and as beautiful as ever, and,
faith, I believe as constant too. You'll never leave
playing the fool with that spiritual creature, till she
draws you into matrimony; ten thousand pounds,
with beauty and virtue, are very great temptations.

Wor. Then do you really think I have any interest
in that dear creature?

Rove. Had you as much with the lords of the admiralty, **you** would be a great man; for she dotes on
you. Could you have but seen the countenance
she put on, when there was a report that you were
killed; the sighs, the agonies, and the groans she had
upon that occasion, were more sincere than those her
religion obliges her to.

B

Wor. I am impatient till I see the dear charmer. But how goes thy affair on with Belinda?

Rove. Much after the manner of the French king's affairs; they have a dismal aspect; we quarrel like man and wife, or high church and low. She knows her ascendant over my heart is so rivetted, that she cann't lose me; and therefore she uses me as tyrannically as if she were the French king, and I one of the Protestants.

Wor. I hope no persecution will make you leave her kingdom.

Rove. To carry on the simile, I am somewhat stubborn; but, rather than lose her money, I shall be a convert.

Wor. But see, the commodore.

Enter FLIP.

Flip. Ha, Rovewell! What cheer, what cheer, my lad?

Rove. Most noble commodore, your humble servant.

Flip. Noble! A pox of nobility, I say! the best commodores that ever went between two ends of a ship, had not a drop of nobility in them, thank Heaven.

Rove. Then you still value yourself for being a brute, and think ignorance a great qualification for a sea-captain.

Flip. I value myself for not being a coxcomb; that is what you call a gentleman captain; which is a new name for our sea-fops, who, forsooth, must wear white linen, have field beds, lie in Holland sheets, and load their noddles with thirty ounces of whores' hair, which makes them hate the sight of an enemy, for fear bullets and gunpowder should spoil the beau wig and laced jacket. They are, indeed, pretty fellows at single rapier, and can, with a little drink in their heads, cut the throats of their best friends; but catch them yard-arm and yard-arm with a Frenchman, and down goes the colours. Oh, it was not so in the Dutch wars! then we valued ourselves upon wooden legs, and stumps of arms, and fought as if heaven and earth were coming together.

Rove. Yes, yes, you fought very gloriously, when you let the Dutch burn the fleet at Chatham.

Flip. That accident was owing to the treachery of some rogues at land, and not to us sea-faring folks.

Wor. Come, leave railing, my good commodore. I believe thou art honest and brave; but wanting sense and good manners, would fain put the world out of conceit with those accomplishments. You old captains, who sit at court-martials, are very envious; and often mulct a young fellow for actions, which were reckoned glorious ones when done by any of your stupid selves.

Flip. By the loadstone, I swear, I am none of those. I have served in every office belonging to a ship, from cook's boy to a commodore; and have all the sea jests by heart, from the forecastle to the great cabin; and I love a sailor.

Wor. Ay, so well as to get drunk with every mess in the ship once a week.

. *Flip.* Why, that makes the rogues love me; my joculousness with them makes them fight for me; they keep me out of a French gaol. I'll follow my old method, till I am superannuated; which I believe I sha'n't petition for these twenty years.

Wor. Since you love your common sailors so well, what reason can you have for using your lieutenant so like a dog?

Flip. Because he sets up for a fine gentleman, and lies in gloves to make his hands white. And, tho' 'tis his watch, when I ring my bell, the rogue is above coming to my cabin. I sent him ashore yesterday to the post-house, with a letter to the admiralty; I ordered him to buy me a quarter of mutton, and three-score cabbages, for my own use; and the land-lubber (for he is no sailor) had the impudence to tell me he would not be my boy. I told him I'd bring him to a court-martial, and he threatened to throw up his commission, and cut my throat.

Rove. Ha, ha! I'm glad thou hast met with a young fellow of life and vigour, that knows how to use you according to your deserts. But see who comes here so gay.

Flip. 'Tis a water-beau. One water-spaniel is worth fifty of such fair-weather fops. Do but observe him now. Oh, monstrous!

. . .   *Enter* MIZEN *and Cockswain.*

Miz. Go you to the perfumer's, buy me a gallon

of orange-flower-water, and a pint of jessamin-oil; let the muslin curtains and furbelow'd toilet be washed out of hand; carry on board a bushel of sweet powder; and tell the purser, I am resolved every man on board my ship shall have a clean white shirt at his charge. Tuesday next is my visiting-day; and I design to let the world see how much I have reformed the navy.

Flip. Ho, ho, ho! here's a fine gentleman for you!

Miz. [*Seeing the company.*] Dear Rovewell! split me on a rock, if I am not transported at the sight of you.

Flip. It would be well for the nation, if such butterflies as you were transported to some of the plantations. I wish you were my bow-man, and the wind blew strong at east, I'd spoil your beauetry.

Miz. Why, Lard, commodore, won't you give a man leave to be decent and clean? Will nothing please you, but what stinks with tar and tobacco?

Flip. Tar and tobacco are sweeter, one would think, than the excrements of a civetty-cat. But I am well assured talking to you is like rowing against wind and tide; and therefore e'en steer your compass your own way. Friend Rovewell, I don't care if you and I toss off a can of Sir Cloudesly before we sail.

Rove. Where do you lodge?

Flip. At the Three Mariners.

Miz. May my ship's anchor come home, if it be

not an arrant bawdy-house! The husband keeps a bom-boat, the wife a brandy-shop, and the two daughters are let out to all comers and goers.

Wor. Indeed, the house is very notorious. Why don't you frequent the India-Arms?

Flip. Because all the fops and beardless boys of the navy go there; besides, I think the husband too blind, and the wife has too much sight. But Tom Cragg and I were boatswain's mates together. As to its being a bawdy-house, that is no offence to me; for all houses in sea-ports have been reckoned so, ever since I pick'd oakum; I suppose, brother Finical, you don't know what that is.

Miz. Why, dear commodore, do you think, because we gentlemen put on clean shirts every day, that we cann't understand the affairs of the navy as well as those who wear their shirts till they are lousy? Do you think nastiness gives you a title to knowledge?

Rove. Ay, as my friend Mizen says, because brutes are sailors, can none be sailors but brutes?

Flip. I don't know what you mean by the word brute; but I can perceive that no animal is so ridiculous as a monkey, except it be his charming imitator, a beau.

Miz. Did you never see an unlick'd bear? He, he, he!

Flip. He, he, he! Yes, I have, booby, what then?

Miz. Oh! dear monster, be civil.

Flip. Bullets and gunpowder, what do you mean ? If the government did but know what a swab thou art, I should be knighted for cutting thy throat.

Rove. Oh! fye, let's have no quarrelling.

Miz. No, no, there's no fear of it ; the commodore knows the length of my sword, and nimble turn of my wrist, too well to pick a quarrel with me.

Flip. Why, thou canst only value thyself for being a fencing-master : were we in a saw-pit together, with each a blunderbuss, I'd try if I could not make a sieve of thy lac'd jacket ; I'd soon singe thy curls so, that thy wig should hang like a parcel of rigging after an engagement.

Wor. This has been the continual diversion of our voyage.

Flip. Ay, ay, you're all alike. A periwig-maker covers your noddles, and a dancing-master gives you a hitch in your pace, but the taylor finishes the fop. I find there's no bringing your folly to an anchor, so long as the wind blows strong in the nonsensical corner ; so fare you well.   [*Exit* Flip.

All. Your humble servant.

Rove. 'Tis a wretched fellow !

Miz. I have not words to express what a miserable plague he has been to me, besides a charge ! Would you believe it ? split me on a rock, if he did not one day break me forty pounds worth of china.

Rove. For Heaven's sake where was it ?

Miz. Why, in my great cabin : I dare affirm it no town lady's withdrawing-room, nor country gentlewoman's closet, is nicer furnished than my cabin; 'tis wainscoted with most charming India Japan, and looking-glass; I have a very noble scrutoire, and the most celebrated screen in Europe: I have an invention, which makes the great guns in my cabin appear to be elbow chairs covered with cloth of tissue; I have six and thirty silver sconces, and every vacancy is cramm'd with china.

Rove. These rarities are worth seeing, indeed.

Wor. Oh, he keeps a visiting day, you and I'll wait on him.

Miz. I shall think myself prodigiously obliged to you: may be you'll see as great a concourse of people as there is at a general's when he returns victorious: barges, pinnaces, deal yawls, and long-boats innumerable.

Rove. Pray who visits you in the long-boats?

Miz. Why, Dutch admirals. You must know I range them in the following order: my barges I call coaches and six, my pinnaces are chariots with two horses, my deal yawls are sedans, and my long-boats hackney-coaches.

Wor. Very nice, indeed.

Miz. All my sconces are loaded with wax tapers; my lieutenants and warrant officers, nicely dressed and perfumed, place themselves on each side of my steerage; my midshipmen and quarteers are ranged from the bulk-head to the gang-way, in my own white shirts; the ship's side is mann'd by my boat's crew, in spruce apparel and clean gloves; and the

rest of the ship's company are ready upon all occasions to give cheers and huzzas, according to the
quality of my visitants.

Rove. Well, and what entertainment are we to
meet with ?   •

Miz. Why, I generally treat with tea, but the most
modern way is to give nothing.

Rove. Pshaw! methinks a bowl of punch would be
most proper.

Wor. Oh, beastly! we at sea always smoke when
we drink, and that would spoil all the gay furniture.

Miz. Oh, wretched! and the **stink** would suffo-
cate me.

Rove. What is your conversation ?

Miz. We imitate the ladies as near as we can, and
therefore scandalize every body : we laugh at the ridiculous management of the Navy-board ; pry into
the rogueries of the Victualling-office ; and tell the
names of those clerks who were ten years ago bare-
foot, and are now twenty thousand pound men : we
hear stories of the scandalous marriages of our captains ; the lewdness of some of their wives, and the
meanness of the rest : sometimes we quarrel about
whose ship sails best, who makes the finest punch ;
or who has the greatest hardships, by having great
mens' favourites put over their heads; and I keep
them within the bounds of good manners and moderation.

Wor. That is a very great point gained.

Miz. May I be keel-hauled if any man in the uni-

verse has more reformed the navy than myself: I am
now compiling a book, wherein I mend the language
wonderfully. I leave out your larboard and starboard, hawsers and swabs: I have no such thing as
haul cat haul, nor belay; silly words, only fit for
Dutchmen to pronounce. I put fine sentences into
the mouths of our sailors, derived from the manliness of the Italian, and the softness of the French :
and by that time I am made an admiral, I doubt not
of bringing every sailor in the navy to be more polite than most of our country gentlemen ; and the
next generation of them may pass very well for people
of the first quality. I'll get an order for removing
them from Wapping into the Pall-Mall: and instead
of frequenting punch, music, and bawdy-houses; the
chocolate houses, eating-houses, and fine taverns
shall be obliged to receive them.

Enter to them a Servant with a Letter.

Serv. Pray which is Captain Worthy?

Wor. Friend, I am he.

Serv. Sir, here's a letter for you.

Wor. Ha! Dorcas Zeal! Oh, let me kiss the hand
ten thousand times.

Rove. How keen a sportsman a long voyage makes
a man!

Wor. [*Reads.*] "Friend Worthy, if thou hast not
forgot thy old acquaintance, give but thyself the
trouble of coming to the north end of the town,

where thou hast often vented **thy** vows of sincerity, and thou wilt most assuredly find thine,

DORCAS ZEAL."

Hark'ee ; let the lady know I'll wait on her instantly.

[*Exit Servant.*

Miz. So, brother, I find you have an intrigue already ; I suppose I sha'n't be much behind-hand with you, for I expect a billet-doux from a ten thousand pounder.

Rove. Pr'ythee, who is she ?

Miz. Why, she's a Quaker : an intimate acquaintance of mine has promised me his assistance in stealing her for me.

Wor. Death and hell ! This is my angel !

Rove. Patience, man !

Miz. Now you must know, if we once get her upon the beach, I whip her into my boat, carry her on board, marry her, lie with her, then come ashore and demand her fortune ; and after that, you know, if I don't like her, 'tis but heaving her out at the cabin window, and give out she had a calenture, and so jump'd overboard. Well, dear gentlemen, I must go and see about this business ; for such a fortune is not to be neglected, especially when a peace is so near. [*Exit.*

Wor. Blood and fire ! What a discovery's here !

Rove. Why, truly, it was a lucky one : I have a merry thought come into my head ; there's a quondam friend of yours and mine, who in our sinful days was very obliging to us.

Wor. What, Jenny Private ?

Rove. The same.

Wor. Alas! poor frailty! that once fair pleasure-boat begins to lower her sails, wears out in her hulk, and sinks both in her price and her credit; besides, the new reformation wind blows so high, that every weather-beaten vessel cann't live in't.

Rove. Now, for that very reason, a sudden charitable design is got into this fruitful noddle, of putting off this very creature to Mizen for a wife, a just punishment upon him for his barbarous designs upon thy Dorcas.

Wor. Nay, but, thanks to Heaven, we have discovered the villany, and I'll instantly to my Dorcas, and give **her** that due caution, as shall blow up his whole conspiracy; and therefore mix a little mercy with thy justice.

Rove. No; I'll not carry on the jest so cruelly as to undo the poor dog neither; a little mortify him, but not ruin him.

Wor. I'll instantly then to my dear Dorcas, and make her our confident in the business: about an hour hence I'll meet you at Daniel's, where we'll take a sneaker of Amy's punch; and afterwards spend our evening with the women: I'll send Dorcas to see Belinda, and there shall be the rendezvous.

[*Exeunt.*

Enter Dorcas Zeal *and* Arabella.

Ara. **Why,** sister, do you ever think to secure

Worthy to yourself, with that senseless religion of yours; he'll certainly laugh at your formal hood.

Dor. Why look thee, Arabella, my religion and dress may seem strange unto thee, because thou art of the church belonging to the wicked; but I tell unto thee, Worthy loveth me so much, that I have hopes of drawing him to be one of the pure ones. 'Tis true, thou art a facetious young creature, and the education my aunt hath given thee, maketh thy thoughts run much upon the vanity of this world; and I suppose the fortune my father left thee will be thrown into the arms of one of the lewd pillars of thy steeple-house.

Ara. Look'ee, I'll have no reflections upon establishments. Liberty of conscience gives you no title to rail. I find you are resolved to persist in your whining faith; 'tis one stubborn article of your cant: but I am well assured Worthy will force you to church; if he don't, I'll part with my maidenhead without a husband.

Dor. And that thou art wild enough to do; but I pray thee, none of this vain raillery before Worthy, if thou hast any expectation of my living in sisterly love and charity with thee.

Ara. Oh, you should have snuffled that thro' the nose. In short, I'll always tease you; you that have sense and beauty, thus to deform those heavenly graces, it makes me mad. If all the kind bewitching airs, the tender looks, and compassionate words that

C

woman can invent, will draw Worthy's love from you, I'll use them, and triumph in the conquest.

Dor. Poor vain creature! thou art handsome it's true; but thou hast not the virtues of the mind to ensnare him with. But **see,** he comes; forbear thy follies, I say, forbear.

Enter WORTHY.

Wor. [*Embraces.*] This is a reward for all my labours; the fatigues of an hundred voyages are forgot whilst I am in these arms.

Dor. Be not vain, flatter not; 'tis base, 'tis mean, 'tis irreligious.

Wor. Dear charmer, I am all ecstasy.

Ara. So much of it, that, methinks you have forgot your friends, good captain.

Wor. Pardon me, madam, [*Salutes her.*] some of my ecstasies are due to you; for the love I have to this lady makes me admire all her relations.

Ara. Ay, wheedle her out of what she has: get her money, then use her like a wife, turn her out of doors, and compound with her for a maintenance.

Dor. Sister, to shew thee that I think it is impossible **for** thee to debauch the principles of my friend Worthy, I now commit myself into his hands.

Wor. Which blessing I receive with all the joy imaginable: this is a reward indeed for all my services.

Dor. Take to thyself my hand, and thus I plight it with my faith. Now, sister, your threatening words are vain, for all your looks and sighs can never take him from me.

Ara. Ha, ha, ha! you see, Worthy, I have done the work for you, reconciled even contradiction it-self, made the flesh and the spirit unite, and joined an unsanctified brother of the wicked to a sanctified sister of the godly ones.

Dor. Fie, sister, do not triumph in my weakness.

Ara. Thy weakness! no, thy shame; with all thy boasted sanctity, to own before my face a carnal in-clination! Nay, and to put thy **hand to pen** and paper to court him to thy arms! Out **on thee!** I am ashamed of thee.

Dor. Nay, **now** thou art scurrilous! I cannot bear this, thou raisest all the blood into my cheeks. Stay thou, dear Worthy, and rebuke her for it, whilst I retire awhile to recover my confusion, and then I'll see thee again.   [*Exit* Dor.

Wor. Fie, Arabella; could you have the heart to treat that innocent thing so roughly? Nay, by Hea-vens, I'm amazed! I cannot guess the meaning **of all** this.

Ara. Fie, stupid Worthy, cann't you apprehend the reason why I study to make a breach betwixt my sister and yourself?

Wor. 'Tis all a mystery to me!

Ara. Spare a virgin's blushes, and let your ap-prehensions tell you what my trembling tongue is loth to utter.

Wor. Fine heroics, truly! I'm too well acquainted

with your manner of bantering, to take notice of any thing you say; yet it would divert me, had not my charming Quaker's last dear words wrapt up my soul to a diviner contemplation.

Ara. Must I then say I love, and be refused? Consider, my fortune's equal to my sister's; **my** face and my religion too, I think, may vie with hers.

Wor. Your words are spoke with a sound of truth; and were I not engaged by ten thousand oaths, I should have manlike vanity enough to think what you say real.

Ara. The inequality of the match between you soon absolves you from such empty vows: I own I long have loved; and, before your last voyage, intended to discover it to you, but you unexpectedly sailed. I never believed you had a real passion for my sister, her religion and her principles being so averse to yours.

Wor. Madam, I know my own unworthiness too well to believe you are in earnest; but were it so, my honour tells me I must not be so base as to wrong your sister. The resolution she has made will soon be void, when I tell her your romantic story, which though I don't believe, I'll strive to make her do it. Pardon my absence, dear madam, for I'm impatient until I undeceive her.   [*Exit.*

Ara. And is my youth, my beauty, and my fortune thus despised! By Heavens, I hate him now, and am resolved to muster up all the spirit of my sex to meditate revenge. The plots of plays, and the designs of injured lovers, I'll instantly peruse, and make them all my own.   [*Exit.*

Enter DORCAS, WORTHY *following.*

Wor. By **all** my honour and my love 'tis true; nay more, she loved, and said she had long.

Dor. Nay, then I am convinced her falsehood's great; I ne'er expressed a satisfaction for thee, but still she strove to cool my friendship, by strange stories of thy inconstancy and unfaithfulness, which I must own I ne'er believed.

Wor. Kind creature! since by envious ways **she strives to** break the cord of our united hearts, let us instantly put it out of hers and fortune's power.

Dor. To-morrow then I will be thine; according to the foolish custom of thy church the priest shall join our hands.

Wor. Then I am completely blessed!—Now I must tell you I have discovered a most villanous design against your person.

Dor. As how?

Wor. This **day** you were to have been stolen by **a** nauseous coxcomb of the navy; 'twas luckily discovered by Rovewell and myself, who hope to counterplot their design so far as to punish the vain fop's intentions: if you meet us about two hours hence at Belinda's, you then shall know the whole story.

Dor. I had thoughts of spending this evening with her; I'll to her instantly, **for** she is **so** much my friend, that she will be overjoyed thou art arrived:

but I think I will not mention the vileness of my sister, lest she becometh a laughing-stock unto the whole town.

Wor. Do as you think fit in that. Adieu, my soul.

Dor. Fare thee well.   [*Exeunt.*

Enter FLIP's *Cockswain; to him a Sailor.*

Sail. Oh, Cockswain, have I found you! Yonder's the Commodore swearing and storming as if the ship had struck on a rock; there's all the boat's crew with him excepting yourself; he sits with as good a bucket of flip before him as e'er was tossed up betwixt the stem and stern of a ship.

Cock. A pox of his kindness, I'd rather be in an engagement of twenty-four hours than mess with him to-night; I know his way well enough, he makes us half-seas over, and then we grow saucy; then after shipping in two or three ladles full more, we fancy we're all before the mast, and so shall go together by the ears: for which, as soon as we come on board, there's whips, pickles, guns, gears, and bilboes for us all.

Sail. Pshaw, pshaw! who would not stand all this, to have their upper and lower tier well stowed with flip? Besides, we shall each of us have a whore at his charge.

Cock. Ay, and so be clapp'd. If he would force the surgeon to cure us at the government's charge, it would be a mighty encouragement to us; but our rogue of a loblolly doctor, being not satisfied with

his two-pences, must have a note for two months pay
for every cure; and the last time the ship was paid,
between the officers and the sailors, he swept above
half the ship's company's money into his own hat.

Sail. That's a grievance truly; but come, pr'ythee
go, for an the commodore gets into his trantrum humours, there's no coming within a cable's length of
him.

Cock. Ay, that's true, therefore bear a hand.

[*Exeunt running.*

ACT II.   SCENE I.

Enter Sir CHARLES PLEASANT, *Lieut.* CRIBBIDGE,
and Lieut. EASY.

Pleasant.

WHY, by your report, old Flip makes your life a
very uneasy one; thank Heaven, my captain has another way of management; with the affable, easy,
and genteel air, he gains applause from all.

Easy. I know he's a gentleman, by being civil to
our corps; 'tis only the brutes of the navy that we
marine officers disagree with.

Crib. Why, I believe I shall frighten the old pimp
into some civility; for that day we came to anchor,
he had some friends aboard: in the height of their
mirth, I was called into the cabin; the negro fills a
glass, and hands it over his shoulder, with a Here,

lieutenant, will you drink? I made as if I would take it, but overset it in his collar, laid the fault upon him, and pretending to be wet myself, went out of the cabin in a passion.

Easy. Pho, these are small faults, and natural to you subs of the navy; but the old dog had the impudence to confine me three months to my cabin, only for knocking down a boatswain's mate that had struck one of my marines; nay, if it had not been for Captain Worthy, would have broke me at a court-martial. If the colonels of our corps don't hinder this rascally imposition upon us, nobody will buy commissions of them.

Plea. That is a new trick put upon you, gentlemen, and I fear will breed ill blood amongst us.

Easy. Hang it, we agree well enough with all the young fellows, 'tis the old sots that hate we should come aboard them.

Crib. We agree well enough upon an equal par; but most of you stay ashore 'till all the money's gone, and then you come aboard and expect to mess with us: who must find fresh provisions for you?

Plea. We often slight them for their poverty, indeed; but, hang it, what a strange want of mercury do we young fellows shew, to have been a ten months voyage, safely return'd, and landed two hours, without having been among the females! There's many a lad in the navy gets a clap before the ship's moored.

Easy. I believe my friend Cribbidge is in a better condition to give than to receive one.

Crib. I could wish a punk of my noble captain's was well peppered with it; I would fain see the old dog snuffle once.

Plea. The design's good; but first let's have a sneaker of punch.

Easy. With all my heart; I'll just go and draw a bill upon our agent, get some necessaries for the men, cheat my captain a little in the sum total, and wait upon you immediately.   [*Exit.*

[Indent *crosses the stage.*

Crib. See, yonder's Indent, our purser, gone to Daniel's; he'll be glad to be of our company.

Plea. A very honest fellow, and keeps a much better character in the navy, than people of his employ generally do.

Crib. Why, the fellow has lived well; he was bred a mercer in Covent-Garden, was ruin'd by a whore of his own, and a bully of his wife's: but managed his matters so well, he cleared himself of a gaol, by a commission of bankrupt, without forswearing himself, which is the only precedent of that nature since the act was made.

Plea. They say his wife's handsome.

Crib. She was, when but eighteen; but whoring, and the misfortunes which commonly follow that, has made her look somewhat hagged, though but three and twenty.

Plea. If the young wenches of fifteen did but consider that the vices of the age ruin their beauty more than the small-pox, their pride would make them virtuous in spite of their inclinations.

Crib. Why, as you say, Sir Charles, a virtuous woman keeps her complexion tolerably well till five and twenty, when a whore is fain to borrow one of Mr. White and Red before she comes of age.

Plea. By the sense that you and I have of the vanities of the world, it looks as if we had a mind to quit our royal mistress, and enter aboard some merchantman for a matrimonial voyage.

Crib. Why, if she's richly laden, I could be content to go chief mate.

Plea. And I suppose mutiny, as Avery did; turn your captain ashore, then set up for a pirate; and, like Drawcansir in the Rehearsal, kill both friends and foes.

Crib. A pretty simile for matrimony and whoring!

Plea. If we chime into harmony so well already, we may expect a bowl of Daniel's punch will make us talk like the music of the spheres.

Crib. Why, methinks, there's a tune in every godown from a punch-bowl.

Plea. I wonder our coxcombly poets don't write some fine encomiums upon that heavenly compound.

Crib. Why, the fellows are damnably poor, and not having money enough to buy victuals, drink the lees of sack to take away their stomachs, which raises their fancies no higher than a lady's fan, her busk, or her lap-dog.

Plea. Faith, the poets of this age are not so poor as those of the last, they have wit enough to write themselves into good places.

Crib. That is, by wheedling a sort of people who love flattery better than wit.

Enter Drawer.

Draw. Gentlemen, Lieutenant Easy, and Purser Indent, would be glad to kiss your hands at our house.

Plea. A polite message : tell them we'll do ourselves the honour immediately.

Draw. I shall, sir.   [*Exit.*

Plea. Come, Cribbidge,

Let's drink away our dismal storms and cares,
Those slavish hardships that a sailor bears :
Whilst proud Britannia may securely boast,
She safely sleeps while we secure her coast. [Exeunt.

Enter ROVEWELL, *meeting* WORTHY.

Rove. So, dear Worthy, once more well met; have you acquainted your little Quaker with our design?

Wor. Part of it.

Rove. As how?

Wor. I'll tell you at Daniel's: but have you engaged Jenny?

Rove. Oh, as you could wish : the jade is as overjoyed, as a dean at the death of a bishop ; and to make our story good, I have invited Mizen to the

India-Arms, where I have ordered her to write to him. Will Dorcas meet us at Belinda's?

Wor. She will.

Rove. Come on then.   [*Exeunt.*

SCENE II.

The Bar at Daniel's, *Drawers, &c. Bar-Maid.* Enter *Sir* CHARLES PLEASANT *and* CRIBBIDGE.

Plea. What! does my pretty bar-maid keep her beauty still? I know thou'rt virtuous, because the blue of the plum is not wore off yet.

Bar. Thanks to my own honesty if I am so then, for here's rakish lieutenants enough come here to debauch all the young virgins in the country, if they had but money; but the government keeps them poor, or we should have a wretched life with them.

Crib. Then nothing but money is able to debauch you; pr'ythee, how great a sum will fit you to lewdness?

Bar. Not your eighteen months pay, added to the pinch of your hat, and dangling of your cane.

Plea. Well said, Nanny, kiss me, and tell him you are meat for his masters.

Bar. Pshaw! I wonder at you; [*Kisses her.*] you are all alike for that.

Crib. Fye, Sir Charles, why did you kiss her? you

see she likes it not; come, my dear, I'll take it off
again.   [*Kisses her.*

Bar. Oh, intolerable! I'll ne'er complain of a fool
again, for fear of being plagued with a worse; shew
a room there.

Draw. Sir, if you please, Purser Indent is this way.
                                          [*They follow.*

Enter MIZEN.

Miz. Thou divine, pretty bud of beauty, one always finds you in your cabin, chalking upon your
logboard there.

Bar. If every body would but mind their own
business, I might sit still here; but we have so many
horsing monsters of the navy use our house, that one
had better be a punk amongst footmen, and ply in the
upper gallery, than be plagued with them.

Miz. Well, you shall see in a few months, how the
navy will be reformed; all the sea-officers will be so
full of manners, that they shall look like a parcel of
beaux in a side-box, or chocolate-house.
                                          [*A noise within.*

Bar. Do but listen, they are got to horse and bear,
the constant diversion of their lives.

Miz. Indeed I blush for them, my dear angel.
                                          [*Kisses her*

Enter ROVEWELL *and* WORTHY.

Wor. Ha! brother tar, what so close, and in pub-

D

lic too! If you take this freedom in the eye of the world, what would you do in private?

Bar. I don't know what he may do in private; but I hope you don't suspect me, captain.

Wor. Not in the least, dear Nanny; thy known virtue, and prudent management, is somewhat above the censure of the world.

Bar. **Oh,** your servant, sir.

Rove. 'Tis a strange thing to see how vice loves to be flattered! There's scarce a punk in town, be she never so notorious, but would fain be thought virtuous: and hates to be called whore, even from the fellow that made her so.

Bar. I never expect your good word, Mr. Rovewell; I have denied you the favour too often.

Rove. Why, I may have asked you the question when drunk; but assure yourself I repented of it when sober.

Bar. Lord, you need not be angry with yourself for it; I have denied several admirals.

Rove. And at the same time have taken up with their cockswains.

Bar. Sir, you grow scurrilous.—Shew a room there.

Wor. Mind him not, he's a splenetic fellow; has my lieutenant, Sir Charles Pleasant, been here?

Bar. He's now in the house with Lieutenant Cribbidge, Easy, and Purser Indent.

Wor. Come, we'll join companies, they're all honest fellows.

Miz. With all my heart; if they're brutish, I'll try to reform them.

Draw. This way, gentlemen.   [*Exeunt.*

2d Draw. A sneaker of punch in the Crown, score.

3d Draw. A can of small beer, a quart of brandy, and a pound of sugar in the kitchen, score.

4th Draw. A box of dice for the Mermaid.

1st Draw. Make the great bowl full for the gentlemen in the Fleecer.

Bar. So, it begins to work in each room, and I must be plagued this whole night.   [*Scene shuts.*

Enter BELINDA *and* ADVOCATE.

Bel. I used to be troubled with the impertinent visits of Rovewell three or four times a day. Pr'ythee, Advocate, what's become of the coxcomb?

Ad. Oh! madam, the Virginia fleet's come in; and Captain Worthy, his old acquaintance, is on shore. They are inseparable friends.

Bel. Why then I hate him: for if he won't sacrifice his all to my humour, I'll ne'er part with the freedom I enjoy, to be that dull insipid thing a wife, to please his humour.

Ad. Well, madam, you play with him as a cat plays with a mouse; you fret and tease him till he'll get away from you at last.

Bel. Impertinent creature! do you think I value the loss of a fellow? The red, the blue, and the white flags die for me.

Ad. Ay, madam, they are married men; but have you a gentleman, whose sense, whose reputation, whose courage, is to be named in a day with that charming man's, Mr. Rovewell?

Bel. How insipidly the fool talks! If a fellow without a nose should bribe thee as much as Rovewell has done, you would say as much in his behalf. Why should we make such unfaithful creatures as our chambermaids are our confidants!

Ad. Why, madam, there's no posts without perquisites; since you ladies have found out the way of trucking your old clothes for china (which was our due time out of mind), I hope you'll pardon us for trucking your hearts away for a much brittler ware.

Bel. Ay, Advocate, I should like that brittle ware, a husband, well enough, if one could but break him, or give him away, as one does china.

Ad. Oh, madam, 'tis easy to break his heart; and if you don't do it effectually whene'er you marry, I'll be content to die a chambermaid. But see, madam, the Fair Quaker is come to visit you.

Enter DORCAS.

Dor. Friend Belinda, I am come resolved to chat away the evening with thee.

Bel. My pretty saint, thou'rt welcome. I need not ask you how Worthy does, I see it in your eyes; the demure aspect is vanished, and you begin to look like one of us.

Dor. Why, I am flesh and blood as well as thou

art; and did not my spirit get the better of my clay, I should be as vain as thou art.

Bel. Come, leave canting, and tell me where is my Arabella?

Dor. Why, I left her at home not well; but may be she may see us anon.—Know, friend Belinda, that I have at last got faith enough to put my trust in man: Worthy and I have plighted troths.

Bel. Why then the flesh has got the better of the spirit.

Dor. If thou wouldst prove a friend indeed, thou must give thyself over unto Rovewell.

Bel. So, because you have done a foolish thing, I must keep you in countenance; no truly, I'll be confined to none of your fellows.

Dor. Come, dissemble not; you know the man is assuredly thy own.

Bel. Why, is it not better to say the fellow's mine, than I his?

Dor. For thee it may be better; but what thinkest thou the world will say?

Bel. Why, not worse of me than I say of the world. But to keep thee no longer in suspense, I won't make a vow of chastity, nor will I forswear having the fellow Rovewell: I don't know but one time or another, when I am in a very maggotty humour, I may marry the creature. Come into my closet, and I'll tell thee more of my mind.   [*Exeunt.*

Ad. It is impossible to tell, whether this mistress of

mine will ever have Rovewell or not; but since he pays me well, I'll tease and wheedle in his behalf; and if he gets her, I hope he'll make her a modern husband. Well, if I **could** get a lover upon the first popping of the question, to fly into his arms, and so good-night maidenhead. It shews a wonderful folly in mankind to whine and snivel after these coy peevish things. Bless me! if they knew the way into a lady's heart so well as I do, there would be no sighing and ogling, no presents or serenading, no dying at a lady's feet: let them take the shortest way with the dissenters, and the business is done. [*The bell rings.*] Coming, coming. [*Exit.*

Enter JENNY PRIVATE *and a Sailor.*

Jen. So, I think I am equipt like one of the righteous; I am overjoyed at the intrigue, and shall be pleased to see myself a real captain's lady; I am sure I have been a sham one to many of them. Let me see, my letter is penn'd in a true canting form: my name is Dorcas Zeal, and my fortune ten thousand pounds. Well, if I do not act the babe of grace, the formal quaking saint, with as much outside sanctity as a new-entered nun, or an old mother abbess, I'll be content to truss up like James Nailor.—Here, sailor, carry this to Captain Mizen; then follow Captain Worthy's orders.

Sail. Ay, friend, I'll hand it to him, and then look out sharp. [*Exit.*

Jen. Now to the place of rendezvous ;
 And there, with look demure, I'll pass for saint :
 No such fair colour as religious paint. [Exit.

SCENE III.

Draws and discovers ROVEWELL, WORTHY, MIZEN,
 Sir CHARLES PLEASANT, EASY, *and Purser* IN-
 DENT.—*A bowl of punch.*

Rove. Come, her majesty's health in a bumper, and
may she live for ever.

Wor. And may all her subjects be as true to her
as we are.

Miz. May they all take as much pains to put her
affairs, civil and military, into as good order as I do.
May I be hoisted over a ship's side, with a tackle
hooked to a running bowling, with a knot under my
left ear, if I don't make her navy one of the greatest
navies in the universe.

Plea. Why, sir, 'tis that already.

Miz. Ay, but Sir Charles, I don't mean a fighting
navy, for that's the least part of our business ; I am
for a polite navy ;——that is, a navy full of sense and
good manners ; a navy of proper, handsome, well-
drest fellows ; that when it appears aboard, may be
the wonder of the world, for glittering, shining coats,
powdered wigs, snuff-boxes, and fashionable airs.

Easy. So then, s r, you are for saluting away the
queen's powder.

Crib. No, he's for turning the gun-powder into sweet powder, and the iron-balls into wash balls.

Miz. Well, gentlemen, you'll have no cause to complain at my design.

Rove. Why, if thou shouldst offer this to an old captain of the navy, he'd bring thee to a court martial, and break thee for being crazy.

Miz. Oh, sir, before I laid my design at the parliament-door, I'd get an order from the admiralty to send all the tar-captains to the West-Indies.

Easy. What then, sir?

Miz. Why then, sir, they would lay down their commissions, and so the navy would be rid of them.

Crib. That last intention I like wonderfully; then we young fellows might have hopes of jumping into fifty-gun ships.

Rove. But, Mizen, I have been thinking if the old captains will not go to the West-Indies; pray, who shall we get to go.

Miz. Why, these young fellows.

Plea. Ay, with all our hearts, faith: but suppose the lot should fall upon yourself, captain?

Miz. Oh, there's no fear of that; I know where to fix a present to somebody, that shall be nameless, to keep me off the list.

Wor. Indeed, that is prudent management; I know men of the party, who quit when they're nominated; but soon after, by the help of friends and merits, they get better ships.

Miz. You may think it friendship if you please;

but there's nothing done in this world without money.

Enter a Sailor.

Sail. Is Captain Mizen here?

Miz. I am he, friend; what want you, sir?

Sail. Why, here's a ticket for you.

Miz. Ha!—Dorcas Zeal! Oh, ecstasy! Oh, transport! [*Reads.*] " Friend, I am informed thou hast a
liking to my person; my neighbour hath informed
me thou art a sober, good man. I am now walking
towards Deal castle, where, if thy pretensions are sincere, we will consult about the matter thy friend spoke
to me of this day. I should not be thus free with
thee, had it not chanced, that passing by me at thy
first landing, I beheld thy comely person, and liked
it; and therefore used this plainness with thee, as
becometh a sister of that congregation that hateth ceremonies. Be secret, for Worthy is thy rival, but
his pretensions will prove vain; for my heart is thine.

DORCAS ZEAL."

Miz. Oh, thou dear creature!——But, hush! no
transports before arrival. Poor Worthy, how thy
weak foundation totters! how sneakingly would the
poor mortal look, if he saw this letter! Well, Dorcas has seen me, and I shot her with a side glance.
What a refined creature is a sweet beau, to a homely
coarse tar; to carry off the prize at one single attack,
which that dull rogue has been laying a whole year's

siege to? But, come, gentlemen, about with the glass.
Here, Worthy, here's thy mistress's health.

Wor. I thank you, sir.

Miz. Nay, don't think I drink to an unknown fair.
Here's honest Rovewell has made me a small piece of
a confidant in thy amour. Well, old boy, when the
consummation-day comes with thy sanctified bride,
I'll make one at throwing the profane stocking—and
to her health.   [*Drinks.*

Rove. Here's a dog!   [*Aside.*

Wor. Well, Mizen, to resume thy compliment,
when that happy day does come, I'll bespeak thee
for a bride-man.

Miz. Nay, that will be too great an honour. But,
cry ye mercy, gentlemen, I have a small affair to dispatch, I must be forced to borrow myself from your
company; but upon my honour, I'll return again in
a very few moments.   [*Exit.*

Wor. Ha, ha, ha! the rogue swallows the bait as
we could wish.

Plea. What, some ridiculous intrigue on foot: pray
let us join with you in your mirth.

Crib. Nothing diverts so much, as using a coxcomb
according to his deserts.

Easy. And so exquisite a coxcomb as this cann't be
used too ill.

Rove. Why, the design is pretty severe; he is gone
to marry Jenny Private, an old quondam punk.

Ind. This will be a noble revenge for his imper-

tinence: oh, lieutenant! would we could clap such
a trick upon our brute of a commodore.

Rove. Ay, that may be done; I have just such another blind bargain for him too.

Wor. Come, to your good success: the marrying
these two coxcombs may provoke them to hang
themselves, which will be a meritorious service to the
navy.

Plea. Oh, for a vacancy, that **dear** delight to us
young fellows: ha, Cribbidge!

Crib. Ay, the two ships would serve us nicely.

Easy. Then we should have commissions to wet.

Rove. So, the bowl sucks; empty is the word.

Ind. Pray, gentlemen, give me leave to pay for this
bowl.

All. Oh, by no means, purser.

Ind. Pray, gentlemen, let it be so. Come, Captain
Worthy, I may be your purser one time or other.

Wor. Why, if you should, **it won**'t be much to your
advantage; for I ne'er allow my purser to oppress
the men; nor will I keep a whole ship's crew miserable, to make one man rich.

Ind. Oh, sir, I don't desire that, sir; but you are
so fine a gentleman, sir, that you won't hinder me
from those common perquisites allowed to all pursers.

Plea. The word perquisite comprehends a great
deal of roguery; and under that notion the government is sufficiently cheated.

Ind. Ay, sir; but all people have regard to the
methods of the navy.

Wor. Why, yes, purser, I own you may plead custom for the abundance of villanies committed in the navy; but we have now got men of honour at the helm, who will not suffer rogues to go unpunished.

Crib. It has been the method to let a stinking butt of beer **stand six** days a-broach; and when complaint has been made, the captain (who should do the sailors **justice**) punishes the complaining rascal for mutiny.

Plea. It has been the method for cooks, with pitch-forks sharp, **to** squeeze the fat from out the meat, **for** fear the grease should rise in poor Jack Sailors' stomachs.

Easy. It has been the method to waste a pound to ounces ten which makes the bread, the butter, and the cheese, a poor allowance for those hard-working men.

Rove. In short, what with chest-money, hospitals, slops, two-pences, groats, and mulcts, they are mere galley-slaves.

Plea. The captain uses them like dogs, which forces them to run away; the chequering clerk puts on the R. and then the purser loads their pay with slops they never had, and so cheats the queen and subjects too.

Ind. Why, you may rail at these proceedings; but when you stand the captain and the purser too, you'll often wish to **be** indenting; half money, and half stores, have **tempted most** of you.

Wor. Come, no more; since we have discovered you, I hope you'll let us pay our clubs.

Ind. No, faith, gentlemen, I'll treat you for all this. You mighty pretenders to honour are not much unlike whores, who rail at that which they most commonly practise.

Rove. Come, Worthy, we must away. Sir Charles, your company is desired too; we must spend this evening at Belinda's. But stay, Cribbidge, I must have one private whisper with thee by the way. Revenge is the word, and I must engage thee in the plot.

Crib. Ay, most willingly, in such a cause.

Rove. If we succeed in this farce, it will be a most noble revenge.

For brutes and fools were only made for sport;
Nothing is like a coxcomb to divert:
They cure the spleen, and make the toils of life
An easy burthen, and a pleasing strife.   [Exeunt.

ACT III.   SCENE I.

Enter JENNY PRIVATE.

Jenny.

SURE the sailor has mistook, and given my letter to a wrong person. My heart goes pit-a-pat, for fear I should not succeed. But see, he comes!

Enter MIZEN.

Miz. So, that must be my Quaker, by her sanctified air——Madam, madam——

E

Jen. Would you ought with me, friend?

Miz. Only to desire the favour of you to give me leave to throw myself at your feet. My name is Mizen; I came hither by appointment from your fair hands—She is very beautiful! board me else. [*Aside.*

Jen. If thy sincerity is answerable to the character my friend has given me of thee, I am content, according to his desire, to be thy help-mate.

Miz. Well, old Scruple is a prevailing rogue, and deserves the fifty guineas, pos. [*Aside.*] Oh, my charmer! I have been long sighing and wishing for this opportunity, and hope you'll now give me leave to make the best of my time.

Jen. Will you change your vain religion then? Will you stand fast to the faith? In perseverance, will you come over to the congregation of the upright? Will you put off these gaudy clothes, those vanity of vanities?

Miz. Yea, verily, I will put off my gaudiness; I will strip myself to the nakedness of the spirit.

Jen. Why, then thou hast overcome me; and verily I will be thine in a few months.

Miz. Oh, thou lovely lamb, set not so terrible a time! the spirit moveth me to make thee flesh of my flesh, and bone of my bone, before the sun shineth again.

Jen. I have some fears upon me, that thy eagerness to my person, may proceed from a desire thou hast to my money.

Miz. Why, I say thy fears are uncharitable; for

hadst thou nothing, nor that neither, my zeal would be as much for thee as it is now.

Jen. Then I am satisfied ; and, accordingly, here is my hand.

Miz. Why, I am transported to the highest ecstasies! Look ye, my boat waiteth on the beach for me; if thy yearnings are great as mine are to thee, thou wilt venture thyself upon the deep along with me. I have on board my ship a man called a chaplain, which, according to our establishment, will link us together——Turn me keel upwards, if ever I carried on an intrigue better in my life. [*Aside.*

Jen. Well, thou art a powerful man, and I submit myself unto thee ; but can help thee to one of thy priests on shore——Admirably well managed! [*Aside.*

Miz. Come, my spirit, my light, my light of my light, and——humph——Let us go then.

[*Exeunt, hugging her.*

Enter ROVEWELL, WORTHY, *and Sir* CHARLES PLEASANT.

Wor. So, off goes the boat, and there's a punk provided for.

Plea. Merry be his heart. This will put such a damp upon his undertakings, that we shall be troubled no more with his nonsensical whimsies about reforming the navy.

Rove. I wish all our friends were as well provided for as Jenny.

Wor. Why, faith, so do I ; for when I enter the sa-

E ij

cred bonds, I'll give a receipt in full to lewdness, shake hands with vice, and bid adieu to immorality.

Rove. And I am resolved to make the best of husbands.

Plea. These are pious designs truly. I begin myself to be out of conceit with wickedness; and could I but succeed in my amour with Arabella, I should willingly bid adieu to all the frail part of mortality. But she has used me so unmercifully, that I quite despair of success.

Wor. Pr'ythee, Sir Charles, matters are not gone so far as to throw thee into desperation.

Rove. Let me alone to make up the match. Sir Charles, 'tis a pretty play-thing in time of peace, which, if some care is not taken, these victorious generals of ours will bring it to; and a sea-lieutenant, with only half a crown a day, will never agree with your quality.

Plea. I am wholly at your devotion.

Rove. Come on, then; let us to Belinda's, where we shall see her.

Wor. I fear her late disappointment will hinder her from appearing abroad this evening. 'Tis only Belinda has interest enough to bring her.　　[*Exeunt.*

Enter CRIBBIDGE, EASY, *and* JILTUP.

Jilt. My dear puppies, if you make me a captain's lady, my husband shall hang himself, that there may be a vacancy for one of you.

Crib. Why, you must make use of all your cunning

to draw him into the noose.   Get him but to the word
parson, and I, like his evil genius, will appear to him.
You won't be the only jilt married **to a** sea-captain
this day.

Jilt. How say you ?

Easy. Why, Mrs. Jenny Private, through the intrigues, instigations, and temptations of Beau Mizen,
is gone on board his ship, in order to be his lawful
spouse.

Jilt. Od's my life, my cousin Jenny ! If such common strumpets as she meet with such good luck, what
must a woman of my known virtue and modest conversation expect ?

Crib. Why, then you make degrees in whoring ?

Jilt. Oh, ever ! She that is a bastard-bearing
whore is the most notorious ; she that lies with half
the town, and does it privately, is a prudent whore ;
she that gets money by it, is a mercenary whore ; she
that does it generously and bare-fac'd, is a whore of
honour.

Crib. Very nice distinctions, truly !

Easy. I wonder, since you are so numerous a body
of people, you don't get a charter ; it will raise a
considerable tax to the government ; they may as
well tolerate you, as wink at great men's keeping
you.

Jilt. Why, really, settlements are very comfortable
things ; and our gentry, how sneaking soever they
are to their creditors, are most generous to our faculty.

Crib. Come, toss up a bowl of the best, to enable us to go through with this great work.   [*Exeunt.*

Enter ARABELLA *and Justice* SCRUPLE.

Scrup. I am somewhat troubled your sister is gone abroad, because I had a business to impart to her of very great consequence.

Ara. If you please to leave your affairs to me, I'll acquaint her with them.

Scrup. Why, upon second thoughts, you might do my business as well as she.

Ara. Suppose it, sir. What is it?

Scrup. Why, there is a friend of mine, who is what the world calleth a fine gentleman; he is endowed with a plentiful estate, and is captain of a good sixty-gun ship; has interest enough to get a good station; has spoke to me to recommend him to your sister. Now, I have considered, that you, being of his religion, may suit better with his temper than your sister.

Ara. His name, his name, sir.

Scrup. Why, people call him Captain Mizen.

Ara. Oh, I have heard of the finical coxcomb! You have lost your labour with me, sir; and therefore, pray, keep him for my sister.

Scrup. Verily, if her sister answereth me so, it's probable I may lose my five hundred guineas which the captain has promised me for making up the match. I will in the morning take her fasting, which

I believe to be the best time to try a woman's inclinations.   [*Aside. Exit.*

Enter ARABELLA'*s Maid.*

Ara. So, the old rascal's gone. These psalm-
singing match-makers are worse than your irreligious
bawds; for the latter only betray our maidenheads
and our reputations, when these religious rogues are
for betraying our fortunes, our freedoms, our pleasures, our every thing.

Maid. Ay; but, madam, to be settled in the world
is what we all aim at, and marriage is honourable.

Ara. So **was the** knighthood formerly; but now
they both grow odious——Have you wrote those letters I gave you to copy?

Maid. I have, madam, and here they are.

Ara. You'll get somebody to deliver this packet to
my sister while she's at Belinda's?

Maid. Yes, madam, I have a small Mercury already prepared for it.

Ara. Well; and this letter, in which I have so
well counterfeited my brother's hand, that my sister
will ne'er discover it——

Maid. But can you **hope,** madam, by this intrigue
to make Captain Worthy yours?

Ara. No, fool; nor were he dying at my feet would
I receive him. My design is to make my sister hate
him; nothing this world calls dear can equal the
pleasure of seeing him ill used by her.

Maid. I fear, madam, 'twill be past your skill to break the lover's knot that rivets them together.

Ara. Fear not, girl; my sister's zeal will over-whelm her carnal passion; and our story is so plausible, she cann't but believe it.

Maid. I wish all may prove as you design it. I'm wholly disposed to follow whatever your commands are pleased to lay upon me.

Ara. Send the letter to my sister by a hand you dare trust, and then come into my chamber.

Maid. I'll instantly about it, madam.   [*Exeunt.*

SCENE II.

Draws, and discovers FLIP, *Cockswain, and six Sailors.*

Flip. Sirrah, don't you flinch your ladle; he that will do that, will run down into the hold in an engagement, or say his prayers in a storm.

1 *Sail.* Why, I am married, sir, and must lie with my wife to-night, which I have not done this eighteen months.

Flip. You rogue, cann't you get drunk first, and lie with her afterwards?

1 *Sail.* Ay, sir, but my ill quality is, when I get drunk, I beat my wife immoderately, and kick her out of doors; which I would not willingly do the first night.

Flip. Oh! I'll save you the trouble of that, hell-bird, you shall go on board to-night, and sha'n't see your wife these two months.

1 Sail. Oh! then, sir, I'll be drunk with all my heart.

Flip. Come; confusion to all the fops and cox-combs of the navy! When I am at the helm, I'll root the rogues from thence: as for you, cockswain, I'll make you captain, and all the boat's crew shall be lieutenants.

2 Sail. Look'e, I'll be no lieutenant; I'll be cap-tain the first stroke.

Flip. Why, what pretensiveness have you to it, sirrah?

2 Sail. My pretensiveness to it is, sir, that I was rated able, when your worship was ordinary.

Flip. That's no rule, sirrah, for at that rate I should be king of the seas now, for I was a midshipman, when some that shall be nameless were swabbers of the upper-gun deck.

3 Sail. And I could say my compass, reef, hand, and splice, when ne'er a commission-officer in our ship could tell starboard from larboard.

4 Sail. I wonder your honourable worship, being so notorious a man with the ambralty, don't get cap-tain of the sufferans.

5 Sail. And I likewise wonder your worshipful ho-nour don't get to be knighted.

6 Sail. 'Tis a wonderful thing, that, Jack, to have the queen's majesty's honour clap a cutlash upon a man's skull, and bid him rise up sir any thing.

Flip. Look'e, rogues, the design is very good, and 'tis a gracious piece of preferment; but it has puffed up so many of our sea-coxcombs, that their pride and vanity will ruin the credit of the navy. But here's to you, cockswain. [*Drinks.*] Fill it up, sirrah.

Cock. I am almost drunk, an like your honour; another cup will make me clap the ship on board to windward.

Flip. Why then, sirrah, I'll clap you in the bilboes to leeward.

Cock. So, now the storm begins to rise.

2 Sail. To be free with your right reverend worship's honour and glory, I must tell you, being you and I were afore the mast together, it would look as it were something clever of your honourableness to throw three things overboard.

Flip. Why, what are those things, sirrah?

2 Sail. The boatswain, the purser, and the bilboes.

All Sail. Ay, overboard with them, i'faith.

Flip. What! do you mutiny, ye dogs? Don't you know there's a court-martial, and that I am presidentum.

Cock. I was sure these rogues would bring themselves into a prim-in-iron.

2 Sail. Why, most worthy captain, and my messmate that was, look'e, we have no design of mutinying, but only by way of telling our grievances to your grace's honour, and so my humbleness to you.

[*Drinks.*

Flip. Well, well, to shew my natural goodness to

you all, give me good reasons for throwing overboard the bilboes; I begin at the latter end of your
propositions, because I intend to ask them all gradu-
ally; and so, sirrah, here's to you.   [*Drinks.*

3 Sail. Thank your monstrousness: the bilboes,
an't like your wonderfulness, is a great stumbling-
block in the way of a sailor's agility; to have our
heels land-lock'd when we have sea-room enough, is
worse than to run ashore where there's no land.

All Sail. Oh! worse by half.

Flip. Come, no more of your nonsensicalness; but
get drunk as fast as you can.

Enter INDENT.

Ind. Sir, a word with you.   [*They go aside.*
Cock. Ah ——when the captain and purser whisper,
our guts ought to grumble.

6 Sail. Ay, cockswain, those whisperations are
many an ounce of butter and cheese out of our way.

3 Sail. Ay! and a great deal of beer **too** : but my
service to you, mess-mate.

Flip. Why, I designed to go and **see** her this evening.   [*To* Indent.

Ind. As I pass'd by the door, she told me she was
impatient to see you, for you was the handsomest man
in the navy, and the best-natured captain in **the**
whole fleet.

Flip. Why, I believe the jade does love me, therefore you and I will go to supper with her; but first
I'll make all the boat's crew drunk, according to an-

cient custom. Come, rogues, clap the bucket to your mouths, and don't stand sipping out of a bowl that don't hold above a pint.

Cock. Well, if we must all be drunk, we must, and so down let it go. Here's to you——If every man stows as much of it as I did in those half dozen gulps, I'll pawn my call on't it won't come round again.

Flip. So, I am in stout heart enough now to venture an engagement with this virgin frigate; and so come along with me.   [*Exeunt* Flip *and Purser.*

6 *Sail.* Well, now we have got rid of the rum duke, being in a very merry humour, let us put it to the vote whether we shall beat the mayor and corporation, and drown the constable; or shall we ravish all the women we meet with, and unwindow the houses?

5 *Sail.* Let us ravish first.

3 *Sail.* No, no, ravish afterwards; for I have as much courage before ravishment as any body; but afterwards I'm as cowardly as a Dutchman that has drank no brandy.

Cock. Hark'e, my lads, I'd have you take care who you ravish; for a great many women in this town don't love to be boarded by force, they will fight you broadside and broadside, and yard-arm and yard-arm, till they sink you; and you may fire as many great guns betwixt wind and water before you make any one of them leaky. Besides, I don't care to attack a fire-ship of better force than any frigate in our squadron; for if they once come to lash you fast to them, you are blow'd up in spite of the ambralty. I will therefore lie down for an hour or two ; call me when the captain's ready to go.

3 Sail. Why, do you think to be left out of the plot ? No, no, Mr. Cockswain, you shall go along with us, or else we'll ravish you.

All Sail. Ay, ay, force him along. [*They haul him.*

Cock. Why, rogues, an't I captain of the boat ?

4 Sail. If you were captain of the ship, we should use you as we do now ; for we have no dispect of persons.

2 Sail. Ay, or if he was ambaral we should make no difference ; for all that there is between an ambaral and a sailor is, a stout sailor will fire ten guns to an ambaral's one.

Cock. Well, well, unhand me, if I must go, I must ; but I am very much mistaken, if we are catch'd a-doing a mischief by the justices, if they don't clap us into the wooden bilboes.

4 Sail. Why, to get the better of that prehension of yours, the first thing we'll go about shall be to pull the stocks up by the roots, launch them into the sea, and let the Goodwin sand be better for them.

All Sail. Done, done, come away. [*Exeunt.*

F

ACT IV. SCENE I.

Enter ROVEWELL, WORTHY, *Sir* CHARLES PLEASANT, BELINDA, *and* DORCAS.

Rovewell.

I AM sorry Arabella comes not; 'tis a disappointment to Sir Charles.

Plea. Methinks I do look a little awkward amongst you billing turtles; I am not a fit companion for lovers.

Bel. I cann't imagine what you mean by lovers; my friend the Quaker **here** has indeed shewn a little foolish fondness for Captain Worthy, but I hope you have suspected no such thing from any action of mine.

Dor. Why, friend Belinda, art thou not ashamed to dissemble so? I must tell thee, my conscience will not let me do it; if thou dost not shew a great deal of kindness to Rovewell forthwith, I will discover what pass'd in thy closet between us just now.

Rove. Oh! tell me but that, and I'll adore thee; give me but a cause to laugh at her impertinent weakness, and I shall be happy.

Bel. How dare you offer at this insolence! Have you any pretensions to me, vain fellow?

Rove. Yes, I have, vain woman: if two years constant courtship, with an awful respect and adoration **paid to you;** if oaths, if vows, if sighs and tender expressions can give a man pretensions, I can justly claim them.

Bel. You might have put in your foolish presents too; your bawbles of China, your Indian umbrella, your hair-ring, and your own picture.

Rove. By Heavens! I'd give the world I could hate thee now: but, Belinda, there's something so bewitching in your form, that I still must love you; tho' ne'er so ill used, like a spaniel, I must fawn upon you.

Plea. Now, faith, Belinda, had I admired you an age, nay, had I **thought** you an angel, and been as much enamoured of you as 'twas possible for a coxcomb to be; I would, at this usage, marry your chamber-maid, that she might take place of you: I'd ridicule you in all companies, quarrel with, and cut the throat of any body that pretended courtship to you, and would make you die a maid in spite of your teeth.

Rove. Whilst I, like a good-natured fool, hug my chains, and think of no heaven but my Belinda.

Wor. For shame, proud creature, let not your vain folly get the better of your sense and reason; take to your arms the man you love. Come, I see good-nature in your eyes: thus I seize your hand, and am resolved to give it him who has your heart.

Bel. Pshaw, what insolence is this! Do you think I am to be forced?

Dor. No, no, there can be no force in the case; thou art a dissembler.

Plea. In short, if she refuses, we'll swear a contract, and make a forc'd marriage on't.

Bel. Had I not some inclination, your force and threats should never do. Here, Rovewell, take my hand; I hope for better usage from you than you have received from me.

Rove. Oh, my Belinda! one pleasing look makes amends for all my pains and agonies.

Dor. Ay, now it is as it should be.

Bel. I know, Rovewell, you'll forgive the folly of my sex, and put a favourable construction on what I've done.

Wor. There, there, kiss her hand eagerly; turn up the whites of your eyes, and fetch your breath very short, and leave her to imagine what you ought to say. To-morrow, one priest will join both couples; now let us spend the night in mirth; by this time Mizen has linked with our sham Quaker. With your leave, Belinda, we'll invite them hither.

Rove. 'Tis ten to one but the vanity of his imaginary conquest will bring him without an invitation.

Bel. Pray make my house your own.

Wor. Pardon, my dear creature, the freedom we have taken in using your name; but this coxcomb might have offered a violence we should have wished undone.

Rove. Belinda, I'll take the freedom of sending for our noble Commodore, and his lady too, who are by this time noosed; we'll first dance, then raise them to the height of mirth, and discover the plot.

Plea. It will be a most pleasant comedy.

Wor. Faith, I fear it will prove a tragedy to poor Mizen.

Enter a Servant.

Serv. Madam, this packet was left for you **by a** sailor.   [*Gives it to* Dorcas.

Dor. Ha!—To Mrs. Dorcas Zeal, and one enclosed to Worthy! Who can this be from? [*Reads.*] " I doubt not but you'll wonder at the villanies of mankind, when I tell you that Worthy, whom you have thoughts of making your husband, is already married to me. I have two children by him. Give him the enclosed ; if, after reading on't, he dares deny it, the next post shall bring to his sight his much injur'd

ELIZABETH WORTHY."

[Dorcas *swoons away.*

Wor. Oh, Heavens, what ails my charmer! she's cold as clay! run for some water, quick !

Bel. Surprising !   [*They all hold her.*

Dor. Oh, false man ! Oh, cruel Worthy !

[*She swoons again.*

Bel. Bless me, she faints again, and mutters something about you !

Wor. I am amazed !

Rove. So, she comes to herself again.

[*They set her in a chair.*

Dor. Oh, read these lines, thou perjur'd man !

Wor. [*Reads the letter, and drops it again in a great surprise.*] What's here? Another, and directed to

F iij

me! [*Reads.*] "Tho' you have been guilty of many villanies, and used me ill, I never thought you would have dar'd to have marry'd another wife; but since I know you so well, I'll appear at Deal, and tear your idol Quaker's heart out. I am your much injur'd

ELIZABETH WORTHY."

Sir Charles, feel me, have I life, am I awake, or do I dream? A dizziness overwhelms my brain, and darkness draws its sable curtains o'er my eyes!

Rove. What a plague means all this romantic stuff? have we got the method of poisoning by letter come into England at last?

Plea. Faith, I am afraid to take the letter up, for fear I should be transmogrified.

Bel. This sudden change is most surprising. Help, lead her to my chamber, a little sleep may bring her to herself again.

Dor. Lead me to death most willingly: horrors and despair will end my days.

[*Exeunt* Dorcas, Belinda, *and Servants.*

Wor. Go, charming fair! I cann't blame thee for this great concern. Death, hell, and devils! am I then at last become a villain! a despicable husband! a betrayer of weak virgins' hearts!——Am I, from a man of honour, sunk to a degenerate slave!——By Heaven, I'm raging mad! What ill-boding spirit could owe me such a spite, and cross at once my full-blown joys?

Rove. Worthy, is the frolic to go round? Are we to be all mad? or must only you and the Quaker carry on the jest?

Wor. Oh, Rovewell, you have known me long, but never saw me in such agonies of grief before; read these, the cause of all my woes.

Rove. [*Takes up the letter, reads, and* Pleasant *over his shoulder.*] " Guilty——Villanies——another wife —at Deal—Quaker's heart out. ELIZ. WORTHY." An intrigue well carried on, i'faith. [*Reads the other letter.*]   " I doubt not——wonder——of man—— Worthy—your husband——two children——the en- closed—next post—to his sight.   ELIZ. WORTHY."

Plea. Why, this lady of yours writes very prettily, captain.

Rove. The woman has a pretty knack, faith; pr'y- thee, Worthy, are these two children of yours boys or girls? ha, ha, ha!

Wor.   Hell and furies! am I become your scorn? Do you laugh at me?

Rove. Ay, faith, do we.   Canst thou be concerned at the stratagem of a woman who loves thee? Look once more upon the scrawl, canst thou not guess whose hand it is?

Wor. Ha!——By this light it looks somewhat like Arabella's! It must be hers.   Fool that I was not to perceive it before; 'twas cunningly performed, I swear: I wonder my charming Quaker discovered it not! I'll in, and undeceive her.   [*Meets* Belinda.

Bel. Make no noise, she's in a slumber, which I hope will compose her.

Wor. Oh, Belinda! this is a trick of Arabella's;

behold, see here the cunning penning of her envious fingers.

Bel. I wish the worst effects on't are past; for she has vow'd never to see you more: I'll watch her slumbers, and when she wakes, I'll tell her the story before her fits return.——Rovewell, you may now see when once our sex resolve to love, 'tis dangerous to disappoint us.

Rove. But 'tis hard, Belinda, that you should so soon believe that men are false; ten thousand letters ne'er could make me alter the rooted passion I have for you.

Bel. Oh! should you be told I am married to a man, who has had two children by me, you'd fly back from promises and vows, and cry, pox take her, she's a jilt.

Rove. So **far from** that, my soul, that I'd stab the inventor of such a story.

Bel. That would be very heroic, indeed; but come, let's comfort the poor captain here, who looks more dejected than a discarded minister.

Plea. Oh, worse than that, madam, he puts me in mind of an English captain taken by a French privateer.

Rove. 'Tis a dismal thing to be first boarded, then stript, and afterwards clapt into a French gaol.

Bel. In short, he looks as if he were married.

Plea. Right, madam, and his countenance shews full of a family concern.

Wor. How can you blame my surprise? Were you to see the fair Belinda, whom I know you love the best of any one on earth; were you, I say, to see her in tears and agonies for something you had done, nay, for something you had not done, some villanous imputation charged upon you, 'twou'd touch your heart as much as mine.

Rove. Why, faith, I have so good an opinion of Belinda, that I fancy she would give herself none of those airs if she heard I had twenty children.

Bel. Nay, more than that, had you **twenty** wives, I should keep my temper : care shall be **taken in** drawing the writings, so as I may not be the worse for you in my fortune; and if you will love a great many of my sex, it's probable I shall find out a way of making reprisals.

Plea. What's all this to my happiness? How am **I** to come by my Arabella?

Bel. Why, she's as easily come at as the rest of her sex.

Plea. But, madam, if she dotes on my captain, how can I expect she'll ever smile on me?

Wor. Oh! her love to me is vanish'd, if e'er she **had** any; this action of hers plainly **shews** her malice.

Bel. Come, I'll write her word what an heroic passion she has put Worthy into, and the fainting condition poor Dorcas lies in; I'll praise her for her well-invented stratagem, and then let her know Sir Charles is here.

Plea. Why, madam, do you think that will bring her?

Bel. Sir Charles, I have heard her say abundance of handsome things of you; I know she likes the word quality much, and would not care if on any terms she could be called her lady'ship; for she is pleased with taking place : that, you must know, is the darling vanity of our sex.

Rove. You may set your heart at rest; you have a fairer prospect of marrying Arabella, than poor Worthy has for marrying her sister.

Bel. **Come,** tease him no more : I'll steal up to her, and convince her of the error she's in. Go into the parlour, there's cards.   [*Exit.*

Rove. Come, what **think** you of ombre, or a pool at piquet.

Wor. I can do nothing with pleasure till I know how I am to be received by my dear charmer.

Plea. Come, pray divert these melancholy whimsies.

Rove. Why, if you don't go to cards, Sir Charles and I shall be very satirical upon you.

Wor. Nay, rather than you should play that game with me, I'll go to cards.   [*Exeunt.*

Enter FLIP *drunk,* INDENT, *and* JILTUP.

Jilt. This was kind, indeed, my dear dog, to make me the first visit, when so many ladies in town die for you.

Flip. Why, you little hussy you, I think all the women in town look like swabs to you.

Ind. Indeed, madam, the commodore does often launch out in your praises.

Flip. Ay, and commendations too: why, I love you so well, that I could be your consort and your mess-mate for ever. When I die 'tis all your own; my houses, my land, my part in ships, and my every thing else come to you by will and deed.

Jilt. Poor good-natured thing, how is it possible for me to return thy kindnesses? I have no land but my own body; take that into thy custody, and make the most on't.

Enter CRIBBIDGE *in a Priest's Habit.*

Flip. What have we here? a priest!

Jilt. Oh, dear cousin Homily, I'm glad to see you.

Flip. Is this your cousin, my dear? You're welcome, as I may say.

Crib. Sir, I thank you. Cousin, I'm glad to see you; I come to stay with you some time; your doctor being gone to make interest for a bishopric, I am to officiate for him until his return.

Ind. Rarely acted i'faith, he looks much modester than most of our sea-chaplains.

Crib. Well, cousin, may I joy you? Have you entered into the holy state of matrimony yet?

Jilt. No, cousin, I am willing to see a little more of the world first.

Crib. A parishioner of mine, that has seen you, seems to have a great mind to make you his wife:

he has a plentiful estate, with a fine house, in a pleasant part of Kent; he is of a very good family, and
is a personal handsome man.

Flip. Heark'e, sir, none of your match-making stories here: this lady is disposed of, and her inclinations are moor'd to my affections; and he that claps
her aboard, must expect to be raked fore and aft with
my partridge double and round.

Crib. Sir, I beg your pardon; if you are the lady's
husband I have done, sir.

Flip. Look'e, sir, I am not at present the lady's
husband, but if **you** understand that part of your
trade, and will splice **us** together, I have a couple of
guineas at your service.

Crib. Sir, if all parties are consenting, I shall not
be a great while performing that ceremony.

Flip. **Why** all parties are consented, Reverendissimo.

Crib. Sir, if I have that from the lady's mouth, and
you can get her a father to give her away, I shall
proceed.

Flip. Oh, as to a father, here's the purser shall
stand that part of the story. Tell him, my dear, how
you love and adore **me.**

Jilt. I must say I have an unalterable affection for
the Commodore; but if I should marry him, and he
should not love me after it, I should be the miserablest
creature nature ever form'd.

Flip. Not love you, my dear! why I'll stick as close
to you as carv'd work to a ship's stern; nothing shall

be done by me without thy consent; you shall have the working of my vessel, and stand at the helm in all weathers.

Ind. Well, madam, since I am chose for your father, give me leave to know what's best for you; I'll engage the Commodore proves the tenderest husband in the navy.

Crib. Truly the gentleman hath the aspect of a man of parts.

Flip. Reverendissimo, I thank you for your good opinion of my outelects; and if you'll **give** yourself the trouble of coming on board my ship, you shall have your skull and guts fill'd so full of brandy and salt-beef, and your ears so alarmed with drums, trumpets, huzzas and guns, that you'll be as drunk in half an hour as you were at the wetting your commission.

Crib. Sir, people of my cloth never launch out beyond the rules of modesty.

Flip. I cann't say any thing to your shore-folks; but I am certain our sea-chaplains (generally speaking) are drunk as often as our sea-captains.

Crib. The more's the pity, that religion should be so abused by such profligates.

Ind. Why, indeed, the sailors are apt enough to be wicked of themselves, and such examples from their guides may be one great reason of so much immorality in the navy.

Flip. Come, my dear, let the doctor do his office, and belay our affair.

G

Jilt. Well, you have overcome me.

Flip. So, very well; then begin Mr. Homily.

Jilt. Oh, **no, we** shall be disturbed here, the next room is more private.

Flip. March away then. I am all over storeship and transport with thy dear person; come, I'll give you a tow, you are my prize now. [*Exeunt.*

ACT V. SCENE I.

Enter ARABELLA *dressed like a Quaker, in Men's Clothes.*

Arabella.

So, my plot succeeds as I could wish. Belinda's letter tells me all. Now must I take care to give my saint-like sister these credentials when she 'wakes. I think I look as like one of the pious brethren as if I had been educated by George Fox. [*Kneels.*

Enter ADVOCATE.

Is Dorcas Zeal within this dwelling-place?

Ad. Yes, she is.

Ara. Wilt thou go and tell unto her, that I would speak with **her** instantaneously?

Ad. If you'll walk in, I'll let my mistress know your message; but the lady is asleep.

Ara. Go, I'll follow thee. [*Exeunt.*

Enter again in the Parlour.

Ad. Sit **down**, while I acquaint my lady. [*Exit.*

Ara. Now for a disguising look, that she may not know me.

Enter BELINDA.

Bel. My servant tells me you would speak with Dorcas Zeal.

Ara. Yea, verily, **she** hath told thee the truth.

Bel. She is laid down and indisposed, I am loth to disturb her.

Ara. Verily, I could **wish** thou couldst dispense with giving her some small disturbance: my business is very urgent; for behold my errand **is** from her brother, and concerneth her much, **and** we must be in private.

Bel. Then follow me.

Ara. So I will.   [*Exeunt.*

SCENE II.

Draws, and discovers DORCAS *on a Couch.* Re-enter
BELINDA *and* ARABELLA.

Dor. How dreadful are the dreams of souls disturbed! Why was I so void of grace to trust to such a monster!

Bel. How does my dear? I feared we should have disturbed your rest; but this young man being very urgent to speak with you, I ventured to bring him up.

Dor. I am much better; but still troubled in mind.

G ij

Bel. Oh, as soon as you have dispatch'd your business, I'll set your mind to rights, I'll warrant you.

[*Exit.*

Ara. May be not. [*Aside.*] Friend, thy brother did send this unto thee ; when thou hast overlooked the contents thereof, thou wilt know my business here.

Dor. May be it contains something of that traitor Worthy.

[*Reads.*

" BELOVED SISTER,

" The bearer hereof, being the son of Ananias, who was an upright member of the cause, I recommend unto thee for a help-mate. He hath two thousand pounds a year, and stiffly adherent to our ways of going; and I send him to thee in good season, that thou may'st be delivered from the wicked designs of the seducing married man Worthy. Thine, in truth and sincerity,   -   SHADRACH ZEAL."

Dor. A comely youth, well worthy my good liking. Besides, how blest an occasion offereth to be revenged of an ungrateful man ! [*Aside.*] Art thou, young man, the subject of this paper ?

Ara. Yea, lovely maiden, I am the chosen man, selected by my friend and thy good brother to greet thee with a holy kiss, and tell thee I love thee, fair one.

Dor. Love me at first sight !——Have a care thou talk not in the language of the world, and play the deceiver; if thou dost, assure thyself I shall rebuke thee for it.

Ara. I have seen thee often before, verily.

Dor. Where didst thou see me?

Ara. In the great London city.

Dor. When there saw'st thou me?

Ara. At the last general assembly of the faithful, met at that season worldly men call Whitsuntide.

Dor. Yea, truly, our good brother Shadrach carried me up to that noisy town of pride and vanity, to greet our brethren friends at the last meeting. But if thou saw'st me there, how chanceth it, that in so long a silence thou hast stifled up the breathings of thy heart from the fifth month even to the ninth?

Ara. Oh! Dorcas, Dorcas,——ah——I saw and loved thee, but, alas! I check'd the moving spirit within. With my green years, methought I was too young to lead a sister.

Dor. Too young! Oh, fie! was that the fault! the younger the sporting lambs, they play more harmlessly: verily, the outward man thou bearest looketh with an honest face.

Ara. My inward man bears the same honest face too. [*Kisses Dorcas's hand.*] Deny me not thine hand.

Dor. Some such like agonies as these I felt from the first touches of the false Worthy.———

Ara. False indeed!—He is one of the profane, alien to our purer flock; and who can tell, were he thy chosen yoke-mate, but he'd force thee to one of his own steeple-houses; nay, and perhaps lead thee in vain foppings to a carnal seat in one of the sad playhouses?

Dor. [*Sighs.*] Ah!——

Ara. But I am, thou know'st, a lamb of thy own fold; me thou may'st mould to what thy own heart liketh: then let us not, like the vain babbling worldly ones, thus lose the precious time in foolish courtship; but let me forthwith wriggle myself into thy inward affections.

Dor. Yea, I do take thee, and, like a backslider who repenteth, I will, with pure zeal and fervency, turn unto thee.

Enter WORTHY, ROVEWELL, *Sir* CHARLES, *and* BELINDA.

Wor. Oh, my dear creature, do I hold thee fast!

Ara. Friend, hast thou any pretensions to this woman, who is the wife of my bosom?

Dor. Stand off, vile man, thou with thy flattering tongue hadst almost betrayed me: but now I defy thee. Go to thy wife and children.

Wor. Furies and fire! I shall run distracted.

Ara. Friend, swear not at all.

Wor. What canting coxcomb's this; that dares usurp my right?

Ara. Thou may'st bluster as much as thou pleasest: but I tell unto thee, this woman is bone of my bone, and flesh of my flesh.

Dor. Thou hast said the truth, and nothing but the truth; I say again and again begone to thy own wife.

Ara. **Ay, go** unto thy wife.

Wor. Rovewell, Sir Charles, Belinda, must I bear all this? Let me but keep my senses!

Bel. I am surprised at you!

Rove. behold, the letters you received were written by Arabella: see here, her very hand.

Ara. Friend, listen not to them, they are deceivers: let us depart from amongst them.

Plea. Look'e, young fellow, none of your impertinent cant here: this lady shall not stir 'till we have undeceived her.

Rove. And when we have done that, good sir, you may troop to the Bull and Mouth again, without this she-friend's money.

Dor. What power hast thou to hinder our departing hence?

Ara. Ay, friend, tell us that.

Rove. How can you be so cruel to a man, whose life's sole happiness is placed in you?

Dor. How can I be cruel enough to one, who would have for ever made me miserable?

Wor. Oh! would you but hear me justify myself, I soon would answer all this villanous forgery, and clear my wounded innocence and honour.

Ara. Friend, hear him not, he hath a vile deluding tongue.

Plea. Hark'e, young fellow, I have something to tell you.

Ara. Friend, I have nothing to say to thee; therefore touch me not, I say.

Dor. Pray, use no rudeness, but let us be gone quietly.

Plea. No struggling, good, sweet, diminutive cox-comb; if thou dost, I shall use the carnal weapon upon thee.

Ara. Begone, fellow.

[*In struggling her hat and wig fall off.*

Bel. How! Arabella!—Then the plot's discovered!

Dor. [*Shrieks.*] How's this! my holy brother in the spirit, turned an arrant sister in the flesh!

Wor. Ha!——my old friend, this was a well-acted tragi-comedy.

Dor. I am in so much confusion and surprise, I know not what to say.

Ara. Now, sir, I suppose you'll let me go; I have no more business here.

Plea. This discovery will make me hold you faster than before.

Rove. Ay, madam, there's no retreating now; we'll be even with you for all your usage.

Dor. Friend Worthy, canst thou forgive me, and once more take my hand?

Wor. Can I live! Not without thee, I'm sure! Oh, had you but once o'erlooked these lines, how had you saved **me** this wild distraction!

Plea. Look'e, madam, no struggling; you are now my prisoner; I shall **not** release you but upon very advantageous terms to myself.

Bel. Those terms, Sir Charles, let me have leave

to make. I know the gentlewoman's mind so well,
that I dare give you her hand.

Ara. Upon what account, Belinda?

Bel. Why upon the account of being my Lady
Pleasant. Pr'ythee don't put on a dissembling look;
consent forthwith, or you shall die a maid. But first
I'll reconcile you to this couple.

Dor. I forgive thee, sister, what excess of passion
moved thee to; but if thou valuest me, accept of the
man Pleasant for thy husband.

Ara. I am a little confounded; let me retire till I
have recovered myself, I'll wait on you again.

[Is going.

Dor. Stay, sister, husband that wouldst have been;
one serious word before thou goest.

Ara. Ay, and two merry ones, if you please.

Dor. If I had taken thee hand in hand to the
steeple-house yoke-maker, wouldst thou have had
the impudence to have said after him; I, a false brother Ananias, take thee a true sister Dorcas, to have
and to hold, to love and to cherish?——Thou love
and cherish me! when thou knowest thyself a woman, and hadst it not in thee, naughty creature!

Ara. No, faith, sister, I should never have pushed
the jest so far neither.

Dor. Go, go thy ways; thou art a sad facetious girl.

[Exit Arabella.

Rove. Follow, Sir Charles, follow her; never let
her go beyond thy reach, till thou hast her safe; and

we'll all go along with thee, to be ready for auxilia-
ries upon occasion.

Bel. Well, I'll take care the breeches shall be delivered, Sir Charles; this shall be the last hour of
your wearing those masculine trophies of tyranny.

[Exeunt all but Worthy and Dorcas.

Dor. Well, this malicious sister of ours had a strange
plot against us; but, I hope, kind Worthy, thou canst
heartily forgive her.

Wor. Ay, and thank the very hand that snatched
thee from me, because it brings me the transporting
joys of this blest restoration.

Enter FLIP, *pulling in* MIZEN, *who holds* JENNY PRI-
VATE *in his other hand, dressed like a Quaker, exactly
like* DORCAS.

Flip. Now, pox on thee, come forwards with thy
fair spouse; as thou hast snapt this rich galleon, and
got the ten thousand pound cargo, never be ashamed
of thy good fortune, but bear up full sail to him, and
lay him athwart with her.

Miz. By my bowsprit, and so I will. Oh, the sweet
pleasure of the mortification I shall give him.—Come
forward, sweeting. [*Enter with her farther upon the
Stage.*] My dear brother Worthy, thou seest I have
made bold. We have signed and sealed, noble captain.

Wor. I see you have.

Flip. Ay, Bully Tar, they are twined together as strong as a first-rate cable.

Miz. Ha!———What's yonder! [*Spying the real* Dorcas.] Is that beautiful Quaker a relation of thine?

Jen. Yea, my dear sister and friend, I greet thee lovingly.

Dor. My sister! Pray, who art thou?

Jen. In my single estate I was called Dorcas Zeal; but in my wedlock bonds my name is Dorcas Mizen.

Dor. Dorcas and Zeal!———Who gave thee those names?

Jen. None of the vain ceremonies of godfathers and godmothers; no verily, it is a name I borrowed to myself, to make this dear man happy in a yoke-mate.

Miz. Borrowed! in the name of Lucifer.

Dor. Nay, in my clothing too! my very likeness.

Wor. I wish you joy, my happy rival!

Flip. Ay, joy, sir, joy in your ten thousand pound Quaker.

Miz. Ten thousand torments! Joy! never was man so cheated, so betrayed and ruined———Spouse, monster, fury, Jezabel, who art thou?

Jen. Shall I answer thee in the language of the sanctified?

Miz. No, answer me in thine own infernal dialect; and tell me, friend, whence camest thou?

Jen. From London, an't please you.

Miz. A woman of the town, I suppose, a walking night-bird, in or about Drury-Lane wards.

Jen. Yes, truly, one of that cloudy generation; But, Heavens be thanked, those dark days are over with me, I shall shine out a captain's lady now.

Miz. Shine out a firebrand, brimstone and smoke! a whore, a common strumpet!

Flip. Oh, fye, brother Mizen, no more hard words, but take her to thy bosom.

Miz. Take her to the devil.

Flip. I tell thee, Mizen, thou couldst not have picked out a wife **so** fit for thee, out of a whole regiment **of doxies. Does** she not own herself a piece of brittle ware? and will so sweetly set off thy cabin with the rest of thy china!

Wor. Ay, Mizen, take the commodore's good coun**sel,** and bear it all with patience; thou art as quarrelsome **as a** game-cock at a looking-glass, and with as little reason for thy passion.

Miz. Not reason for my passion, when I'm tied to such a limb of hell!

Wor. No, not when thou hast deserved to be so tied!

Miz. Deserved!

Wor. Ay, sir, deserved. Didst not thou know my claim to this fair creature? And with thy treacherous designs to play so poor a game, to invade my sacred right, art thou not justly punished?

Dor. Yea, naughty man, thou hast thy just reward.

Miz. Ay, noble Worthy, I own myself a villain, and the hand of Heaven has reached me for it.

Flip. Hang thee, who pities thee. You wanted a

ten thousand pounder, and must set up downright buccaneer, and pirate for a wife ; no prize but Wor-hy's Dorcas! now I have married a girl——

Wor. Thou married !

Flip. Ay, this very morning. But my fubbs-yacht pretends to no thousands ; a pox of portions, I have yellow-bows enow (thanks to a harvest in her ma-esty's service) to make the white and red in the fair cheeks of an honest smiling bed-fellow look lovely, with neither paint nor patch.

Wor. Where is this white and red, with neither paint nor patch ? Troth, Flip, thou keepest thy rus-tic humour still ; to have taken a young bride, and be seen thus long out of her company, on the very nuptial morning, is not over modish, let me tell you.

Flip. Hang ceremonies. Look you, sir, the wench I have taken is a plain country pinnace, with no gay gildings, either at poop or stern ; but her plain trim so neat, that at first sight, as she sailed by me, a puff of love sprung up so brisk a gale, that I immediately tacked round, and boarded her.

Wor. That is to say, you wedded her.

Flip. Right, sir ; and when the job was done, I was obliged to put her in a little more modish rigging fit for the she-mate of a commodore ; my landlady and she are gone together to the milliner's and the semp-stress's, and so forth——but I expect them——see, here they are ! Oh, my sweet spouse !

Enter JILTUP *and* CRIBBIDGE.

Wor. Joy, happy sir.

Miz. The like **to you,** fair bride!

Jilt. I thank you, gentlemen and ladies: thanks to the whole fair company. Ha!——my sweet cousin here! Dear Jenny——   [*Embracing her.*

Flip. Her cousin, say you?

Jilt. Ay, my best dear, though I have the honour to be a commodore's lady, I must not grow proud, and forget my old friends and acquaintance. This young lady and I were bred up play-fellows together.

Flip. Not at her game, I hope.

Jilt. Oh! yes, sir; we were two such intimates, two such sworn friends, that our delights, our joys, our very lives were **all** wound up together.

Flip. Where, where, my pretty lady-bird, was thy acquaintance with that play-fellow?

Jilt. At London, sir.

Flip. What part of London?

Jilt. The neighbourhood of Covent-Garden.

Flip. Sink and Sodom!

Jilt. Both lodgers in one house; nay, and when either of us had room for a she-bedfellow, we were those loving fools, we always slept together.

Flip. Oh——

Jilt. This frank confession is, I hope, my virtue, not my fault: I have lived in a bad world, and played the hypocrite so long, that I am now quite weary on't; besides, you're a plain-dealing honest gentleman, and it would be barbarous to tell you lies upon your wedding-day. You frankly married me for better for worse, perform your vow then, and take me as you find me.

Flip. Take a succubus;—diseases, poxes, leprosy! Oh, fool! sot! dotard! lunatic!—Death! I'll run mad; turn the muzzle of a gun down in the powder-room, and blow myself up to the devil.

Wor. Hold, Flip, no treason!—Blow up her majesty's ship.

Flip. Blow the world up!

Miz. Ay, brother sufferer, married to two such miscreants, so hardened in their shame, they make it even their glory to proclaim it.—Oh, Worthy, if thou bearest a human soul, as basely as I plotted to betray thee, even thou thyself must pity me.

Wor. I do pity thee, pity both of you; and to prove I do so, what will you say to me, if I release you, knock off your chains, and free you both from slavery?

Miz. What will we say!——We'll kneel to thee.

Flip. Worship thee.

Miz. Thou shalt command our lives, we'll fight for thee.

Flip. Hang for thee.

Miz. Drown for thee.   [*Kneeling.*

Wor. No more of this romantic stuff. What will you do for these poor creatures?

Flip. Do for them!—Why, friend, I'll give a leg or an arm for composition.

Wor. A leg or an arm!——A haunch of common swine's flesh would do them twice the service. What bread will you give them, to take them off from their lewd lives, and make two honest women of them?

Flip. Troth, I'll give my boatswain's pay, settled for life upon her.

Wor. That shall satisfy. Say, girl, art thou contented.

Jilt. So well contented, sir, that on my knees I'll thank you.

Flip. Sayest thou so, girl? Then, faith, I'll throw thee in one twenty brace of pounds to rig an honest house up of thy own, and roost no more in whores nests.

Wor. Well, sign this parchment, which entitles her to fifty pounds a year for life, and I'll release you.—— And what says Mizen?

Miz. Faith, I'll treat my Jenny [*Pulls out a large rich purse.*] with this purse of gold, the weighty stowage of a fair hundred guineas, and give her the same settlement into the bargain.

Wor. Come, come, sign, sign them.——Now, gentlemen, in order to your deliverance, first, I must tell you both, these sweet wedlock-nooses were my handy work, your friend and servant Worthy, the head match-maker.

Flip. and Miz. Thou!

Wor. Not to ruin you, but reform you! And now for a safe cure to all fears and dangers, the reverend man in black that linked you both was only an honest tar, your good friend Cribbidge in pious masquerade; and since there has been neither lawful matrimony nor consummation, the knot will soon be loosed.

Crib. You see, noble captain, I'm ready to serve you in all capacities.

Flip. I thought indeed the canonical rascal had a hanging look, somewhat like my lieutenant.

Miz. Ay, hang him, rogue, a halter would better become his neck for a collar, than a surcingle his whoreson hide for a girdle.

Wor. No murmurs, thou knowest how thou deservest it.

Miz. Touch my past shame no more, I'm a true penitent.

Wor. And for thee, Flip, I knew thee such a rake, that the least mad drunken fit would run thee headlong into irrevocable shame and ruin; and therefore, even for thy mere preservation, I put this innocent cheat upon thee, only to stand a warning sea-mark to thee against all future shipwrecks on this quicksand.

Flip. By Neptune, and by **Mars,** you are a brave fellow.

Wor. And, gentlemen, to sign your full redemption, these ladies shall seal articles of release.

Jilt. The strongest you can ask, or law can bind; and since you have provided so handsomely for us, we are resolved to change our course of lives, and live honestly for the future. What thousands of wretched creatures, like ourselves, would willingly——

The follies of their ill-spent lives recall,
Turn, and live honest, could they live at all.

Jen. Yes, female frailty first made them sinners, but from necessity they live and die so,

To their dark cells and midnight revels led,
Not from their thirst to man, but hunger for his bread.

Wor. Well, though I have made your purses smart a little, you see I have made you do some good in your generation, put a helping hand to two poor sinners' conversion.

Flip. Ay, and my own conversion too. Henceforward I'll keep such honest fellows as thee company, cast off my old, dull, rascally conversation, and learn good sense and manners.

Miz. Nay, dear Worthy, take one new convert more, for from this hour I'll play the effeminate fool no more, but bear the face of a man like thee, strip my fop-cabin of all my china baubles, toys for girls, and **shew my**self a true hero for my glorious queen.

Wor. Nay, now, dear gentlemen, you'll make me proud of this day's happy work.

Enter Sir CHARLES, *and* ARABELLA *in her own Dress,* ROVEWELL *and* BELINDA.

Wor. Well, dear Sir Charles, how stand the affairs of love?

Plea. Faith, very well: generous Arabella has

hung out her white **flag, and** given her promise she'll seal the speedy articles of surrender.

Wor. Nay then, sir, we shall see you **shine a conqueror.**

Plea. When this fair hand has crowned me one.

Ara. Yes, Worthy, no more of my wild airs, no more mad frolics; as I have studied to plague thee, I'll play a soberer part, and study now————

[*Giving her hand to Sir* Charles.

Plea. To bless the happiest of mankind.

Wor. But what says Rovewell?

Rove. What I am proud to say; Belinda's kind at last, and crowns my love.

Bel. Yes, Worthy, I have at last played the true woman, not always able to hold out invincible.

Wor. Well, ladies, since the whole preliminaries of the soft peace of love are all adjusted, what if, according to old laudable custom, we have a little music and a dance.

Plea. Nothing more *à-propos.*

Rove. Madam, you are my partner.

Dor. Oh, fie, friend Rovewell! the females of our congregation think it vanity of vanities.

Rove. Yes, in the country they may do't; but your London friends have all the gaiety imaginable; they sing, they dance, wear patches, and keep visiting-days.

Dor. Well, rather than spoil your mirth, I will walk about.

A DANCE.

After the Country Dance, enter a Servant.

Serv. Your cockswain and boat's crew, hearing you had got the music, desire they may present you with a little of their agility.

A DANCE *of Sailors.*

Dor. Well, dear Worthy, since I have heard the affected sanctity and friendly cant, not only from my sister Arabella, but even from that carnal vessel of pollution; to make our marriage-yoke more cheerful still, from this blessed hour I'll join thy holy worship.

Wor. Now I have all my utmost wish could ask.

Miz. Hold, Worthy, do not boast too proud a triumph in making this fair proselyte. Flip and I have there outdone you : you have only made a sister convert from one faith to another; but we have converted a fair brace of infidels, a work of reformation far beyond you.

Wor. Ay, there you have outdone me : and I think, gentlemen, you have set a good example for the world in general to follow.

Oh! what a happy change this age would find,
In all the looser part of womankind,
Would all their cullies do as you have done,
And every fool, like you, reform but one.

[Exeunt omnes.

EPILOGUE.

*F*RIENDS, *doth it please you that this trifle pass?*
Are you contented not to damn the ass?
Or doth it to your wiser judgment seem
More fit this leading folly to condemn,
For fear of being charg'd with more of them?
Sedately think, and let your equal zeal
Weigh both the public and his private weal.
First then, i' th' public name, debate it whether
Ye can subsist, **keep** *life and soul together,*
Without the privilege of coming hither.
If that you can spin out your life-long days,
Without the vanity of seeing plays,
Down with this scribbler's **hopes,** *this house and all,*
Let both these marts for lewdness, tumble, fall.
For, ah! it cutteth, it provoketh passion,
To think you should indulge abomination.
But if you're harden'd, stung, as I may say,
With moral madness like tarantula,
That nothing else but noise and dance can cure you;
Then pray encourage what you have before you,
For as these triflers now-a-days do write,
No mirth's more innocent than this to-night.

Now, **sirs,** *I come* **to plead our** *strippling's* **cause,**
All the young fellow wants, is your applause.
Poet's *a sounding, empty name,*
Born on Parnassus' cliffs, he pants for fame;
Not ev'n your third night's bounty would content him,
If of the grand Sophies you should prevent him;
That word my skill in languages has **lent** *him.*
Nay, for my own sake I demand this grace,
Because with much constraint I've set my face,
To carry on a quaker's dull grimace:
And ill, *my friends, you would reward my pains,*
If I should suffer for his want of brains;
For where the luckless poet feels your hate,
The undistinguish'd players share your fate.

De Wilde pinx.   Monkum

Mr. HOLMAN as TANCRED.

How! is she not my lord, the late king's sister.
Heir to the crown of Sicily?

London, Printed for J. Bell, British Library, Strand, April 28, 1792.

TANCRED AND SIGISMUNDA.

A

TRAGEDY,

BY MR. JAMES THOMSON.

ADAPTED FOR

THEATRICAL REPRESENTATION,

AS PERFORMED AT THE

THEATRES-ROYAL,

DRURY-LANE AND COVENT-GARDEN.

REGULATED FROM THE PROMPT-BOOKS,

By Permission of the Managers.

LONDON :

Printed for the Proprietors, under the Direction of
JOHN BELL, British Library, STRAND,
Bookseller to His Royal Highness the Prince of Wales.

M DCC XCII.

HIS ROYAL HIGHNESSS
FREDERICK,
PRINCE OF WALES.

SIR,

THE honour your Royal Highness has done me in the protection you was pleased to give to this Tragedy, emboldens me to lay it now at your feet, and beg your permission to publish it under Royal Patronage. The favouring and protecting of letters has been, in all ages and countries, one distinguishing mark of a great prince; and that with good reason, not only as it shews a justness of taste, and elevation of mind, but as the influence of such a protection, by exciting good writers to labour with more emulation in the improvement of their several talents, not a little contributes to the embellishment and instruction of society. But of all the different species of writing, none has such an effect upon the lives and manners of men, as the dramatic; and therefore, that of all others most deserves the attention of princes; who, by a judicious approbation of such pieces as tend to promote all public and private virtue, may more than by any coercive methods, secure the purity of the stage, and in consequence thereof, greatly advance the morals and politeness of their people. How eminently your Royal Highness has always

A iij

extended your favour and patronage to every art and science, and in a particular manner to dramatic performances, is too well known to the world for me to mention it here. Allow me only to wish, that what I have now the honour to offer to your Royal Highness, **may** be judged not unworthy of your protection, at least in the sentiments which it inculcates. A warm and grateful sense of your goodness to me, makes me desirous to seize every occasion of declaring in public, with what profound respect and dutiful attachment, I am,

Sir,

Your Royal Highness's

most obliged,

most obedient, and

most devoted servant,

JAMES THOMPSON.

TANCRED AND SIGISMUNDA.

THIS is the only play of THOMSON's that has been of late performed upon our theatres. The genius of this amiable Poet did not naturally lead him to Tragedy : the desire of profit seems to have induced him to become a Tragic Poet, in which walk of literature his superiors are much more numerous, than in the descriptive and the allegoric.

Drawing, however, from a master so consummate as LE SAGE, the present play could not but be interesting and busy ; displaying events suitable to the ends of Tragedy, as calling forth terror, and demanding pity.

It is singular that THOMSON should not have hinted at the source from which TANCRED was derived. His age, however, might have scrupled a drama drawn from GIL BLAS. The incidents therein are closely followed, and there appears to be much poetic address, and classical purity, in the disposition of the circumstances, and the colouring of the sentiments.

BOLD is the man! who, in this nicer age,
Presumes to tread the chaste corrected stage,
Now, with gay tinsel arts, we can no more
Conceal the want of nature's sterling ore.
Our spells are vanish'd, broke our magic wand,
That us'd to waft you over sea and land.
Before your light the fairy people fade,
The demons fly---the ghost itself is laid.
In vain of martial scenes the loud alarms,
The mighty prompter thundering out to arms,
The playhouse posse clattering from afar,
The close-wedg'd battle, and the din of war.
Now, even the senate seldom we convene ;
The yawning fathers nod behind the scene.
Your taste rejects the glittering false sublime,
To sigh in metaphor, and die in rhime.
High rant is tumbled from his gallery throne :
Description, dreams—nay, similies are gone.

What shall we then ? to please you how devise,
Whose judgment sits not in your ears nor eyes ?
Thrice happy! could we catch great Shakspere's art,
To trace the deep recesses of the heart :
His simple, plain sublime, to which is given
To strike the soul with darted flame from heaven :

Could *we* awake soft Otway's tender woe,
The pomp of verse and golden lines of Rowe.

   We to your hearts apply : let them attend ;
Before their silent, candid bar we bend.
If warm'd, they listen, 'tis our noblest praise :
If cold, they wither all the muse's bays.

Dramatis Personae.

DRURY-LANE.

Men.

TANCRED, *Count of Lecce,* - - -	Mr. Kemble.
MATTEO SIFFREDI, *Lord High Chancellor of Sicily,* - - -	Mr. Bensley.
EARL OSMOND, *Lord High Constable of Sicily,* - - -	Mr. Barrymore.
RODOLPHO, *Friend to* Tancred, *and Captain of the Guards,* - -	Mr. Benson.

Women.

SIGISMUNDA, *Daughter of* Siffredi, -	Mrs. Powell.
LAURA, *Sister of* Rodolpho, *and Friend to* Sigismunda.	Mrs. Kemble.

Barons, **Officers,** *Guards, &c.*

SCENE, the City of Palermo in Italy.

COVENT-GARDEN.

Men.

TANCRED, *Count of Lecce,* - -	Mr. Holman.
MATTEO SIFFREDI, *Lord High Chancellor of Sicily,* - - -	Mr. Hull.
EARL OSMOND, *Lord High Constable of Sicily,* - - -	Mr. Farren.
RODOLPHO, *Friend to* Tancred, *and Captain of the Guards,* - -	Mr. Macready.

Women.

SIGISMUNDA, *Daughter of* Siffredi, -	Mrs. Merry.
LAURA, *Sister of* Rodolpho, *and Friend to* Sigismunda, - - -	Mrs. Mountain.

Barons, Officers, Guards, &c.

SCENE, the City of Palermo in Italy,

3

TANCRED AND SIGISMUNDA.

ACT I. SCENE I.

The Palace. *Enter* SIGISMUNDA *and* LAURA.

Sigismunda.

AH, fatal day to Sicily! the king
Touches his last moments!

Laura. So 'tis fear'd.

Sig. " The death of those distinguish'd by their
    station,
" But by their virtue more, awakes the mind
" To solemn dread, and strikes a saddening awe:
" Not that we grieve for them, but for ourselves,
" Left to the toil of life—And yet the best
" Are, by the playful children of this world,
" At once forgot, as they had never been."
Laura, 'tis said, the heart is sometimes charged
With a prophetic sadness: such, methinks,
Now hangs on mine. The king's approaching death
Suggests a thousand fears. What troubles thence
May throw the state once more into confusion,

What sudden changes in my father's house
May rise, and part me from my dearest Tancred,
Alarms my thoughts.

 Laura. The fears of love-sick fancy!
Perversely busy to torment itself.
But be assured, your father's steady friendship,
Join'd to a certain genius, that commands,
Not kneels to fortune, will support and cherish,
Here in the public eye of Sicily,
This, I may call him, his adopted son,
The noble Tancred, form'd to all his virtues.

 Sig. Ah, form'd to charm his daughter!—This fair
   morn
Has tempted far the chase. Is he not yet
Return'd?

 Laura. No.—When your father to the king,
Who now expiring lies, was call'd in haste,
He sent each way his messengers to find him;
With such a look of ardour and impatience,
As if this near event was to Count Tancred
Of more importance than I comprehend.

 Sig. There lies, my Laura, o'er my Tancred's birth
A cloud I cannot pierce. With princely accost,
Nay, with respect, which oft I have observ'd,
Stealing at times submissive o'er his features,
In Belmont's woods my father rear'd this youth—
Ah, woods! where first my artless bosom learn'd
The sighs of love.—He gives him out the son
Of an old friend, a baron of Apulia,
Who in the late crusado bravely fell.

But then 'tis strange ; is all his family
As well as father dead ? and all their friends,
Except my sire, the generous good Siffredi ?
Had he a mother, sister, brother left,
The last remain of kindred ; with what pride,
What rapture, might they fly o'er earth and sea,
To claim this rising honour of their blood !
This bright unknown ! this all-accomplish'd youth !
Who charms too much, the heart of Sigismunda !
" Laura, perhaps your brother knows him better,
" The friend and partner of his freest hours."
What says Rodolpho ? Does he truly credit
This story of his birth ?

   Laura. He has sometimes,
Like you, his doubts ; yet, when maturely weigh'd,
Believes it true. As for Lord Tancred's self,
He never entertain'd the slightest thought
That verg'd to doubt ; but oft laments his state,
By cruel fortune so ill pair'd to yours.

   Sig. Merit like his, the fortune of the mind,
Beggars all wealth—Then, to your brother, Laura,
He talks of me ?

   Laura. Of nothing else. Howe'er
The talk begin, it ends with Sigismunda.
Their morning, noontide, and their evening walks,
Are full of you, and all the woods of Belmont
Enamour'd with your name———

   Sig. Away, my friend ;
You flatter———yet the dear delusion charms.

   Laura. No, Sigismunda, 'tis the strictest truth,

Nor half the truth, I tell you. Even with fondness
My brother talks for ever of the passion
That fires young Tancred's breast. So much it
       strikes him,
He praises love as if he were a lover.
" He blames the false pursuits of vagrant youth,
" Calls them gay folly, a mistaken struggle
" Against best judging nature." Heaven, he says,
In lavish bounty form'd the heart for love ;
In love included all the finer seeds
Of honour, virtue, friendship, purest bliss——
    Sig. Virtuous Rodolpho !
    Laura. Then his pleasing theme
He varies to the praises of your lover——
    Sig. And what, my Laura, says he on the subject ?
    Laura. He says that, though he was not nobly born,
Nature has form'd him noble, generous, brave,
" Truly magnanimous, and warmly scorning
" Whatever bears the smallest taint of baseness ;
" That every easy virtue is his own ;
" Not learnt by painful labour, bnt inspir'd,
" Implanted in his soul."—Chiefly one charm
He in his graceful character observes ;
That though his passions burn with high impatience,
And sometimes, from a noble heat of nature,
Are ready to fly off ; yet the least check
Of ruling reason brings them back to temper,
And gentle softness.
    Sig. True ! Oh, true, Rodolpho !
Blest be thy kindred worth for loving his !
He is all warmth, all amiable fire,

All quick heroic ardour! temper'd soft
With gentleness of heart, and manly reason!
If virtue were to wear a human form,
To light it with her dignity and flame,
Then soft'ning mix her smiles and tender graces;
Oh, she would choose the person of my Tancred!
Go on my friend, go on, and ever praise him;
The subject knows no bounds, nor can I tire,
While my breast trembles to that sweetest music!
The heart of woman tastes no truer joy,
Is never flattered with such dear enchantment——
" 'Tis more than selfish vanity"—as when
She hears the praises of the man she loves——

    Laura. Madam, your father comes.

Enter SIFFREDI.

    Sif. [*To an attendant as he enters.*] Lord Tancred
Is found?
    At. My lord, he quickly will be here.
" I scarce could keep before him, though he bid me
" Speed on, to say he would attend your orders."
    Sif. 'Tis well——retire——You too, my daughter,
        leave me.
    Sig. I go, my father—But how fares the king?
    Sif. He is no more. Gone to that awful state,
Where kings the crown wear only of their virtues.
    Sig. How bright must then be his!—This stroke is
        sudden;
He was this morning well, when to the chase
Lord Tancred went.

B

Sif. 'Tis true. But at his years
Death gives short notice—Drooping nature then,
Without a gust of pain to shake it, falls,
His death, my daughter, was that happy period
Which few attain. The duties of his day
Were all discharg'd, " and gratefully enjoy'd
" Its noblest blessings;" calm as evening skies
Was his pure mind, and lighted up with hopes
That open heaven; when, for his last long sleep
Timely prepar'd, a lassitude of life,
A pleasing weariness of mortal joy,
Fell on his soul, and down he sunk to rest.
Oh, may my death be such!——He but one wish
Left unfulfill'd, which was to see Count Tancred—

Sig. To see Count Tancred!—Pardon me, my
lord—

Sif. For what, my daughter?—But, with such
emotion,
Why did you start at mention of Count Tancred?

Sig. Nothing—I only hop'd the dying king
Might mean to make some generous just provision
For this your worthy charge, this noble orphan.

Sif. And he has done it largely—Leave me now—
I want some private conference with Lord Tancred.

[*Exeunt* Sigismunda *and* Laura.

My doubts are but too true—If these old eyes
Can trace the marks of love, a mutual passion
Has seiz'd, I fear, my daughter and this prince,
My sovereign now—Should it be so? Ah, there,
There lurks a brooding tempest, that may shake

My long concerted scheme, to settle firm
The public peace and welfare, which the king
Has made the prudent basis of his will——
Away, unworthy views! you shall not tempt me!
Nor interest, nor ambition shall seduce
My fix'd resolve——Perish the selfish thought,
Which our own good prefers to that of millions!
He comes, my king, unconscious of his fortune.

Enter TANCRED.

Tan. My lord Siffredi, in your looks I read,
Confirm'd, the mournful news that fly abroad
From tongue to tongue—We then, at last have lost
The good old king?

Sif. Yes, we have lost a father!
The greatest blessing Heaven bestows on mortals,
" And seldom found amidst these wilds of time."
A good, a worthy king!—Hear me, my Tancred,
And I will tell thee, in a few plain words,
How he deserv'd that best, that glorious title.
" 'Tis nought complex, 'tis clear as truth and virtue."
He lov'd his people, deem'd them all his children;
The good exalted, and depress'd the bad.
" He spurn'd the flattering crew, with scorn rejected
" Their smooth advice that only means themselves,
" Their schemes to aggrandize him into baseness;
" Nor did he less disdain the secret breath,
" The whisper'd tale, that blights a virtuous name."
He sought alone the good of those for whom
He was entrusted with the sovereign power:

Well knowing that a people in their rights
And industry protected; living safe
Beneath the sacred shelter of the laws,
" Encouraged in their genius, arts and labours,
" And happy each as he himself deserves,"
Are ne'er ungrateful. With unsparing hand
They will for him provide : their filial love
And confidence are his unfailing treasure,
And every honest man his faithful guard.

   Tan. A general face of grief o'erspreads the city.
I mark'd the people, as I hither came,
In crowds assembled, struck with silent sorrow,
And pouring forth the noblest praise of tears.
" Those, whom remembrance of their former woes,
" And long experience of the vain illusions
" Of youthful hope, had into wise consent
" And fear of change corrected, wrung their hands,
" And, often casting up their eyes to heav'n,
" Gave sign of sad conjecture. Others shew'd,
" Athwart their grief, or real or affected,
" A gleam of expectation, from what chance
" And change might bring." A mingled murmur ran
Along the streets; and from the lonely court
Of him who can no more assist their fortunes,
I saw the courtier-fry, with eager haste,
All hurrying to Constantia.

   Sif. Noble youth !
I joy to hear from thee these just reflections,
Worthy of riper years—But if they seek
Constantia, trust me, they mistake their course.

Tan. How! Is she not, my Lord, the late king's
    sister,
Heir to the crown of Sicily? the last
Of our fam'd Norman line, and now our queen?

Sif. Tancred, 'tis true; she is the late king's sister,
The sole surviving offspring of that tyrant
William the Bad—" so for his vices stil'd;
" Who spilt much noble blood, and sore oppress'd
" Th' exhausted land: whence grievous wars arose,
" And many a dire convulsion shook the state.
" When he, whose death Sicilia mourns to-day,
" William, who has and well deserved the name
" Of Good, succeeding to his father's throne,
" Reliev'd his country's woes—But to return;
" She is the late king's sister," born some months
After the tyrant's death, but not next heir.

Tan. You much surprise me—May I then presume
To ask who is?

Sif. Come nearer, noble Tancred,
Son of my care. I must, on this occasion,
Consult thy generous heart; which, when conducted
By rectitude of mind and honest virtues,
Gives better counsel than the hoary head—
Then know, there lives a prince, here in Palermo,
The lineal offspring of our famous hero,
Roger the First.

Tan. Great Heaven! How far remov'd
From that our mighty founder?

Sif. His great grandson:

B iij

Sprung from his eldest son, who died untimely,
Before his father.

Tan. Ha! the prince you mean,
Is he not Manfred's son? The generous, brave,
Unhappy Manfred! whom the tyrant William,
You just now mention'd, not content to spoil
Of his paternal crown, threw into fetters,
And infamously murder'd?

Sif. Yes, the same.

Tan. " By heavens, I joy to find our Norman reign,
" The world's sole light amidst these barbarous ages,
" Yet rears its head; and shall not, from the lance,
" Pass to the feeble distaff."—But this prince,
Where has he lain conceal'd?

Sif. The late good king,
By noble pity mov'd, contriv'd to save him
From his dire father's unrelenting rage,
And had him rear'd in private, as became
His birth and hopes, with high and princely nurture,
Till now, too young to rule a troubled state,
By civil broils most miserably torn,
He in his safe retreat has lain conceal'd,
His birth and fortune to himself unknown;
But when the dying king to me intrusted,
As to the chancellor of the realm, his will,
His successor he nam'd him.

Tan. Happy youth!
He then will triumph o'er his father's foes,
O'er haughty Osmond, and the tyrant's daughter.

Sif. Ay, that is what I dread—the heat of youth;

There lurks, I fear, perdition to the state,
I dread the horrors of rekindled war :
Though dead, the tyrant still is to be fear'd ;
His daughter's party still is strong and numerous :
Her friend, Earl Osmond, Constable of Sicily,
Experienc'd, brave, high-born, of mighty interest.
Better the prince and princess should by marriage
Unite their friends, their interest, and their claims !
Then will the peace and welfare of the land
On a firm basis rise.

  Tan. My Lord Siffredi,
If by myself I of this prince may judge,
That scheme will scarce succeed—Your prudent age
In vain will counsel, if the heart forbid it—
But wherefore fear ? The right is clearly his ;
" And, under your direction, with each man
" Of worth, and stedfast loyalty, to back
" At once the king's appointment and his birthright,
" There is no ground for fear. They have great odds,
" Against th' astonished sons of violence,
" Who fight with awful justice on their side."
All Sicily will rouse, all faithful hearts,
Will range themselves around Prince Manfred's son.
For me, I here devote me to the service
Of this young prince ; I every drop of blood
Will lose with joy, with transport in his cause—
" Pardon my warmth—but that, my lord, will never
" To this decision come"—Then find the prince ;
Lose not a moment to awaken in him
The royal soul. Perhaps he, now desponding,

Pines in a corner, and laments his fortune;
That in the narrower bounds of private life
He must confine his aims, those swelling virtues
Which from his noble father he inherits.

Sif. Perhaps, regardless, in the common bane
Of youth he melts, in vanity and love.
But if the seeds of virtue glow within him,
I will awake a higher sense, a love
That grasps the loves and happiness of millions.

Tan. Why that surmise? Or should he love, Siffredi,
I doubt not, it is nobly, which will raise
And animate his virtues—Oh, permit me
To plead the cause of youth—Their virtue oft,
In pleasure's soft enchantment lull'd a while,
Forgets itself; it sleeps and gayly dreams,
Till great occasion rouse it; then, all flame,
It walks abroad, with heighten'd soul and vigour,
And by the change astonishes the world.
" Even with a kind of sympathy, I feel
" The joy that waits this prince; when all the powers,
" Th' expanding heart can wish, of doing good;
" Whatever swells ambition, or exalts
" The human soul into divine emotions,
" All crowd at once upon him.
    " *Sif.* Ah, my Tancred,
" Nothing so easy as in speculation,
" And at a distance seen, the course of honour,
" A fair delightful champaign strew'd with flowers.
" But when the practice comes; when our fond
        passions,

" Pleasure and pride, and self-indulgence, throw
" Their magic dust around, the prospect roughens ;
" Then dreadful passes, craggy mountains rise,
" Cliffs to be scal'd, and torrents to be stem'd ;
" Then toil ensues, and perseverance stern ;
" And endless combats with our grosser sense,
" Oft lost, and oft renew'd ; and generous pain
" For others felt ; and, harder lesson still !
" Our honest bliss for others sacrific'd ;
" And all the rugged task of virtue quells
" The stoutest heart of common resolution.
" Few get above this turbid scene of strife.
" Few gain the summit, breathe that purest air,
" That heavenly ether, which untroubled sees
" The storm of vice and passion rage below.
  " *Tan.* Most true, my lord.   But why thus au-
        gur ill ?
" You seem to doubt this prince.   I know him not.
" Yet, oh, methinks, my heart could answer for him !
" The juncture is so high, so strong the gale
" That blows from Heaven, as through the deadest
        soul
" Might breathe the godlike energy of virtue."
  Sif. Hear him, immortal shades of his great fa-
        thers !—
Forgive me, Sir, this trial of your heart.
Thou ! thou, art he !
  Tan. Siffredi !
  Sif. Tancred, thou !
Thou art the man of all the many thousands

That toil upon the bosom of this isle,
By Heaven elected to command the rest,
To rule, protect them, and to make them happy!
  Tan. Manfred my father! I the last support
Of the fam'd Norman line, that awes the world!
I, who this morning wander'd forth an orphan,
Outcast of all but thee, my second father!
Thus call'd to glory! to the first great lot
Of human kind!—Oh, wonder-working hand,
That, in majestic silence, sways at will
The mighty movements of unbounded nature;
Oh, grant me, Heaven, the virtues to sustain
This awful burden of so many heroes!
Let me not be exalted into shame,
Set up the worthless pageant of vain grandeur.
Meantime I thank the justice of the king,
Who has my right bequeath'd me. Thee Siffredi,
I thank thee—Oh, I ne'er enough can thank thee!
Yes, thou hast been—thou art—shalt be my father!
Thou shalt direct my unexperienc'd years,
Shalt be the ruling head, and I the hand.
  Sif. It is enough for me—to see my sovereign
Assert his virtues, and maintain his honour.
  Tan. I think, my lord, you said the king com-
      mitted
To you his will. I hope it is not clogg'd
With any base conditions, any clause,
To tyrannize my heart, and to Constantia
Enslave my hand devoted to another.
The hint you just now gave of that alliance,

You must imagine, wakes my fear.   But know,
In this alone I will not bear dispute,
Not even from thee, Siffredi!—Let the council
Be strait assembled, and the will there open'd :
Thence issue speedy orders to convene,
This day ere noon, the senate : where those barons,
Who now are in Palermo, will attend,
To pay their ready homage to the king,
" Their rightful king, who claims his native crown,
" And will not be a king by deeds and parchments."

Sif. I go, my liege.   But once again permit me,
To tell you——Now, is the trying crisis,
That must determine of your future reign.
Oh, with heroic rigour watch your heart!
And to the sovereign duties of the king,
Th' unequall'd pleasures of a god on earth,
Submit the common joys, the common passions,
Nay, even the virtues of the private man.

Tan. Of that no more.   They not oppose, but aid,
Invigorate, cherish, and reward each other.
" The kind all-ruling wisdom is no tyrant."

[*Exit* Siffredi.

Tan. Now, generous Sigismunda, comes my turn
To shew my love was not of thine unworthy,
When fortune bade me blush to look to thee.
But what is fortune to the wish of love ?
A miserable bankrupt!   " Oh, 'tis poor,
" 'Tis scanty all, whate'er we can bestow !
" The wealth of kings is wretchedness and want!"
Quick, let me find her! taste that highest joy,

Th' exalted heart can know, the mix'd effusion
Of gratitude and love!—Behold, she comes!

Enter SIGISMUNDA.

Tan. My fluttering soul was all on wing to find thee,
My love, my Sigismunda!

Sif. Oh, my Tancred!
Tell me, what means this mystery and gloom
That lowers around? Just now, involv'd in thought,
My father shot athwart me—You, my lord,
Seem strangely mov'd—I fear some dark event,
From the king's death to trouble our repose,
That tender calm we in the woods of Belmont
So happily enjoy'd——Explain this hurry,
What means it? Say.

Tan. It means that we are happy!
Beyond our most romantic wishes happy!

Sig. You but perplex me more.

Tan. It means, my fairest,
That thou art queen of Sicily; and I
The happiest of mankind! " than monarch more!"
Because with thee I can adorn my throne.
Manfred, who fell by tyrant William's rage,
Fam'd Roger's lineal issue, was my father. [*Pausing.*
You droop, my love; dejected on a sudden;
You seem to mourn my fortune—The soft tear
Springs in thy eye—Oh, let me kiss it off——
Why this, my Sigismunda?

Sig. Royal Tancred,
None at your glorious fortune can like me

Rejoice ;—yet me alone, of all Sicilians,

It makes unhappy.

   Tan. I should hate it then !

Should throw, with scorn, the splendid ruin from
       me !—

No, Sigismunda, 'tis my hope with thee

To share it, whence it draws its richest value.

   Sig. You are my sovereign—I at humble distance—

   Tan. Thou art my queen! the sovereign of my soul!

" **You** never reign'd with such triumphant lustre,

" **Such** winning charms as now ; yet, thou art still"

The dear, the tender, generous Sigismunda !

" Who, with a heart exalted far above

" Those selfish views that charm the common breast,

" Stoop'd from the height of life and courted beauty,

" Then, then, to love me, when I seem'd of fortune

" The hopeless outcast, when I had no friend,

" None to protect and own me, but thy father.

" And wouldst thou claim all goodness to thyself ?

" Canst thou thy Tancred deem so dully form'd,

" Of such gross clay, just as I reach'd the point—

" A point my wildest hopes could ne'er imagine—

" In that great moment, full of every virtue,

" That I should then so mean a traitor prove

" To the best bliss and honour of mankind,

" So much disgrace the human heart, as then,

" For the dead form of flattery and pomp,

' The faithless joys of courts, to quit kind truth,

' The cordial sweets of friendship and of love,

" The life of life ! my all, my Sigismunda !

" I could upbraid thy fears, call them unkind,

" Cruel, unjust, an outrage to my heart,

" Did they not spring from love.

   " *Sig.* Think not, my lord,

" That to such vulgar doubts I can descend."

Your heart, I know, disdains the little thought

Of changing with the vain, external change

Of circumstance and fortune. " Rather thence

" It would, with rising ardour, greatly feel

" A noble pride, to shew itself the same."

But, ah! the hearts of kings are not their own.

" There is a haughty duty that subjects them

" To chains of state, to wed the public welfare,

" And not indulge the tender, private virtues."

Some high-descended princess, who will bring

New power and interest to your throne, demands

Your royal hand—perhaps Constantia——

   Tan. She!

Oh, name her not! were I this moment free

And disengag'd as he who " never felt,

" The powerful eye of beauty," never sigh'd

For matchless worth like thine, I should abhor

All thoughts of that alliance. Her fell father

Most basely murder'd mine; " and she, his daughter,

" Supported by his barbarous party still,

" His pride inherits, his imperious spirit,

" And insolent pretensions to my throne."

And canst thou deem me, then, so poorly tame,

So cool a traitor to my father's blood,

As from the prudent cowardice of state

E'er to submit to such a base proposal?
" Detested thought! Oh, doubly, doubly hateful!
" From the two strongest passions; from aversion
" To this Constantia—and from love to thee.
" Custom, 'tis true, a venerable tyrant,
" O'er servile man extends a blind dominion:
" The pride of kings enslaves them; their ambition,
" Or interest, lords it o'er the better passions.
" But vain their talk, mask'd under specious words
" Of station, duty, and of public good."
They whom just Heaven has to a throne exalted,
To guard the rights and liberties of others,
What duty binds them to betray their own!
" For me, my free-born heart shall bear no dictates,
" But those of truth and honour; wear no chains,
" But the dear chains of love, and Sigismunda!"
Or if indeed, my choice must be directed
By views of public good, whom shall I choose
So fit to grace, to dignify a crown,
And beam sweet mercy on a happy people,
As thee, my love? Whom place upon my throne
But thee, descended from the good Siffredi?
" 'Tis fit that heart be thine, which drew from him
" Whate'er can make it worthy thy acceptance."
    Sig. Cease, cease to raise my hopes above my duty.
Charm me no more, my Tancred!—Oh, that we
In those blest woods, where first you won my soul,
Had pass'd our gentle days; far from the toil
And pomp of courts! Such is the wish of love;
" Of love that, with delightful weakness, knows

C ij

" No bliss, and no ambition but itself.
" But in the world's full light, those charming
   dreams,
" Those fond illusions vanish.   Awful duties !
" The tyranny of men, even your own heart,
" Where lurks a sense your passion stifles now,
" And proud imperious honour call you from me."
'Tis all in vain—you cannot hush a voice
That murmurs here——I must not be persuaded !

 Tan. [*Kneeling.*] Hear me, thou soul of all my
   hopes and wishes !
And witness Heaven, prime source of love and joy !
Not a whole warring world combin'd against me ;
" Its pride, its splendor, its imposing forms,
" Nor interest, nor ambition, nor the face
" Of solemn state, not even thy father's wisdom,"
Shall ever shake my faith to Sigismunda !
     [*Trumpets and acclamations heard.*
But, **hark** ! the public voice to duties call me,
Which with unwearied zeal I will discharge ;
And thou, yes, thou, shalt be my bright reward——
Yet—ere I go—to hush thy lovely fears,
Thy delicate objections——[*Writes his name.*] Take
   this blank,
Sign'd with my name, and give it to thy father :
Tell him, 'tis my command, it be fill'd up
With a most strict and solemn marriage-contract.
How dear each tie ! how charming to my soul !
That more unites me to my Sigismunda.

For thee, and for my people's good to live,
Is all the bliss which sovereign power can give.

[*Exeunt.*

ACT II.   SCENE I.

A grand Saloon. *Enter* SIFFREDI.

Siffredi.

So far 'tis well——The late king's will proceeds
Upon the plan I counsel'd; that Prince Tancred
Shall make Constantia partner of his throne.
Oh, great, oh, wish'd event! " whence the dire seeds
" Of dark intestine broils, of civil war,
" And all its dreadful miseries and crimes,
" Shall be for ever rooted from the land.
" May these dim eyes, long blasted by the rage
" Of cruel faction and my country's woes,
" Tir'd with the toils and vanities of life,
" Behold this period, then be clos'd in peace!"
But how this mighty obstacle surmount,
Which love has thrown betwixt? " Love, that dis-
          turbs
" The schemes of wisdom still; that, wing'd with
          passion,
" Blind and impetuous in its fond pursuits,
" Leaves the grey-headed reason far behind.
" Alas, how frail the state of human bliss!
" When even our honest passions oft destroy it.

C iij

" I was to blame, in solitude and shades,
" Infectious scenes! to trust their youthful hearts.
" Would I had mark'd the rising flame, that now
" Burns out with dangerous force!"—My daughter
          owns
Her passion for the king; she trembling own'd it,
With prayers, and tears, and tender supplications,
That almost shook my firmness—And this blank,
Which his rash fondness gave her, shews how much,
To what a wild extravagance he loves—
I see no means—it foils my deepest thought—
How to controul this madness of the king,
That wears the face of virtue, and will thence
Disdain restraint, " will, from his generous heart,
" Borrow new rage, even speciously oppose
" To reason reason"——But it must be done.
" My own advice, of which I more and more
" Approve, the strict conditions of the will,
" Highly demand his marriage with Constantia;
" Or else her party has a fair pretence——
" And all at once is horror and confusion——
" How issue from this maze?"——The crowding
          barons
Here summon'd to the palace, meet already,
To pay their homage, and confirm the will.
On a few moments hang the public fate,
On a few hasty moments——Ha! there shone
A gleam of hope—Yes, with this very paper
I yet will save him——" Necessary means,
" For good and noble ends, can ne'er be wrong.

" In that resistless, that peculiar case,
" Deceit is truth and virtue——But how hold
" This lion in the toil ?——Oh, I will form it
" Of such a fatal thread, twist it so strong
" With all the ties of honour and of duty,
" That his most desperate fury shall not break
" The honest snare."——Here is the royal hand—
I will beneath it write a perfect, full,
And absolute agreement to the will ;
Which read before the nobles of the realm
Assembled, in the sacred face of Sicily,
Constantia present, every heart and eye
Fix'd on their monarch, every tongue applauding,
He must submit, his dream of love must vanish—
It shall be done——To me, I know, 'tis ruin ;
But safety to the public, to the king.
I will not reason more, " I will not listen
" Even to the voice of honour."—No—'tis fix'd !
I here devote me for my prince and country ;
Let them be safe, and let me nobly perish !
Behold, Earl Osmond comes, without whose aid
My schemes are all in vain.

Enter OSMOND.

Osm. My Lord Siffredi,
I from the council hasten'd to Constantia,
And have accomplish'd what we there propos'd.
The princess to the will submits her claims.
She with her presence means to grace the senate,
And of your royal charge, young Tancred's hand,

Accept. " At first, indeed, it shock'd her hopes
" Of reigning sole, this new, surprising scene
" Of Manfred's son, appointed by the king,
" With her joint heir——But I so fully shew'd
" The justice of the case, the public good,
" And sure establish'd peace which thence would rise,
" Join'd to the strong necessity that urg'd her,
" If on Sicilia's throne she meant to sit,
" As to the wise disposal of the will
" Her high ambition tam'd." Methought, besides,
I could discern, that not from prudence merely
She to this choice submitted.

    Sif. Noble Osmond,
You have in this done to the public great
And signal service. Yes, I must avow it;
This frank and ready instance of your zeal,
In such a trying crisis of the state,
" When interest and ambition might have warp'd
" Your views, I own this truly generous virtue"
Upbraids the rashness of my former judgment.

    Osm. Siffredi, no. To you belongs the praise;
" The glorious work is yours. Had I not seiz'd,
" Improv'd the wish'd occasion to root out
" Division from the land, and sav'd my country,
" I had been base and infamous for ever."
'Tis you, my lord, to whom the many thousands,
That by the barbarous sword of civil war
Had fallen inglorious, owe their lives; " to you
" The sons of this fair isle, from her first peers
" Down to the swain who tills her golden plains,

" Owe their safe homes, their soft domestic hours,
" And through late time posterity shall bless you,
" You who advis'd this will."—I blush to think
I have so long oppos'd the best good man
In Sicily——" With what impartial care
" Ought we to watch o'er prejudice and passion,
" Nor trust too much the jaundic'd eye of party !
" Henceforth its vain delusions I renounce,
" Its hot determinations, that confine
" All merit and all virtue to itself."
To yours I join my hand ; with you will own
No interest and no party but my country.
Nor is your friendship only my ambition :
There is a dearer name, the name of father,
By which I should rejoice to call Siffredi.
Your daughter's hand would to the public weal
Unite my private happiness.

Sif. My lord,
You have my glad consent.   To be allied
To your distinguish'd family and merit,
I shall esteem an honour.   From my soul
I here embrace Earl Osmond as my friend
And son.

Osm. You make him happy.   This assent,
" So frank and warm, to what I long have wish'd,
" Engages all my gratitude ; at once,
" In the first blossom, it matures our friendship."
I from this moment vow myself the friend
And zealous servant of Siffredi's house.

Enter an Officer belonging to the Court.

Off. [*To* Siffredi.] The king, my lord, demand
     your speedy presence.

Sif. I will attend him strait—Farewell, my lord;
The senate meets : there, a few moments hence,
I will rejoin you.

Osm. There, my noble lord,
We will complete this salutary work ;
Will there begin a new auspicious era.

                         [*Exeunt* Siffredi *and Officer*

Siffredi gives his daughter to my wishes—
But does she give herself ? Gay, young, and flatter'd,
Perhaps engag'd, will she her youthful heart
Yield to my harsher, uncomplying years ?
I am not form'd, by flattery and praise,
By sighs and tears, and all the whining trade
Of love, to feed a fair-one's vanity ;
To charm at once and spoil her. These soft arts
Nor suit my years nor temper ; these be left
To boys and doting age. A prudent father,
By nature charg'd to guide and rule her choice,
Resigns his daughter to a husband's power,
Who with superior dignity, with reason,
And manly tenderness, will ever love her ;
Not first a kneeling slave, and then a tyrant.

Enter Barons.

" My lords, I greet you well. This wondrous day
" Unites us all in amity and friendship.

' We meet to-day with open hearts and looks,
' Not gloom'd by party, scowling on each other,
' But all the children of one happy isle,
' The social sons of liberty.   No pride,
' No passion now, no thwarting views divide us :
' Prince Manfred's line, at last to William's join'd,
' Combine us in one family of brothers.
' This to the late good king's well-ordered will,
" And wise Siffredi's generous care, we owe.
" I truly give you joy.   First of you all,
" I here renounce those errors and divisions
" That have so long disturb'd our peace; and seem'd,
" Fermenting still, to threaten new commotions——
" By time instructed, let us not disdain
" To quit mistakes.   We all, my lords, have err'd.
" Men may, I find, be honest, though they differ.
   " 1st *Baron.* Who follows not, my lord, the fair
       example
" You set us all, whate'er be his pretence,
" Loves not with single and unbias'd heart,
" His country as he ought.
   " 2nd *Baron.* Oh, beauteous peace !
" Sweet union of a state ! what else but thou
" Gives safety, strength, and glory to a people ?
" I bow, lord constable, beneath the snow
" Of many years ; yet in my breast revives
" A youthful flame.   Methinks, I see again
" Those gentle days renew'd, that bless'd our isle,
" Ere by this wasteful fury of division,
" Worse than our Ætna's most destructive fires,

" It desolated sunk. I see our plains
" Unbounded waving with the gifts of harvest;
" Our seas with commerce throng'd ; our busy ports
" With cheerful toil. , Our Enna blooms afresh ;
" Afresh the sweets of thymy Hybla flow.
" Our nymphs and shepherds sporting in each vale,
" Inspire new song, and wake the pastoral reed—
" The tongue of age is fond—Come, come, my sons ;
" I long to see this prince, of whom the world
" Speaks largely well—His father was my friend,
" The brave unhappy Manfred—Come, my lords ;
" We tarry here too long.

Enter two Officers keeping off the Crowd.

" *One of the Crowd.* Shew us **our** king,
" The valiant Manfred's son, who lov'd the people—
" We must, we will behold him—Give us way.

" *1st Off.* **Pray,** gentlemen, give back—it must
        not be—
" Give back, I pray——on such a glad occasion,
" I would not ill entreat the lowest of you.

" *2nd Man of the Crowd.* Nay, **give us** but a glimpse
        of our young king.

" We, more than any Baron of them all,
" Will pay him due allegiance.

" *2nd Off.* Friends—indeed
" You cannot pass this way——We have strict orders,
" To keep for him himself, and for the Barons,
" All these apartments clear——Go to the gate
" That fronts the sea, you there will find admission.

" *Omnes.* Long live king Tancred! Manfred's son
—huzza!   [*Crowd goes off.*"

Enter 1st *Officer.*

1st Off. *My lord, the king is rob'd, the senate sits,*
And waits your presence.   [*Exeunt* Osmond *and Barons.*
                    [*Shouts within.*

Enter 2nd *Officer.*

2nd Off. *I have not seen*
So wild a tumult; the town is mad with transport;
Shew us our king, they cry, our Norman king,
The valiant Manfred's son, who lov'd the people.
In vain I told 'em, that we had strict orders
To keep for him himself, and for the Barons,
All these apartments clear.   Nought could
Appease their storm **of zeal**; *'till at*
The northern gate, that fronts the sea,
I promis'd them admittance.

1st *Off.* I do not marvel at their rage of joy:
He is a brave and amiable prince.
When in my Lord Siffredi's house I liv'd,
Ere by his favour I obtain'd this office,
I there remember well the young Count Tancred.
To see him and to love him were the same;
He was so noble in his ways, yet still
So affable and mild——Well, well, old Sicily,
Yet happy days await **thee !**

2nd *Off.* Grant it, Heaven!
" We have seen sad and troublesome times enough."

D

He is, they say, to wed the late king's sister,
'Constantia.

   1*st Off.* Friend, **of** that I greatly doubt.
Or I mistake, or Lord Siffredi's daughter,
The gentle Sigismunda, has his heart.
If one may judge by kindly cordial looks,
And fond assiduous care **to** please each other,
Most certainly they love——Oh, be they blest,
As they deserve! It were great pity aught
Should part **a** matchless pair; the glory he,
And she the blooming grace of Sicily!

   2*nd Off.* My Lord Rodolpho comes.

      Enter RODOLPHO *from the Senate.*

  Rod. **My** honest friends,
You may retire. [*Officers go out.*] A storm is in the
      wind.
This will perplexes all. No, Tancred never
Can stoop to these conditions, which at once
Attack his rights, his honour, and his love.
" Those wise old men, those plodding, grave, state
      pedants,
" **Forget the** course of youth; their crooked pru-
      dence,
" To baseness verging still, forgets to take
" Into their fine-spun schemes the generous heart,
" That, through the cobweb system bursting, lays
" Their labours waste—So will this business prove,
" **Or** I mistake the king—back from the pomp
" He seem'd at first to shrink, and round his brow

" I mark'd a gath'ring cloud, when, by his side,
" As if design'd to share the public homage,
" He saw the tyrant's daughter. But confess'd,
" At least to me the doubling tempest frown'd,
" And shook his swelling bosom," when he heard
Th' unjust, the base conditions of the will.
Uncertain, tost in cruel agitation,
He oft, methought, address'd himself to speak,
And interrupt Siffredi; who appear'd,
With conscious haste, to dread that interruption,
And hurry'd on——But hark! I hear a noise,
As if th' assembly rose—" Ha! Sigismunda,
" Oppress'd with grief, and wrapp'd in pensive
   sorrow,
" Passes along.

  " [Sigismunda *and attendants pass through the back
  scene.*]"

Enter LAURA.

Laura. Your high-prais'd friend, the king,
Is false, most vilely false. The meanest slave
Had shewn a nobler heart; " nor grossly thus,
" By the first bait ambition spread, been gull'd."
He Manfred's son! away! it cannot be!
The son of that brave prince could ne'er " betray
" Those rights so long usurp'd from his great father,
" Which he, this day, by such amazing fortune,
" Had just regain'd; he ne'er could" sacrifice
All faith, all honour, gratitude, and love,
" Even just resentment of his father's fate,

" And pride itself; whate'er exalts a man
" Above the groveling sons of peasant mud,"
All in a moment—And for what? why, truly,
For kind permission, gracious leave, to sit
On his own throne with tyrant William's daughter!

 Rod. I stand amaz'd—You surely wrong him,
   Laura.
There must be some mistake.

 Laura. There can be none!
Siffredi read his full and free consent
Before th' applauding senate.   True indeed,
A small remain of shame, a timorous weakness,
Even dastardly in falsehood, made him blush
To act this scene in Sigismunda's eye,
Who sunk beneath his perfidy and baseness.
Hence, till to-morrow he adjourn'd the senate!
To-morrow, fix'd with infamy to crown him!
Then, leading off his gay, triumphant princess,
He left the poor unhappy Sigismunda
To bend her trembling steps to that sad home
His faithless vows will render hateful to her——
He comes—Farewell——I cannot bear his presence!
        [*Exit* Laura.

  Enter TANCRED *and* SIFFREDI, *meeting.*

 Tan. Avoid me, hoary traitor! Go, Rodolpho,
Give orders that all passages this way
Be shut—Defend me from a hateful world,
The bane of peace and honour—then return—
        [*Exit* Rodolpho.

What! dost thou haunt me still? Oh, monstrous
      insult!
Unparallel'd indignity! Just Heaven!
Was ever king, was ever man so treated;
So trampled into baseness?
  Sif. Here, my liege,
Here strike! I nor deserve, nor ask for mercy.
  " *Tan.* Distraction!—Oh, my soul!—Hold, rea-
      son, hold
" Thy giddy seat—Oh, this inhuman outrage
" Unhinges thought!
  " *Sif.* Exterminate thy servant."
  Tan. All, all but this I could have borne—but this!
This daring insolence beyond example!
This murderous stroke, that stabs my peace for ever!
That wounds me there—there! where the human
      heart
Most exquisitely feels———
  Sif. Oh, bear it not,
My royal lord; appease on me your vengeance!
  Tan. Did ever tyrant image aught so cruel!
The lowest slave that crawls upon the earth,
Robb'd of each comfort Heaven bestows on mortals,
On the bare ground has still his virtue left,
The sacred treasure of an honest heart,
Which thou hast dar'd, with rash, audacious hand,
And impious fraud, in me to violate———
  Sif. Behold, my lord, that rash, audacious hand,
Which not repents its crime—Oh, glorious, happy!
If by my ruin I can save your honour.

Tan. Such honour I renounce; with sovereign scorn
Greatly detest it, and its mean adviser!
Hast thou not dar'd beneath my name to shelter,
" My name, for other purposes design'd,
" Given from the fondness of a faithful heart,
" With the best love o'erflowing!—Hast thou not"
Beneath thy sovereign's name, basely presum'd
To shield a lie—a lie, in public utter'd,
To all deluded Sicily? But know,
This poor contrivance is as weak as base.
" In such a wretched toil none can be held
" But fools and cowards——Soon thy flimsy arts,
" Touch'd by my just, my burning indignation,
" Shall burst like threads in flame—Thy doating
          , prudence
" But more secures the purpose it would shake.
" Had my resolves been wavering and doubtful,
" This would confirm them, make them fix'd as fate;
" This adds the only motive that was wanting
" To urge them on through war and desolation."
What! marry her! Constantia! her! the daughter
Of the fell tyrant who destroy'd my father!
The very thought is madness! Ere thou seest
The torch of Hymen light these hated nuptials,
Thou shalt behold Sicilia wrapt in flames,
Her cities raz'd, her vallies drench'd with slaughter—
Love set aside, my pride assumes the quarrel;
My honour now is up; in spite of thee,
A world combin'd against me, I will give
This scatter'd will in fragments to the winds,

Assert my rights, the freedom of my heart,
Crush all who dare oppose me to the dust,
And heap perdition on thee!

Sif. Sir, 'tis just.
Exhaust on me thy rage; I claim it all.
But for these public threats thy passion utters,
'Tis what thou canst not do.

Tan. I cannot! ha!
" Driven to the dreadful brink of such dishonour,
" Enough to make the tamest coward brave,
" And into fierceness rouse the mildest nature,"
What shall arrest my vengeance? Who?

Sif. Thyself.

Tan. Away! Dare not to justify thy crime!
That, that alone can aggravate its horror,
Add insolence to insolence—perhaps
May make my rage forget——

Sif. Oh, let it burst
On this grey head, devoted to thy service!
But when the storm has vented all its fury,
Thou then must hear—nay more, I know thou wilt—
Wilt hear the calm, yet stronger voice of reason.
" Thou must reflect that a whole people's safety,
" The weal of trusted millions, should bear down,
" Thyself the judge, the fondest partial pleasure."
Thou must reflect that there are other duties,
" A nobler pride, a more exalted honour,
" Superior pleasures far, that will oblige,
" Compel thee, to abide by this my deed,
" Unwarranted perhaps in common justice,

" But which necessity, ev'n virtue's tyrant,
" With awful voice commanded"—Yes, thou must,
In calmer hours, divest thee of thy love,
These common passions of the vulgar breast,
This boiling heat of youth, and be a king,
The lover of thy people!

Tan. " Truths, ill employ'd,
" Abus'd to colour guilt!——A king! a king!"
Yes, I will be a king, but not a slave;
In this will be a king; in this my people
Shall learn to judge how I will guard their rights,
When they behold me vindicate my own.
But have I, say, been treated like a king?---
Heavens! could I stoop to such outrageous usage!
I were a mean, a shameless wretch, unworthy
To wield a sceptre in a land of slaves,
A soil abhorr'd of virtue; should belie
My fathers blood, belie those very maxims,
At other times you taught my youth——Siffredi!

[*In a softened tone of voice.*

Sif. Behold, my prince, thy poor old servant,
Whose darling care, these twenty years, has been
To nurse thee up to virtue; " who, for thee,
" Thy glory and thy weal, renounces all,
" All interest or ambition can pour forth;
" What many a selfish father would pursue
" Through treachery and crimes:" behold him here,
Bent on his feeble knees, to beg, conjure thee,
With tears to beg thee to controul thy passion,
And save thyself, thy honour, and thy people!

Kneeling with me, behold the many thousands
To thy protection trusted; fathers, mothers,
The sacred front of venerable age,
The tender-virgin, and the helpless infant ;
" The ministers of Heav'n, those who maintain,
" Around thy throne, the majesty of rule ;
" And those whose labour, scorch'd by winds and sun,
" Feeds the rejoicing public ;" see them all
Here at thy feet conjuring thee to save them
From misery and war, from crimes and rapine !
" Can there be aught, kind Heaven, in self-indul-
         gence
" To weigh down these, this aggregate of love,
" With which compar'd, the dearest private passion
" Is but the wafted dust upon the balance ?"
Turn not away——Oh, is there not some part
In thy great heart, so sensible to kindness,
And generous warmth, some nobler part, to feel
The prayers and tears of these, the mingled voice
Of heaven and earth ?
  Tan. There is, and thou hast touch'd it.
Rise, rise, Siffredi——Oh, thou hast undone me !
Unkind old man !——Oh, ill-entreated Tancred !
Which way soe'er I turn, dishonour rears
Her hideous front—and misery and ruin.
" Was it for this you took such care to form me !
" For this imbu'd me with the quickest sense
" Of shame ; these finer feelings, that ne'er vex
" The common mass of mortals, dully happy
" **In** bless'd insensibility ? Oh, rather

"' You should have sear'd my heart, taught me that
            power
" And splendid interest lord it still o'er virtue ;
" That, gilded by prosperity and pride,
" There is no shame, no meanness ; temper'd thus,
" I had been fit to rule a venal world.
" Alas ! what meant thy wantonness of prudence ?"
Why have you rais'd this miserable conflict
Betwixt the duties of the king and man ? `
Set virtue against virtue ?——" Ah, Siffredi !
" 'Tis thy superfluous, thy unfeeling wisdom,
" That has involv'd me in a maze of error
" Almost beyond retreat"——But hold, my soul,
Thy steady purpose——Tost by various passions
To this eternal anchor keep——There is,
Can be no public without private virtue——
Then, mark me well, observe what I command ;
" It is the sole expedient now remaining——"
To-morrow, when the senate meets again,
Unfold the whole, unravel the deceit ;
" Nor that alone ; try to repair its mischief ;
" There all thy power, thy eloquence and interest
" Exert to reinstate me in my rights,
" And from thy own dark snares to disembroil me."——
Start not, my lord—This must and shall be done !
Or here our friendship ends—Howe'er disguis'd,
Whatever thy pretence, thou art a traitor.

  Sif. I should indeed deserve the name of traitor,
And even a traitor's fate, had I so slightly,

From principles so weak, done what I did,
As e'er to disavow it———

Tan. Ha!

Sif. My liege,

Expect not this———Though practis'd long **in courts,**
I have not so far learn'd their subtle trade,
To veer obedient with each gust of passion.
I honour thee, I venerate thy orders,
But **honour more my duty.**   Nought on earth
Shall ever shake me from that solid rock,
Nor smiles, nor frowns.———

Tan. You will not then?

Sif. I cannot.

Tan. Away! begone!—Oh, my Rodolpho, **come,**
And save me from this traitor! Hence, I say.
" Avoid my presence strait! and know, old man,
" Thou, my worst foe beneath the mask of friendship,
" Who, not content to trample in the dust
" My dearest rights, dost with cool insolence
" Persist, and call it duty; **hadst** thou not
" A daughter that protects thee, thou shouldst feel
" The vengeance thou deservest."———No reply!
Away!   [*Exit* Siffredi.

Enter RODOLPHO.

Rod. What can incense my prince so highly
Against his friend Siffredi!

Tan. Friend! Rodolpho?
When I have told thee what this friend has done,
How play'd me like a boy, a base-born wretch,

Who had nor heart nor spirit, thou wilt stand
Amaz'd, and wonder at my stupid patience.

" *Rod.* I heard, with mix'd astonishment and grief,
" The king's unjust, dishonourable will,
" Void in itself—I saw you stung with rage,
" And writhing in the snare ; just as I went,
" At your command to wait you here—but that
" Was the king's deed, not his.

" *Man.* Oh, he advis'd it !
" These many years he has in secret hatch'd
" This black contrivance, glories in the scheme,
" And proudly plumes him with his traiterous virtue.
" But that was nought, Rodolpho, nothing, nothing !
" Oh, that was gentle, blameless to what follow'd !
" I had, my friend, to Sigismunda given,
" To hush her fears, in the full gush of fondness,
" A blank sign'd with my hand—and he, Oh,
               heavens !
" Was ever such a wild attempt !—he wrote
" Beneath my name an absolute compliance
" To this detested will , nay, dar'd to read it
" Before myself, on my insulted throne
" His idle pageant plac'd——Oh, words are weak
" To paint the pangs, the rage, the indignation,
" That whirl'd from thought to thought my soul in
               tempest,
" Now on the point to burst, and now by shame
" Repress'd——But in the face of Sicily,
" All mad with acclamation, what, Rodolpho,
" What could I do ? the sole relief that rose

" To my distracted mind, was to adjourn
" Th' assembly till to-morrow—But to-morrow
" What can be done ?—Oh, it avails not what !
" I care not what is done—My only care
" Is how to clear my faith with Sigismunda.
" She thinks me false ! She cast a look that kill'd me !
" Oh ! I am base in Sigismunda's eye !
" The lowest of mankind, the most perfidious !
   " *Rod.* This was a strain of insolence indeed,
" A daring outrage of so strange a nature
" As stuns me quite——
   " *Tan.* Curs'd be my timid prudence,
" That dash'd not back, that moment in his face,
" The bold presumptuous lie !—and curs'd this hand,
" That from a start of poor dissimulation,
" Led off my Sigismunda's hated rival.
" Ah, then ! what, poison'd by the false appearance,
" What, Sigismunda, were thy thoughts of me ?
" How, in the silent bitterness of soul,
" How didst thou scorn me ! hate mankind, thyself,
" For trusting to the vows of faithless Tancred ?
" For such I seem'd—I was—the thought distracts
            me !
" I should have cast a flattering world aside,
" Rush'd from my throne, before them all avow'd
            her,
" The choice, the glory of my free-born heart,
" And spurn'd the shameful fetters thrown upon it —
" Instead of that—confusion !—what I did

E

" Has clinch'd the chain, confirm'd Siffredi's crime,
" And fix'd me down to infamy!
  " *Rod.* My Lord,
" Blamé not the conduct which your situation
" Tore from your tortur'd heart—What could you
            do?
" Had you, so circumstanc'd, in open senate,
" Before th' astonish'd public, with no friends
" Prepar'd, no party form'd, affronted thus
" The haughty Princess and her powerful faction,
" Supported by this will, the sudden stroke,
" Abrupt and premature, might have recoil'd
" Upon yourself, even your own friends revolted,
" And turn'd at once the public scale against you.
" Besides, consider, had you then detected
" In its fresh guilt this action of Siffredi,
" You must with signal vengeance have chastis'd
" The treasonable deed—Nothing so mean
" As weak insulted power that dares not punish.
" And how would that have suited with your love;
" His daughter present too? Trust me, your conduct,
" Howe'er abhorrent to a heart like yours,
" Was fortunate and wise—Not that I mean
" E'er to advise submission———
  " *Tan.* Heavens! submission———
" Could I descend to bear it, even in thought,
" Despise me, you, the world, and Sigismunda!
" Submission!—No!—To morrow's glorious light
" Shall flash discovery on the scene of baseness.
" Whatever be the risque, by heavens, to-morrow,

" I will o'erturn the dirty lie-built schemes
" Of these old men, and shew my faithful senate,
" That Manfred's son knows to assert and wear,
" With undiminish'd dignity, that crown
" This unexpected day has plac'd upon him."
But this, my friend, " these stormy gusts of pride
" Are foreign to my love——Till Sigismunda
" Be disabus'd, my breast is tumult all,
" And can obey no settled course of reason.
" I see her still, I feel her powerful image,
" That look, where with reproach complaint was
            mix'd,
" Big with soft wo, and gentle indignation,
" Which seem'd at once to pity and to scorn me——
" Oh, let me find her! I too long have left
" My Sigismunda to converse with tears,
" A prey to thoughts that picture me a villain.
" But ah! how, clogg'd with this accursed state,
" A tedious world, shall I now find access?
" Her father too—Ten thousand horrors crowd
" Into the wild, fantastic eye of love——
" Who knows what he may do? Come then, my
            friend,
" And by thy sister's hand, oh, let me steal
" A letter to her bosom—I no longer
" Can bear her absence, by the just contempt
" She now must brand me with, inflam'd to madness.
" Fly, my Rodolpho, fly! engage thy sister
" To aid my letter." *This black, unheard of outrage,*
I cannot now impart——'Till Sigismunda

Be disabus'd, my breast is tumult all.
Come, then, my friend, and by the hand of Laura,
Oh, let me steal a letter to her bosom,
And this " very" evening
Secure an interview—I would not bear
This rack another day, not for my kingdom.
" Till then, deep plung'd in solitude and shades,
" I will not see the hated face of man."
 Thought drives on thought, on passions passions roll;
 Her smiles alone can calm my raging soul. [*Exeunt.*

ACT III. SCENE I.

A Chamber. SIGISMUNDA *alone, sitting in a disconso-*
late Posture.

Ah, tyrant prince! ah more than faithless Tancred!
Ungenerous and inhuman in thy falsehood!
Hadst thou this morning, when my hopeless heart,
Submissive to my fortune and my duty,
Had so much spirit left, as to be willing
To give thee back thy vows, ah! hadst thou then
Confess'd the sad necessity thy state
Impos'd upon thee, and with gentle friendship,
Since we must part at last, our parting soften'd;
I should indeed—I should have been unhappy,
But not to this extreme—" Amidst my grief,
" I had, with pensive pleasure, cherish'd still
" The sweet remembrance of thy former love,

" Thy image still had dwelt upon my soul,
" And made our guiltless woes not undelightful.
" But coolly thus—How couldst thou be so cruel?—
" Thus to revive my hopes, to sooth my love,
" And call forth all its tenderness, then sink me
" In black despair—What unrelenting pride
" Possess'd thy breast, that thou couldst bear unmov'd
" To see me bent beneath a weight of shame?
" Pangs thou canst never feel! How couldst thou
         drag me,
" In barbarous triumph at a rival's car?
" How make me witness to a sight of horror?
" That hand, which, but a few short hours ago,
" So wantonly abus'd my simple faith,
" Before th' attesting world given to another,
" Irrevocably given!—There was a time,
" When the least **cloud** that hung upon my brow,
" Perhaps imagin'd only, touch'd thy pity.
" Then, brighten'd often by the ready tear,
" Thy looks were softness all; then the quick heart,
" In every nerve alive, forgot itself,
" And for each other then we felt alone.
" **But now, alas! those tender** days are fled;
" Now thou canst see me wretched, pierc'd with an-
         guish,
" With studied anguish of thy own creating,
" Nor wet thy harden'd eye—Hold, let me think—
" I wrong thee sure; thou canst not be so base,
" As meanly in my misery to triumph—
" What is it then!—'Tis fickleness of nature,

E iij

" 'Tis sickly love extinguish'd by ambition——"
Is there, kind Heaven, no constancy in man ?
No stedfast truth, no generous fix'd affection,
That can bear up against a selfish world ?
No, there is none—Even Tancred is inconstant !

                                        [*Rising.*

Hence ! let me fly this scene !—Whate'er I see,
These roofs, these walls, each object that surrounds
        me,
Are tainted with his vows—But whither fly ?
The groves are worse, the soft retreat of Belmont,
Its deepening glooms, gay lawns, and airy summits,
Will wound my busy memory to torture,
And all its shades will whisper—faithless Tancred !—
My father comes—How, sunk in this disorder,
Shall I sustain his presence ?

                Enter SIFFREDI.

  Sif. Sigismunda,
My dearest child ! I grieve to find thee thus
A prey to tears. " I know the powerful cause
" From which they flow, and therefore can excuse
        them,
" But not their wilful obstinate continuance.
" Come, rouse thee then, call up thy drooping spirit,"
Awake to reason from this dream of love,
And shew the world thou art Siffredi's daughter.
  Sig. Alas ! I am unworthy of that name.
  Sif. Thou art indeed to blame ; thou hast too rashly
Engag'd thy heart, without a father's sanction.

But this I can forgive. " The king has virtues,
" That plead thy full excuse ; nor was I void
" Of blame, to trust thee to those dangerous virtues.
" Then dread not my reproaches. Though he blames,
" Thy tender father pities more than blames thee.
" Thou art my daughter still ;" and, if thy heart
Will now resume its pride, assert itself,
And greatly rise superior to this trial,
I to my warmest confidence again
Will take thee, and esteem thee more my daughter.

Sig. Oh, you are gentler far than I deserve !
It is, it ever was, my darling pride,
To bend my soul to your supreme commands,
Your wisest will ; and though by love betray'd—
Alas ! and punish'd too—I have transgress'd
The nicest bounds of duty, yet I feel
A sentiment of tenderness, a source
Of filial nature springing in my breast,
That, should it kill me, shall controul this passion,
And make me all submission and obedience
To you my honour'd lord, the best of fathers.

Sif. Come to my arms, thou comfort of my age !
Thou only joy and hope of these grey hairs !
Come, let me take thee to a parent's heart ;
There, with the kindly aid of my advice,
Even with the dew of these paternal tears,
Revive and nourish this becoming spirit————
Then thou dost promise me, my Sigismunda————
Thy father stoops to make it his request—
Thou wilt resign thy fond presumptuous hopes,

And henceforth never more indulge one thought
That in the light of love regards the king?

Sig. Hopes I have none!—Those by this fatal day
Are blasted all—But from my soul to banish,
While weeping memory there retains her seat,
Thoughts which the purest bosom might have che-
   rish'd,
Once my delight, now even in anguish charming,
Is more, my lord, than I can promise.

Sif. Absence, and time, the softener of our passions,
Will conquer this. Meantime, I hope from thee
A generous great effort ; that thou wilt now
Exert thy utmost force, nor languish thus
Beneath the vain extravagance of love.
Let not thy father blush to hear it said,
His daughter was so weak, e'er to admit
A thought so void of reason, that a king
Should to his rank, his honour, and his glory,
The high important duties of a throne,
Even to his throne itself, madly prefer
A wild romantic passion, the fond child
Of youthful dreaming thought and vacant hours ;
That he should quit his Heaven-appointed station,
Desert his awful charge, the care of all
" The toiling millions which this isle contains ;
" Nay more, should plunge them into war and ruin,
" And all to sooth a sick imagination,
" A miserable weakness"—*What*, must for thee,
To make thee blest, Sicilia be unhappy ?
" The king himself, lost to the nobler sense

" Of manly praise, become the piteous hero
" Of some soft tale, and rush on sure destruction ?
" Canst thou, my daughter, let the monstrous thought
" Possess one moment thy perverted fancy ?"
Rouse thee, for shame ! and if a spark of virtue
Lies slumb'ring in thy soul, bid it blaze forth ;
Nor sink unequal to the glorious lesson,
This day thy lover gave thee from his throne.

Sig. Ah, that was not from virtue !—Had, my father,
That been his aim, I yield to what you say ;
" 'Tis powerful truth, unanswerable reason.
" Then, then, with sad but duteous resignation,
" I had submitted as became your daughter;
" But in that moment, when my humbled hopes
" Were to my duty reconcil'd, to raise them
" To yet a fonder height than e'er they knew,
" Then rudely dash them down——There is the sting !
" The blasting view is ever present to me——"
Why did you drag me to a sight so cruel ?

Sif. It was a scene to fire thy emulation.

Sig. It was a scene of perfidy !—But know,
I will do more than imitate the king—
For he is false !—I, though sincerely pierc'd
With the best, truest passion, ever touch'd
A virgin's breast, here vow to Heaven and you,
Though from my heart I cannot, from my hopes
To cast this prince—What would you more, my
        father ?

Sif. Yes, one thing more—thy father then is happy—
" Though by the voice of innocence and virtue

" Absolv'd, we live not to ourselves alone :
" A rigorous world with peremptory sway,
" Subjects us all, and even the noblest most."
This world from thee, my honour and thy own,
Demands one step ; a step, by which, convinc'd,
The king may see thy heart disdains to wear
A chain which his has greatly thrown aside.
" 'Tis fitting too, thy sex's pride commands thee,
" To shew th' approving world thou canst resign,
" As well as he, nor with inferior spirit,
" A passion fatal to the public weal."
But above all, thou must root out for ever
From the king's breast the least remain of hope,
And henceforth make his mentioned love dishonour.
These things, my daughter, that must needs be done
Can but this way be done—by the safe refuge,
The sacred shelter of a husband's arms.
And there is one——

   Sig. Good heavens ! what means my lord ?

   Sif. One of illustrious family, high rank,
Yet still of higher dignity and merit,
Who can and will protect thee ; one to awe
The king himself—Nay, hear me, Sigismunda—
The noble Osmond courts thee for his bride,
And has my plighted word—This day—

   Sig. [*Kneeling.*] My father !
Let me with trembling arms embrace thy knees !
Oh, if you ever wish to see me happy ;
If e'er in infant years I gave you joy,
When, as I prattling twin'd around your neck,

You snatch'd me to your bosom, kiss'd my eyes,
And melting said you saw my mother there;
Oh, save me from that worst severity
Of fate! Oh, outrage not my breaking heart
To that degree!—I cannot!—'tis impossible!——
So soon withdraw it, give it to another—
" Hear me, my dearest father; hear the voice
" Of nature and humanity, that plead
" As well as justice for me!——Not to choose
" Without your wise direction may be duty;
" But still my choice is free—that is a right,
" Which even the lowest slave can never lose.
" And would you thus degrade me?—make me base?
" For such it were to give my worthless person
" Without my heart, an injury to Osmond,
" The highest can be done"—Let me, my lord—
Or I shall die, shall, by the sudden change,
Be to distraction shock'd—Let me wear out
My hapless days in solitude and silence,
Far from the malice of a prying world;
At least—you cannot sure refuse me this——
Give me a little time—I will do all,
All I can do, to please you!—" Oh, your eye
" Sheds a kind beam——"

  Sif. My daughter! you abuse
The softness of my nature—

  Sig. Here, my father,
'Till you relent, here will I grow for ever!

  Sif. Rise, Sigismunda.—Though you touch my
      heart,

Nothing can shake th' inexorable dictates
Of honour, duty, and determin'd reason.
Then by the holy ties of filial love,
Resolve, I charge thee, to receive Earl Osmond,
As suits the man who is thy father's choice,
And worthy of thy hand—I go to bring him—

Sig. Spare me, my dearest father!

Sif. [*Aside.*] I must rush.
From her soft grasp, or nature will betray me!
" Oh, grant us, Heaven! that fortitude of mind,
" Which listens to our duty, not our passions"—
Quit me, my child!

Sig. You cannot, oh, my father!
You cannot leave me thus!

Sif. Come hither, Laura,
Come to thy friend.   Now shew thyself a friend.
Combat her weakness; dissipate her tears;
Cherish, and reconcile her to her duty. [*Exit* Siffredi.

Enter LAURA.

Sig. Oh, wo on wo! distress'd by love and duty!
Oh, every way unhappy Sigismunda!

Laura. Forgive me, Madam, if I blame your grief.
How can you waste your tears on one so false?
Unworthy of your tenderness; to whom
Nought but contempt is due and indignation?

Sig. You know not half the horrors of my fate!
I might perhaps have learn'd to scorn his falsehood;
Nay, when the first sad burst of tears was past,
I might have rous'd my pride and scorn'd himself—

But 'tis too much, this greatest last misfortune—
Oh, whither shall I fly? Where hide me, Laura,
From the dire scene my father now prepares?

Laura. What thus alarms you, Madam?

Sig. Can it be?
Can I——ah, no!——at once give to another
My violated heart? in one wild moment?
He brings Earl Osmond to receive my vows.
Oh, dreadful change! for Tancred, haughty Osmond.

Laura. Now, on my soul, 'tis what an outrag'd heart
Like yours should wish!——I should, by heavens,
         esteem it
Most exquisite revenge!

Sig. Revenge! on whom?
On my own heart, already but too wretched!

Laura. On him! this Tancred! who has basely sold,
For the dull form of despicable grandeur,
His faith, his love!—At once a slave and tyrant!

Sig. Oh, rail **at me,** at my believing folly,
My vain ill-founded hopes, but spare him, Laura.

Laura. Who rais'd these hopes? who triumphs o'er
         that weakness?
Pardon the word—You greatly merit him;
Better than him, with all his giddy pomp;
You rais'd him by your smiles when he was nothing.
Where is your woman's pride, that guardian spirit
Given us to dash the perfidy of man?
Ye powers! I cannot bear the thought with patience—
" Yet recent from the most unsparing vows
" The tongue of love e'er lavish'd; from your hopes

F

" So vainly, idly, cruelly deluded ;"
Before the public thus, before your father,
By an irrevocable solemn deed,
With such inhuman scorn, to throw you from him :
To give his faithless hand yet warm from thine,
With complicated meanness, to Constantia.
And, to complete his crime, when thy weak limbs
Could scarce support thee, then, of thee regardless,
To lead her off.

  Sig. That was indeed a sight
To poison love ; to turn it into rage
And keen contempt.—What means this stupid weak-
           ness
That hangs upon me ? Hence, unworthy tears
Disgrace my cheek no more ! No more, my heart,
For one so coolly false or meanly fickle——
" Oh, it imports not which"—dare to suggest
The least excuse !—Yes, traitor, I will wring
Thy pride, will turn thy triumph to confusion !
" I will not pine away my days for thee,
" Sighing to brooks and groves ; while, with vain pity,
" You in a rival's arms lament my fate——
" No, let me perish ! ere I tamely be
" That soft, that patient, gentle Sigismunda,
" Who can console her with the wretched boast,
" She was for thee unhappy !——If I am,
" I will be nobly so !"——Sicilia's daughters
Shall wondering see in me a great example
Of one who punish'd an ill-judging heart,
Who made it bow to what it most abhorr'd !

Crush'd it to misery! for having thus
So lightly listen'd to a worthless lover!

Laura. At last it mounts, the kindling pride of virtue;
Trust me, thy marriage will embitter his——

Sig. Oh, may the furies light his nuptial torch!
Be it accurs'd as mine! for the fair peace,
The tender joys of hymeneal love,
May jealousy awak'd, and fell remorse,
Pour all their fiercest venom through his breast!——
Where the fates lead, and blind revenge, I follow.——
Let me not think—By injur'd love! I vow,
Thou shalt, base prince! perfidious and inhuman!
Thou shalt behold me in another's arms;
In his thou hatest! Osmond's!

Laura. " That will grind
" His heart with secret rage:" Ay, that will sting
His soul to madness; " set him up a terror,
" A spectacle of wo to faithless lovers!"——
Your cooler thought, besides, will of the change
Approve, and think it happy. Noble Osmond
" From the same stock with him derives his birth,
" First of Sicilian barons, prudent, brave,
" Of strictest honour, and by all rever'd——"

Sig. Talk not of Osmond, but perfidious Tancred!
Rail at him, rail! invent new names of scorn!
Assist me, Laura; lend my rage fresh fuel;
Support my staggering purpose, which already
Begins to fail me—Ah, my vaunts how **vain!**
How have I ly'd to my own heart!—Alas,
My tears return, the mighty flood o'erwhelms me!

" Ten thousand crowding images distract
" My tortur'd thought——And is it come to this?
" Our hopes, our vows, our oft repeated wishes,
" Breath'd from the fervent soul, and full of heaven,
" To make each other happy——come to this!"

Laura. If thy own peace and honour cannot keep
Thy resolution fix'd, yet, Sigismunda,
Oh, think, how deeply, how beyond retreat,
Thy father is engag'd.

Sig. Ah, wretched weakness!
That thus enthrals my soul, " that chases thence
" Each nobler thought, the sense of every duty;"
And have I then no tears for thee, my father?
Can I forget **thy** cares, from helpless years,
Thy tenderness for me? " an eye still beam'd
" With love; a brow that never knew a frown;
" Nor a harsh word thy tongue?" Shall I for these
Repay thy stooping venerable age
With shame, disquiet, anguish, and dishonour?
It must not be!—Thou first of angels! come,
Sweet filial piety, and firm my breast!
Yes, let one daughter to her fate submit,
Be nobly wretched—but her father happy!——
Laura!—they come! Oh, heavens, I cannot stand
The horrid trial!—Open, open earth!
And hide me from their view.

Laura. Madam.

Enter SIFFREDI *and* OSMOND.

Sif. My daughter,

Behold my noble friend who courts thy hand,
And whom to call my son I shall be proud ;
" Nor shall I less be pleas'd in this alliance,
" To see thee happy."

Osm. Think not, I presume,
Madam, on this your father's kind consent,
To make me blest.   I love you from a heart,
That seeks your good superior to my own ;
And will by every art of tender friendship,
Consult your dearest welfare.   May I hope,
Yours does not disavow your father's choice ?

Sig. I am a daughter, Sir—and have no power
O'er my own heart—I die—Support me, Laura.

[Faints.

Sif. Help—Bear her off—She breathes—my daughter !

Sig. Oh,
Forgive my weakness—soft—my Laura, lead me—
To my apartment.   [*Exeunt* Sigismunda *and* Laura.

Sif. Pardon me, my Lord,
If by this sudden accident alarm'd,
I leave you for a moment.   [*Exit* Siffredi.

Osm. Let me think——
What can this mean ?——Is it to me aversion ?
Or is it, as I fear'd, she loves another ?
Ha !—yes—perhaps the king, the young Count Tan-
cred ;
They were bred up together——Surely that,
That cannot be—Has he not given his hand,

F iij

In the most solemn manner, to Constantia?
Does not his crown depend upon the deed?
" No—If they lov'd, and this old statesman knew it,
" He could not to a king prefer a subject.
" His virtues I esteem—nay more, I trust them——
" So far as virtue goes—but could he place
" His daughter on the throne of Sicily——
" Oh, 'tis a glorious bribe, too much for man!"
What is it then? I care not what it be.
" My honour now, my dignity demands,
" That my propos'd alliance, by her father,
" And even herself accepted, be not scorn'd.
" I love her too—I never knew till now
" To what a pitch I love her. Oh, she shot
" Ten thousand charms into my inmost soul!
" She look'd so mild, so amiably gentle,
" She bow'd her head, she glow'd with such con-
            fusion,
" Such loveliness of modesty! She is,
" **In** gracious mind, in manners, and in person,
" The perfect model of all female beauty!"
She must be mine—She is!—If yet her heart
Consents not to my happiness, her duty,
Join'd to my tender cares, will gain so much
Upon her generous nature—That will follow.

> *The man of sense, who acts a prudent part,*
> *Not flattering steals, but forms himself the heart.*

[*Exit.*

ACT IV. SCENE I.

The Garden belonging to SIFFREDI's *House.*   **Enter**
SIGISMUNDA *and* LAURA.

Sigismunda, with a letter in her hand.

'Tis done!—I am a slave!—The fatal vow
Has pass'd my lips!—Methought in those sad mo-
  ments,
The tombs around, the saints, the darken'd altar,
And all the trembling shrines with horror shook.
But here is still new matter of distress.
Oh, Tancred, cease to persecute me more!
Oh, grudge me not some calmer state of woe;
Some quiet gloom to shade my hopeless days,
Where I may never hear of love and thee!——
Has Laura, too, conspired against my peace?
Why did you take this letter?—Bear it back——
I will not court new pain. [*Giving her the letter.*
 Laura. Madam, Rodolpho
Urg'd me so much, nay, even with tears conjur'd me,
But this once more to serve th' unhappy king——
For such he said he was——that though enrag'd,
Equal with thee, at his inhuman falsehood,
I could not to my brother's fervent prayers
Refuse this office——Read it——His excuses
Will only more expose his falsehood.
 Sig. No:

It suits not Osmond's wife to read one line
From that contagious hand—she knows too well!

   Laura. He paints him out distress'd beyond ex-
      pression ;
Even on the point of madness. "Wild as winds,
" And fighting seas, he raves. His passions mix,
" With ceaseless rage, all in each giddy moment."
He dies to see you, and to clear his faith.

   Sig. Save me from that!—That would be worse
      than all!

   Laura. I but report my brother's words; who then
Began to talk of some dark imposition,
That had deceiv'd us all ; when interrupted,
We heard your father and Earl Osmond near,
As summon'd to Constantia's court they went.

   Sig. Ha! imposition ?——Well, if I am doom'd
To be, o'er all my sex, the wretch of love,
In vain I would resist——Give me the letter——
To know the worst is some relief——Alas,
It was not thus, with such dire palpitations,
That, Tancred, once I us'd to read thy letters.

     [*Attempting to read the letter, but gives it to* Laura.
Ah, fond remembrance blinds me !—Read it, Laura.

   Laura. [*Reads.*] " Deliver me, Sigismunda, from
" that most exquisite misery which a faithful heart
" can suffer—To be thought base by her, from whose
" esteem even virtue borrows new charms. When
" I submitted to my cruel situation, it was not false-
" hood you beheld, but an excess of love. Rather
" than endanger that, I for a while gave up my ho-

" nour. Every moment till I see you stabs me with
" severer pangs than real guilt itself can feel.   Let
" me then conjure you to meet me in the garden, to-
" wards the close of the day, when I will explain this
" mystery.   We have been most inhumanly abused;
" and that by the means of the very paper which I
" gave you, from the warmest sincerity of love, **to**
" assure to you the heart and hand of

" TANCRED."

Sig. There, Laura, there, the dreadful secret
     sprung!
That paper! ah, that paper! it suggests
A thousand horrid thoughts—I to my father
Gave it! and he perhaps—I dare not cast
A look that way—If yet indeed you love me,
Oh, blast me not, kind Tancred, with the truth!
Oh, pitying keep me ignorant for ever.
What strange peculiar misery is mine?
Reduc'd to wish the man I love were false!
" Why was I hurry'd to a step so rash?
" Repairless wo!—I might have waited, sure,
" A few short hours—No duty that forbade—
" I ow'd thy love that justice; till this day
" Thy love an image of all perfect goodness!
" A beam from heaven that glow'd with every virtue!
" And have I thrown this prize of life away?
" The piteous wreck of one distracted moment?
" Ah, the cold prudence of remorseless age!
" Ah, parents, traitors to your children's bliss!

" Ah, curs'd, ah, blind revenge !—On every hand
" I was betray'd—You, Laura, too, betray'd me!
   " *Laura.* Who, who but he, whate'er he writes,
        betray'd you?
" Or false or pusillanimous. For once,
" I will with you suppose, that his agreement
" To the king's will was forg'd—Though forg'd by
        whom?
" Your father scorns the crime—Yet what avails it?
" This, if it clears his truth, condemns his spirit.
" A youthful king, by love and honour fir'd,
" Patient to sit on his insulted throne,
" And let an outrage, of so high a nature,
" Unpunish'd pass, uncheck'd, uncontradicted—
" **Oh, 'tis a meanness equal even to falsehood.**
   " *Sig.* Laura, no more—We have already judg'd
" Too largely without knowledge. Oft, what seems
" A trifle, a mere nothing, by itself,
" In some nice situation turns the scale
" Of fate, and rules the most important actions.
" Yes, I begin to feel a sad presage!
" I am undone, from that eternal source
" Of human woes——the judgment of the passions.
" But what have I to do with these excuses?
" Oh, cease, my treacherous heart, to give them
       'room!
" It suits not thee to plead a lover's cause:
" Even to lament my fate is now dishonour.
" Nought now remains, but with relentless purpose,
" To shun all interviews, all clearing up

" Of this dark scene ; to wrap myself in gloom,
" In solitude and shades ; there to devour
" The silent sorrows ever swelling here ;
" **And** since I must be wretched—for I must—
" To claim the mighty misery myself,
" Engross it all, and spare a hapless father.
" Hence, let me fly !—The hour approaches——
Laura. Madam,
Behold he comes—the king—
Sig. Heavens ! how escape ?
No—I will stay—This one last meeting—Leave me.

[*Exit* Laura.

Enter TANCRED.

Tan. And are these long, long hours of torture past ?
My life ! my Sigismunda !

[*Throwing himself at her feet.*

Sig. Rise, my lord.
To see my sovereign thus no more becomes me.

Tan. Oh, let me kiss the ground on which you tread !
Let me exhale my soul in softest transport !
Since I again behold my Sigismunda !   [*Rising.*
Unkind ! how couldst thou ever deem me false ?
How thus dishonour love ?—" Oh, I could much
" Embitter my complaint !---how low were then
" Thy thoughts of me ? How didst thou then affront
" The human heart itself ?" After the vows,
The fervent truth, the tender protestations,
Which mine has often pour'd, to let thy breast,
Whate'er th' appearance was, admit suspicion ?

Sig. How! when I heard myself your full consent
To the late king's so just and prudent will?
Heard it before you read, in solemn senate?
When I beheld you give your royal hand,
To her, whose birth and dignity of right
Demands that high alliance? Yes, my lord,
You have done well. The man whom heaven appoints
To govern others, should himself first learn
To bend his passions to the sway of reason.
In all, you have done well; but when you bid
My humbled hopes look up to you again,
And sooth'd with wanton cruelty my weakness—
That too was well—My vanity deserv'd
The sharp rebuke, " whose fond extravagance
" Could ever dream to balance your repose,
" Your glory, and the welfare of a people."
Tan. Chide on, chide on. Thy soft reproaches now,
Instead of wounding, only sooth my fondness.
No, no, thou charming consort of my soul!
I never lov'd thee with such faithful ardour,
As in that cruel miserable moment
You thought me false; " when even my honour stoop'd
" **To** wear for thee a baffled face of baseness."
It was thy barbarous father, Sigismunda,
Who caught me in the toil. He turn'd that paper,
Meant for th' assuring bond of nuptial love,
To ruin it for ever; he, he wrote
That forg'd consent, you heard, beneath my name,
" Nay, dar'd before my outrag'd throne to read it!"

Had he not been thy father——Ha! my love!
You tremble, you grow pale!

Sig. Oh, leave me Tancred!

Tan. No!—Leave thee!—Never! never till you set
My heart at peace, till these dear lips again
Pronounce thee mine! Without thee, I renounce
Myself, my friends, the world—Here on this hand—

Sig. My lord, forget that hand, which never now
Can be to thine united——

Tan. Sigismunda!
What dost thou mean?—Thy words, thy look, thy
          manner,
Seem to conceal some horrid secret—Heavens!——
No—that was wild—Distraction fires the thought!—

Sig. Inquire no more——I never can be thine.

Tan. What, who shall interpose? Who dares attempt
To brave the fury of an injur'd king,
Who, ere he sees thee ravish'd from his hopes,
Will wrap all blazing Sicily in **flames** ?——

Sig. In vain your power, my lord--'Tis fatal error,
Join'd to my father's unrelenting will,
Has plac'd an everlasting bar betwixt us——
I am——Earl Osmond's——wife.

Tan. Earl Osmond's wife!——
[*After a long pause, during which they look at one another
    with the highest agitation, and most tender distress.*
Heavens! did I hear thee right? What! marry'd?
          marry'd!
Lost to thy faithful Tancred? lost for ever!
Couldst thou then doom me to such matchless wo,

G

Without so much as hearing me ?—Distraction !——
Alas! what hast thou done ? Ah, Sigismunda !
Thy rash credulity has done a deed,
Which, of two happiest lovers that e'er felt
The blissful power, has made two finish'd wretches I
But—madness !—Sure, thou know'st it cannot be !
This hand is mine ! a thousand thousand vows——

Enter OSMOND.

Osm. [*Snatching her hand from the king.*] Madam,
        this hand, by the most solemn rites,
A little hour ago, was given to me,
And did not sovereign honour now command me,
Never but with my life to quit my claim,
I would renounce it——thus !

    Tan. Ha, who art thou ?
Presumptuous man !

    Sig. [*Aside.*] Where is my father ? Heavens !
                                        [*Goes out.*

    Osm. One thou shouldst better know—Yes—view
        me, one
Who can and will maintain his rights and honour,
Against a faithless prince, an upstart king,
Whose first base deed is what a harden'd tyrant
Would blush to act.

    Tan. Insolent Osmond! know,
This upstart king will hurl confusion on thee,
And all who shall invade his sacred rights,
Prior to thine—thine, founded on compulsion,
On infamous deceit, " while his proceed.

                    3

" From mutual love, and free long-plighted faith.
" She is, and shall be mine!"—I will annul
By the high power with which the laws invest me,
Those guilty forms in which you have entrap'd,
" Basely entrap'd, to thy detested nuptials,"
My queen betroth'd, who has my heart, my hand,
And shall partake my throne—If, haughty lord,
If this thou didst not know, then know it now ;
And know, besides, as I have told thee this,
Shouldst thou but think to urge thy treason further—
" Than treason more ! treason against my love !"—
Thy life shall answer for it.

Osm. Ha ! my life !———
It moves my scorn to hear thy empty threats.
When was it that a Norman baron's life
Became so vile, as on the frown of kings
To hang ?—Of that, my lord, the law must judge :
Or if the law be weak, my guardian sword———

Tan. Dare not to touch it, traitor, lest my rage
Break loose, and do a deed that misbecomes me.

Enter SIFFREDI.

Sif. My gracious lord, what is it I behold !
My sovereign in contention with his subjects ?
Surely this house deserves from royal Tancred
A little more regard, than to be made
A scene of trouble, and unseemly jars.
" It grieves my soul, it baffles every hope,
" It makes me sick of life, to see thy glory

" Thus blasted in the bud."—Heavens! can your
    highness
From your exalted character descend,
" The dignity of virtue ; and, instead
" Of being the protector of our rights,
" The holy guardian of domestic bliss,"
Unkindly thus disturb the sweet repose,
The secret peace of families, for which
Alone the free-born race of man to laws
And government submitted ?
  Tan. My lord Siffredi,
Spare thy rebuke.   The duties of my station
Are not to me unknown.   But thou, old man,
Dost thou not blush to talk of rights invaded ;
And of our best our dearest bliss disturb'd ?
Thou, who with more than barbarous perfidy
Hast trampled all allegiance, justice, truth,
Humanity itself, beneath thy feet ?
Thou know'st thou hast—I could, to thy confusion,
Return thy hard reproaches ; but I spare thee
Before this lord, for whose ill-sorted friendship
Thou hast most basely sacrific'd thy daughter.
Farewell, my lord.—For thee, lord constable,
Who dost presume to lift thy surly eye
To my soft love, my gentle Sigismunda,
I once again command thee on thy life——
Yes—chew thy rage—but mark me—on thy life,
No further urge thy arrogant pretensions ! [*Exit* Tan.
  Osm. Ha! Arrogant pretensions! Heaven and earth!
What! arrogant pretensions to my wife ?

My wedded wife! Where are we? in a land
Of civil rule, of liberty and laws?——
Not, on my life, pursue them?—Giddy prince!
My life disdains thy nod. It is the gift
Of parent Heaven, who gave me too an arm,
A spirit to defend it against tyrants.
" The Norman race, the sons of mighty Rollo,
" Who rushing in a tempest from the north,
" Great nurse of generous freemen, bravely won
" With their own swords their seats, and still possess
                ,them
" By the same noble tenure, are not us'd
". To hear such language——If I now desist,
" Then brand me for a coward! deem me villain!
" A traitor to the public! By this conduct
" Deceiv'd, betray'd, insulted, tyranniz'd."
Mine is a common cause. My arm shall guard,
Mix'd with my own, the rights of each Sicilian,
" Of social life, and of mankind in general."
Ere to thy tyrant rage they fall a prey,
I shall find means to shake thy tottering throne,
" Which this illegal, this perfidious usage
" Forfeits at once," and crush thee in the ruins!——
Constantia is **my** queen!

   Sif. Lord constable,
Let us be stedfast in the right; but let us
Act with cool prudence, and with manly temper,
As well as manly firmness. " True, I own,
" Th' indignities you suffer are so high,
" As might even justify what now you threaten.

" But if, my lord, we can prevent the woes,
" The cruel horrors of intestine war,
"-Yet hold untouch'd our liberties and laws ;
" Oh, let us, rais'd above the turbid sphere
" Of little selfish passions, nobly do it !
" **Nor** to our hot, intemperate pride, pour out
" A dire libation of Sicilian blood.
" 'Tis godlike magnanimity to keep,
" When most provok'd, our reason calm and clear,
" And execute her will from a strong sense
" Of what is right, without the vulgar aid
" Of heat and passion, which, though honest, bears us
" Often too far.". Remember that my house
Protects my daughter still ; and ere I saw her
Thus ravish'd from us, by the arm of power,
This hand should act the Roman father's part.
Fear not ; be temperate ; all will yet be well.
I know the king. " At first his passions burst
" Quick as the lightning's flash ; but in his breast
" Honour and justice dwell"——Trust me, to reason
He will return.

   Osm. **He** will !—By heavens, he shall !——
You know the king—I wish, my lord Siffredi,
That you had deign'd to tell me all you knew——
And would you have me wait, with duteous patience,
Till he return to reason ? Ye just powers !
When he has planted on our necks his foot,
And trod us into slaves ; when his vain pride
Is cloy'd with our submission ; " if, at last,
" He finds his arm too weak to shake the frame

" **Of** wide-establish'd order out of joint,
" And overturn all justice; then, perchance,
" He, in a fit of sickly kind repentance,
" May make a merit to return to reason."
No, no, my lord! there is a nobler way,
To teach the blind oppressive fury reason:
Oft has the lustre of avenging steel
Unseal'd her stupid eyes—The sword is reason!

Enter RODOLPHO *with Guards.*

Rod. My lord high constable of Sicily,
In the king's name, and by his special **order,**
I here arrest you prisoner of state.

Osm. What king? I know no king of Sicily,
Unless he be the husband of Constantia.

Rod. Then know him now—behold his royal orders
To bear you to the castle of Palermo.

Sif. Let the big torrent foam its madness off.
Submit, my lord—No castle long can hold
Our wrongs—This, more than friendship or alliance,
Confirms me thine; **this** binds **me to** thy fortunes,
By the strong tie of common injury,
Which nothing can dissolve——I grieve, Rodolpho,
To see the **reign in such** unhappy **sort**
Begin.

Osm. The reign! the usurpation call it!
This meteor king may blaze a while, but soon
Must spend his idle terrors—Sir, lead on——
Farewell, my lord——more than my life and fortune,
Remember well, is in your hands——my honour!

Sif. Our honour is the same. My son, farewell—
We shall not long be parted, On these eyes
Sleep shall not shed his balm, till I behold thee
Restor'd to freedom, or partake thy bonds.
    Even noble courage is not void of blame,
   Till nobler patience sanctifies its flame.

ACT V. SCENE I.

A Chamber.

Siffredi alone.

THE prospect lowers around. I found the king,
Though calm'd a little, with subsiding tempest,
As suits his generous nature, yet in love
Abated nought, most ardent in his purpose;
Inexorably fix'd, whate'er the risk,
To claim my daughter, and dissolve this marriage—
I have embark'd, upon a perilous sea,
A mighty treasure. " Here the rapid youth,
" Th' impetuous passions of a lover-king,
" Check my bold purpose; and there, the jealous
       pride,
" Th' impatient honour of a haughty lord,
" Of the first rank, in interest and dependance
" Near equal to the king, forbid retreat.
" My honour too, the same unchang'd conviction,
" That these my measures were, and still remain,
" Of absolute necessity to save

" The land from civil fury, urge me on.
" But how proceed ?——I only faster rush
" Upon the desperate evils I would shun.
" Whate'er the motive be, deceit, I fear,
" And harsh unnatural force, are not the means
" Of public welfare, or of private bliss"——
Bear witness, Heaven! thou mind-inspecting eye!
My breast is pure. I have prefer'd my duty,
The good and safety of my fellow-subjects,
To all those views that fire the selfish race
Of mortal men, and mix them in eternal broils.

Enter an Officer belonging to SIFFREDI.

Off. My lord, a man of noble port, his face
Wrapp'd in disguise, is earnest for admission.

Sif. Go, bid him enter——   [*Officer goes out.*
Ha! wrapp'd in disguise!
And at this late unseasonable hour!
" When o'er the world tremendous midnight reigns,
" By the dire gloom of raging tempest doubled——
Who can it be?

Enter OSMOND *discovering himself.*

Sif. " What! ha!" Earl Osmond, you ?—Wel-
            come, once more,
To this glad roof!——But why in this disguise?
Would I could hope the king exceeds his promise!
I have his faith, soon as to-morrow's sun
Shall gild Sicilia's cliffs, you shall be free.——
Has some good angel turn'd his heart to justice?

Osm. It is not by the favour of Count Tancred
That I am here. As much I scorn his favour,
As I defy his tyranny and threats————
Our friend Goffredo, who commands the castle,
On my parole, ere dawn to render back
My person, has permitted me this freedom.
Know then; the faithless outrage of to-day,
By him committed whom you call the king,
Has rous'd Constantia's court. Our friends, the friends
Of virtue, justice, and of public faith,
Ripe for revolt, are in high ferment all.
" This, this, they say, exceeds whate'er deform'd
" The miserable days we saw beneath
" William the Bad. This saps the solid base,
" At once, of government and private life :
" This shameless imposition on the faith,
" The majesty of senates, this lewd insult,
" This violation of the rights of men,
" Added to these, his ignominious treatment
" Of her, th' illustrious offspring of our kings,
" Sicilia's hope, and now our royal mistress.
" You know, my lord, how grossly these infringe
" The late king's will, which orders, if count Tancred
" Make not Constantia partner of his throne,
" That he be quite excluded the succession,
" And she to Henry given, king of the Romans,
" The potent emperor Barbarossa's son,
" Who seeks with earnest instance her alliance."
I thence of you, as guardian of the laws,
As guardian of this will, to you intrusted, -

Desire, nay more, demand your instant aid,
To see it put in vigorous execution.

  Sif. You cannot doubt, my lord, of my concur-
      rence.
Who, more than I, have labour'd this great point?
'Tis my own plan; and if I drop it now,
I should be justly branded with the shame
Of rash advice, or despicable weakness.
But let us not precipitate the matter.
Constantia's friends are numerous and strong;
Yet Tancred's, trust me, are of equal force:
E'er since the secret of his birth was known,
The people all are in a tumult hurl'd,
Of boundless joy, " to hear there lives a prince
" Of mighty Guiscard's line. Numbers, besides,
" Of powerful barons, who at heart had pin'd,
" To see the reign of their renown'd forefathers,
" Won by immortal deeds of matchless valour,
" Pass from the gallant Normans to the Suevi,
" Will with a kind of rage espouse his cause——
" 'Tis so, my lord——be not by passion blinded—
" 'Tis surely so"——Oh, if our prating virtue
Dwells not in words alone—Oh, let us join,
My generous Osmond, to avert these woes,
And yet sustain our tottering Norman kingdom!

  Osm. But how, Siffredi, how?——If by soft means
We can maintain our rights, and save our country,
May his unnatural blood first stain the sword,
Who with unpitying fury first shall draw it!

  Sif. I have a thought—The glorious work be thine.

" But it requires an awful flight of virtue,
" Above the passions of the vulgar breast,
" And thence from thee I hope it, noble Osmond"—
Suppose **my** daughter, to her God devoted,
Were plac'd within some convent's sacred verge,
Beneath the dread protection of the altar————

 Osm. Ere then, by heavens! I would " devoutly
   shave
" My holy scalp," turn whining monk myself,
And pray incessant for the tyrant's safety.————
What! How! because an insolent invader,
A sacrilegious tyrant, " in contempt
" **Of all** those noblest rights, which to maintain
" Is man's peculiar pride," demands my wife;
" That I shall thus betray the common cause
" Of human kind."
What! shall I tamely yield her up,
Even in the manner you propose ?————Oh, then
I were supremely vile! degraded! sham'd!
The scorn of manhood! and abhorr'd of honour!

 Sif. There is, my lord, an honour, the calm child
Of reason, of humanity, and mercy,
Superior far to this punctilious demon,
That singly minds itself, and oft embroils
With proud barbarian niceties the world.

 Osm. My lord, my lord, I cannot brook your pru-
   dence ;
It holds a pulse unequal to my blood————
Unblemish'd honour is the flower of virtue !

The vivifying soul! and he who slights it,
Will leave the other dull and lifeless dross.

Sif. No more——You are too warm.

Osm. You are too cool.

Sif. Too cool, my lord? I were indeed too cool,
Not to resent this language, and to tell thee——
I wish Earl Osmond were as cool as I
To his own selfish bliss—ay, and as warm
To that of others——But of this no more——
My daughter is thy wife——I gave her to thee,
And will, against all force, maintain her thine.
But think not I will catch thy headlong passions,
Whirl'd in a blaze of madness o'er the land ;
Or, till the last extremity compel me,
Risk the dire means of war——The king, to-morrow,
Will set you free ; and, if by gentle means
He does not yield my daughter to your arms,
And wed Constantia, as the will requires,
Why then expect me on the side of justice——
Let that suffice.

Osm. It does—Forgive my heat.
My rankled mind, by injuries inflam'd,
May be too prompt to take, and give offence.

Sif. 'Tis past—Your wrongs, I own, may well
         transport
The wisest mind——But henceforth, noble Osmond,
Do me more justice, honour more my truth,
Nor mark me with an eye of squint suspicion——
" These jars apart—You may repose your soul
" On my firm faith, and unremitting friendship.

H

" Of that I sure have given exalted proof,
" And the next sun we see shall prove it further."—
Return, my son, and from your friend Goffredo
Release **your word.** There try, by soft repose,
To calm your breast.

   Osm. Bid the vext ocean sleep,
Swept by the pinions of the raging north——
But **your** frail age, by care and toil exhausted,
Demands the balm of all-repairing rest.

   Sif. Soon as to-morrow's dawn shall streak the skies,
I, with my friends in solemn state assembled,
Will **to** the palace, and demand your freedom,
Then **by** calm reason, **or** by higher means,
The king shall quit his claim, and in the face
Of Sicily, my daughter shall be yours.
Farewel.

   Osm. My lord, **good** night.   [*Exit* Siffredi.
[*After a long pause.*] I like him not——
Yes—I have mighty matter of suspicion.
" 'Tis plain. I see it lurking in his breast,
" He has a foolish fondness for this king"——
My honour is not safe, while here my wife
Remains——Who knows but he this very night
May bear her to some convent, as he mentioned——
The king too—though I smother'd up my rage,
I mark'd it well—will set me free to-morrow.
Why not to-night? He has some dark design——
By heavens, he has!—I am abus'd most grossly;
Made the vile tool of this old statesman's schemes;
" Marry'd to one—ay, and he knew it—one

" Who loves young Tancred ! Hence her swooning,
    tears,
" And all her soft distress, when she disgrac'd me,
" By basely giving her perfidious hand
" Without her heart—Hell and **perdition !** this,
" This is the perfidy !—this is the fell,
" The keen envenom'd, exquisite disgrace,
" Which, to a man of honour, even exceeds
" The falsehood of the person—But I now
" Will rouse me from the poor tame lethargy,
" By my believing fondness cast upon me."
I will not wait his crawling timid motions,
" Perhaps to blind me meant, which he to-morrow
" **Has** promis'd to pursue.   No ! ere his eyes
" Shall open on to-morrow's orient beam,"
I will convince him that Earl Osmond never
Was form'd **to** be his dupe—" I know full well
" Th' important weight and danger of the deed :
" But to a man, whom greater dangers press,
" Driven to the brink of infamy and horror,
" Rashness itself, and utter desperation,
" Are the best prudence."—I will bear her off
This night, and lodge her in a place of safety :
I have a trusty band that waits not far.
Hence ! let me lose no time—One rapid moment
Should ardent form, at once, and execute
A **bold** design—'Tis fix'd—" 'Tis done !—yes, then,
" When I have seiz'd the prize of love and honour,
" And with a friend secur'd her ; to the castle
" I will repair, and claim Goffredo's promise

" To rise with all his garrison—My friends
" With **brave** impatience wait."   The mine is laid,
And only wants my kindling touch to spring.

                         [*Exit* Osm.

SCENE II.

SIGISMUNDA's *Apartment.*   *Enter* SIGISMUNDA *and*
             LAURA.   [*Thunder.*

 Laura. Heavens! 'tis a fearful night!

  Sig. Ah! the black rage
Of midnight tempest, or th' assuring smiles
Of radiant morn, are equal all to me.
Nought now has charms or terrors to my breast,
The seat of stupid woe!—Leave me, my Laura.
Kind rest, perhaps, may hush my woes a little.
Oh, for that quiet sleep that knows no morning!

  Laura. Madam, indeed I know not how to go.
Indulge my fondness—Let me watch a while
By **your** sad bed, 'till these dread hours shall pass.

  Sig. Alas! what is the toil of elements, [*Thunder.*
This idle perturbation of the sky,
To what I feel within ?—Oh, that the fires
Of pitying heaven would point their fury here!
Good night, my dearest Laura.

  Laura. Oh, I know not
What this oppression means—But 'tis with pain,
With tears, I can persuade myself to leave you——

Well then—Good night, my dearest Sigismunda.

[*Exit.*

Sig. And am I then alone ?—The most undone,
Most wretched being now beneath the cope
Of this affrighting gloom that wraps the world——
I said I did not fear—Ah, me ! I feel
A shivering horror run through all my powers !
Oh, I am nought but tumult, fears and weakness !
And yet how idle fear when hope is gone,
Gone, gone for ever !—Oh, thou gentle scene

[*Looking towards her bed.*

Of sweet repose, where, by th' oblivious draught
Of each sad toilsome day, to peace restor'd,
Unhappy mortals lose their woes awhile,
Thou hast no peace for me !—What shall I do ?
How pass this dreadful night, so big with terror ?—
Here, with the midnight shades, here will I sit,

[*Sitting down.*

A prey to dire despair, and ceaseless weep
The hours away—Bless me—I heard a noise——

[*Starting up.*

No—I mistook—nothing but silence reigns
And awful midnight round—Again !—Oh, heavens !
My lord the king !

Enter TANCRED.

Tan. Be not alarm'd, my love !
Sig. My royal lord, why at this midnight hour,
How came you hither ?
Tan. By that secret way

H iij

My love contriv'd, when we, in happier days,
Us'd to devote these hours, so much in vain,
To vows of love, and everlasting friendship.

  Sig. Why will you thus persist to add new stings
To her distress, who never can be thine?
Oh, fly me! fly! you know——

  Tan. I know too much.
Oh, how I could reproach thee, Sigismunda!
Pour out my injur'd soul in just complaints!
But now the time permits not, these swift moments——
I told thee how thy father's artifice
Forc'd me to seem perfidious in thy eyes.
" Ah, fatal blindness! not to have observ'd
" The mingled pangs of rage and love that shook me:
" When by my cruel public situation
" Compell'd, I only feign'd consent, to gain
" A little time, and more secure thee mine."
E'er since—a dreadful interval of care!
My thoughts have been employ'd, not without hope,
How to defeat Siffredi's barbarous purpose.
But thy credulity has ruin'd all,
Thy rash, thy wild—I know not what to name it——
Oh, it has prov'd the giddy hopes of man
To be delusion all, and sick'ning folly!

  Sig. Ah, generous Tancred! ah, thy truth de-
           stroys me!
Yes, yes, 'tis I, 'tis I alone am false!
My hasty rage, join'd to my tame submission,
More than the most exalted filial duty
Could e'er demand, has dash'd our cup of fate

With bitterness unequal'd—But, alas!
What are thy woes to mine?—to mine! just Heaven!
Now is thy turn of vengeance—hate, renounce me!
Oh, leave me to the fate I well deserve,
To sink in hopeless misery!—at least,
Try to forget the worthless Sigismunda!

Tan. Forget thee! No! Thou **art** my soul itself!
I have no thought, no hope, **no** wish but thee!
" Even this repented injury, the fears,
" That rouse me all to madness, at **the** thought
" Of losing thee, the whole collected pains
" Of my full heart, serve but to make **thee** dearer."
Ah, how, forget thee!—Much must be forgot,
Ere Tancred can forget his Sigismunda!

Sig. But you, my lord, must make that great effort.

Tan. Can Sigismunda make it?

Sig. Ah, **I know not**
With what success—But all that feeble **woman**
And love-entangled reason **can** perform,
I, to the utmost, will exert to do it.

" *Tan.* Fear not—'Tis done!—If thou canst form
    the thought,
" Success is **sure—I am** forgot already.
    " *Sig.* Ah, Tancred!—But, my lord, respect me
    more.
" Think who **I** am—What can you now propose?
    " *Tan.* To claim the plighted vows which Heaven
    has heard,
" To vindicate the rights of holy love
" By faith and honour bound, to which compar'd

" These empty forms, which have ensnar'd thy hand,

" Are impious guile, abuse, and profanation——

"·Nay, as a king, whose high prerogative

" By this unlicens'd marriage is affronted,

" To bid the laws themselves pronounce it void.

  " *Sig.* Honour, my lord, is much too proud to
    catch

" At every slender twig of nice distinctions.

" These for th' unfeeling vulgar may do **well :**

" But those, whose souls are by the nicer rule

" Of virtuous delicacy nobly sway'd,

" Stand at another bar than that of laws.

" Then cease to urge me——Since I am not born

" To that exalted fate to be your queen——

" Or, yet a dearer name——to be your wife !——

" I am the wife of an illustrious lord

" Of your **own princely** blood ; and what I am,

" I will with proper dignity remain.

" Retire, my royal lord.——There is no means

" To cure the wounds this fatal day has given.

" We meet no more !"

  Tan. Oh, barbarous Sigismunda!

And canst thou talk thus steadily ; thus treat me

With such unpitying, unrelenting rigour ?

Poor is the love, that rather than give up

A little pride, a little formal pride,

The breath of vanity, can bear to see

The man, **whose heart** was once so dear to thine,

By many **a tender vow** so mix'd together,

A prey to anguish, fury and distraction !

Thou canst not surely make me such a wretch,
Thou canst not, Sigismunda!—Yet relent,
Oh, save us yet!—Rodolpho, with my guards,
Waits in the garden—Let us seize the moments
We ne'er may have again—With more than power
I will assert thee mine, with fairest honour.
The world shall even approve; each honest bosom
Swell'd with a kindred joy to see us happy.

Sig. The world approve! what is the world to me!
The conscious mind is its own awful world.——
And mine is fix'd—Distress me then no more ;
Not all the heart can plead, (and it, alas,
Pleads but too much)
" And yet, perhaps, if thou wert not a king,
" I know not, Tancred, what I might have done,
" Then, 'then, my conduct, sanctify'd by love,
" Could not be deem'd, by the severest judge,
" The mean effect of interest or ambition.
" But now not all my partial heart can plead,"
Shall ever shake th' unalterable dictates
That tyrannize my breast.

Tan. 'Tis well—No more—
I yield me to my fate—Yes, yes, inhuman!
Since thy barbarian heart is steel'd by pride,
Shut up to love and pity, here behold me
Cast on the ground, a vile and abject wretch!
Lost to all cares, all dignities, all duties!
Here will I grow, breathe out my faithful soul,
Here at thy feet—Death, death alone shall part us!

Sig. Have you then vow'd to drive me to perdition!

What can I more?—Yes, Tancred! once again
I will forget the dignity my station
Commands me to sustain—for the last time
Will tell thee, that, I fear, no ties, no duty,
Can ever root thee from my hapless bosom.
Oh, leave me! fly me! were it but in pity!—
To see what once we tenderly have lov'd,
Cut off from every hope—cut off for ever!
Is pain thy generosity should spare me.
Then rise, my lord; and if you truly love me,
If you respect my honour, nay, my peace,
Retire! for though th' emotions of my heart
Can ne'er alarm my virtue; yet, alas!
They tear it so, they pierce it with such anguish—
Oh, 'tis too much!—I cannot bear the conflict!

Enter OSMOND.

Osm. Turn, tyrant, turn! and answer to my honour,
For this thy base insufferable outrage!

Tan. Insolent traitor! think not to escape
Thyself my vengeance!   [*They fight*, Osmond *falls.*
Sig. Help, here! Help!—Oh, heavens!
                          [*Throwing herself down by him.*
Alas, my lord, what meant your headlong rage?
That faith, which I this day, upon the altar,
To you devoted, is unblemish'd, pure
As vestal truth; was resolutely yours,
Beyond the power of ought on earth to shake it.

Osm. Perfidious woman! die!—[*Shortening his sword,*
  he plunges it into her breast.] and to the grave
Attend a husband, yet but half aveng'd!

Tan. Oh, horror! horror! execrable villain!

Osm. And, tyrant! thou!—thou shalt not o'er my
  tomb
Exult—'Tis well—'Tis great!—I die content!—[*Dies.*

Enter RODOLPHO *and* LAURA.

Tan. [*Throwing himself down by* Sigismunda.] Quick!
  here! bring aid!—" All in Palermo bring,
" Whose skill can save her!"—Ah, that gentle bosom
Pours fast the streams of life.

Sig. All aid is vain,
I feel the powerful hand of death upon me—
But, oh! it sheds a sweetness through my fate,
That I am thine again; and without blame
May in my Tancred's arms resign my soul!

Tan. Oh, death is in that voice! so gently mild,
So sadly sweet, as mixes even with mine
The tears of hovering angels!—Mine again!——
And is it thus the cruel fates have join'd us?
Are these the horrid nuptials they prepare
For love like ours?—" Is virtue thus rewarded?
" Let not my impious rage accuse just Heaven!
" Thou, Tancred, thou, hast murdered Sigismunda!
" That furious man was **but** the tool of fate,
" I, I the cause!—But I will do thee justice
" **On this** deaf heart! that to thy tender wisdom
" Refus'd an ear"—Yes, death shall soon unite us.

Sig. Live, live, my Tancred!—Let my death suffice
To expiate all that may have been amiss.
May it appease the fates, avert their fury
From thy propitious reign! " Mean-time, of me
" And of thy glory mindful, live, I charge thee,
" To guard our friends, and make thy people happy—"

Enter SIFFREDI *fixed in astonishment* **and** *grief.*

My father !——Oh, how shall I lift my eyes
To thee, my sinking father !
    Sif. Awful Heaven !
I am chastis'd——My dearest child !——
    Sig. Where am I ?
A fearful darkness closes all around—
My friends ! We needs must part—I must obey
Th' impetuous call,—Farewel, my Laura ! " cherish
" My poor afflicted father's age—Rodolpho,
" Now is the time to watch the unhappy king,
" With all the care and tenderness of friendship."—
Oh, my dear father, bow'd beneath the weight
Of age and grief—the victim even of virtue,
Receive my last adieu !—Where art thou, Tancred ?
Give me thy hand—But, ah,—it cannot save me
From the dire king of terrors, whose cold power
Creeps o'er my heart——Oh !
    Tan. How these pangs distract me !
Oh, lift thy gracious eyes ;——Thou leav'st me then !
Thou leav'st me, Sigismunda !
    Sig. " Yet a moment——
" I had, my Tancred, something more to say——

" Yes——but thy love and tenderness for me,
" Sure makes it needless—Harbour no resentment
" Against my father; venerate his zeal,
" That acted from a principle of goodness,
" From faithful love to thee—Live, and maintain
" My innocence embalm'd, with holiest care
" Preserve my spotless memory!" Oh,——I die——
Eternal Mercy take my trembling soul!
Oh, 'tis the only sting of death to part
From those we love—from thee—farewel, my Tan-
     cred!   [*Dies.*

   Tan. Thus then!
           [*Flying to his sword, is held by* Rodolpho.
   Rod. Hold, hold, my lord!—Have you forgot
Your Sigismunda's last request already?

   Tan. Off! set me free! Think not to bind me down,
With barbarous friendship, to the rack of life!
What hand can shut the thousand thousand gates
Which death still opens to the woes of mortals?—
" I shall find means—No power in earth or heaven
" Can force me to endure the hateful light,
" Thus robb'd of all that lent it joy and sweetness!"
Off, traitors, off! or my distracted soul
Will burst indignant from this jail of nature,
To where she beckons yonder—No, mild seraph,
Point not to life——I cannot linger here,
Cut off from thee, the miserable pity,
The scorn of human kind!——A trampled king!
" Who let his mean poor-hearted love, one moment,
" To coward prudence stoop! who made it not

" The first undoubting action of his reign,
" To snatch thee to his throne, and there to shield thee,
" Thy helpless bosom, from a ruffian's fury !"——
Oh, shame ! Oh, agony ! Oh, the fell stings
Of late, of vain repentance !——Ha, my brain
Is all on fire ! a wild abyss of thought !
Th' infernal world discloses ! See ! Behold him !
Lo ! with fierce smiles he shakes the bloody steel,
And mocks my feeble tears.——Hence, quickly, hence !
Spurn his vile carcass ! give it to the dogs !
Expose it to the winds and screaming ravens !
" Or hurl it down that fiery steep to hell,
" There with his soul to toss in flames for ever."
Ah, impotence of rage !

 Rod. *Preserve him, Heaven !*

 Tan. What am I ? Where ?
Sad, silent, all ?——The forms of dumb despair,
Around some mournful tomb.——What do I see ?
This soft abode of innocence and love
Turn'd to the house of death ! a place of horror !——
Ah, that poor corse ! pale ! pale ! deform'd with murder !
Is that my Sigismunda ?　[*Throws himself down by her.*

 Sif. [*After a pathetic pause, looking on the scene before him.*
Have I liv'd
To these enfeebled years, by Heaven reserv'd
To be a dreadful monument of justice ?——
Rodolpho, raise the king, and bear him hence
From this distracting scene of blood and death.
" Alas, I dare not give him my assistance ;
" My care would only more inflame his rage.

" *Behold the fatal work of my dark hand,*
" *That by rude force the passions would command,*
" *That ruthless thought to root them from the breast ;*
" *They may be rul'd, but will not be opprest."*
Taught hence, ye parents, who from nature stray,
And the great ties of social life betray ;
Ne'er with your children act a tyrant's part :
'Tis yours to guide, not violate the heart.
Ye vainly wise, who o'er mankind preside,
Behold my righteous woes, and drop your pride ;
Keep virtue's simple path before your eyes,
Nor think from evil good can ever rise.

EPILOGUE.

CRAMM'D *to the throat with wholesome moral stuff,*
Alas, poor audience! you have had enough.
Was ever hapless heroine of a play
In such a piteous plight as ours to-day?
Was ever woman so by love betray'd?
Match'd with two husbands, and yet—die a maid.
But bless me!—hold—what sounds are these I hear—
I see the Tragic Muse herself appear.

> [The back-scene opens, and discovers a romantic
> sylvan landscape; from which the Tragic
> Muse advances slowly to music, and speaks
> the following lines:

Hence with your flippant epilogue, that tries
To wipe the virtuous tear from British eyes;
That dares my moral, tragic scene profane,
With strains—at best, unsuiting, light and vain.
Hence from the pure unsully'd beams that play
In yon fair eyes where virtue shines—away!

Britons, to you from chaste Castalian groves,
Where dwell the tender, oft unhappy loves;
Where shades of heroes roam, each mighty name,
And court my aid to rise again to fame;

To you I come, to freedom's noblest seat,
And in Britannia fix my last retreat.

In Greece and Rome, I watch'd the public weal;
The purple tyrant trembled at my steel:
Nor did I less o'er private sorrows reign,
And mend the melting heart with softer pain.
On France and You then rose my brightning star,
With social ray—The arts are ne'er at war.
Oh, as your fire and genius strongly blaze,
As yours are generous freedom's bolder lays,
Let not the Gallic taste leave yours behind;
In decent manners and in life refin'd;
Banish the motly mode, to tag low verse,
The laughing ballad to the mournful herse.
When through five acts your hearts have learn'd to glow,
Touch'd with the sacred force of honest woe;
Oh, keep the dear impression on your breast,
Nor idly lose it for a wretched jest.

THE END.

De Wilde pinxt.   Audinet.

M.ʳ JOHN PALMER Jun.ʳ as G. BARNWELL

London Printed for J. Bell, British Library, Strand, June 1ˢᵗ 1792.

GEORGE BARNWELL.

A

TRAGEDY,

By GEORGE LILLO.

ADAPTED FOR

THEATRICAL REPRESENTATION,

AS PERFORMED AT THE

THEATRES-ROYAL,

DRURY-LANE AND COVENT-GARDEN.

REGULATED FROM THE PROMPT-BOOKS,
By Permission of the Managers.

LONDON :

Printed for the Proprietors, under the Direction of
JOHN BELL, British-Library, STRAND,
Bookseller to His Royal Highness the PRINCE of WALES.

M DCC XCII.

TO

SIR JOHN EYLES, BART.

Member of Parliament for, and Alderman of, the City of
LONDON, and Sub-Governor of the SOUTH-SEA Company.

SIR,

*IF tragic poetry be, as Mr. Dryden has somewhere
said, the most excellent and most useful kind of
writing; the more extensively useful the moral of any
tragedy is, the more excellent that piece must be of
its kind.*

*I hope I shall not be thought to insinuate, that
this, to which I have presumed to prefix your name,
is such: that depends on its fitness to answer the end
of tragedy, the exciting of the passions, in order to
the correcting such of them as are criminal, either in
their nature, or through their excess. Whether the
following scenes do this in any tolerable degree, is,
with the deference that becomes one who would not be
thought vain, submitted to your candour and impartial judgment.*

*What I would infer is this, I think, evident truth;
that tragedy is so far from losing its dignity by being
accommodated to the circumstances of the generality*

A ij

of mankind, that it is more truly august, in proportion to the extent of its influence, and the numbers that are properly affected by it : as it is more truly great to be the instrument of good to many who stand in need of our assistance, than to a very small part of that number.

If princes, &c. were alone liable to misfortunes arising from vice or weakness in themselves or others, there would be good reason for confining the characters in tragedy to those of superior rank ; but since the contrary is evident, nothing can be more reasonable than to proportion the remedy to the disease.

I am far from denying, that tragedies founded on any instructive and extraordinary events in history, or well-invented fables, where the persons introduced are of the highest rank, are without their use, even to the bulk of the audience. The strong contrast between a Tamerlane and a Bajazet may have its weight with an unsteady people, and contribute to the fixing of them in the interest of a prince of the character of the former ; when thro' their own levity, or the arts of designing men, they are rendered factious and uneasy, though they have the highest reason to be satisfied. The sentiments and example of a Cato may inspire his spectators with a just sense of the value of liberty, when they see that honest patriot prefer death to an obligation from a tyrant, who would sacrifice the constitution of his country, and the liberties of mankind, to his ambition or revenge. I have attempted, indeed, to enlarge the province of the graver kind of poetry, and should be glad to see it carried on by some abler hand. Plays founded on moral tales in private life may be of admirable use, by carrying conviction to the mind with such irresistible force as to engage all the faculties and power of the soul in the cause of virtue, by stifling vice in its first principles. They who imagine this to be too much to be attributed to tragedy, must be strangers to the energy of that noble species of poetry. Shakspere, who has given such amazing proofs of his genius, in that as well as in comedy, in his Hamlet has the following lines:

Had he the motive and the **cause** for passion
That I have, he would drown the stage with tears,
And cleave the gen'ral ear with horrid speech:
Make mad the guilty, and appall the free,
Confound the ign'rant, and amaze indeed
The very faculty of eyes and **ears.**

And farther, in the same speech:

I've heard that guilty creatures at a play
Have, by the very cunning of the scene,
Been so struck to the soul, that presently
They have proclaim'd their malefactions.

Prodigious! yet strictly just. But I shall not take up your valuable time with my remarks: only give me

leave just to observe, that he seems so firmly persuaded of the power of a well-written piece to produce the effect here ascribed to it, as to make Hamlet
venture his soul on the event, and rather trust that,
than a messenger from the other world, tho' it as-
sumed, as he expresses it, his noble Father's form,
and assured him, that it **was** his spirit. I'll have,
says Hamlet, grounds more relative;

————— the play's the thing,
Wherein I'll catch the conscience of the king.

Such plays are the best answers to them who deny
the lawfulness of the stage.

Considering the **novelty of this** attempt, I thought
it would be expected from me to say something in its
excuse; and I was unwilling to lose the opportunity
of saying something of the usefulness of tragedy in
general, and what may be reasonably expected from
the farther improvement of this excellent kind of
poetry.

SIR,
I hope you will not think I have said too much of
an art, a mean specimen of which I am ambitious
enough to recommend to your favour and protection.
A mind, conscious of superior worth, as much de-
spises flattery, as it is above it. Had I found in
myself an inclination to so contemptible a vice, I

should not have chosen Sir JOHN EYLES *for my patron.* And indeed the best written panegyric, tho'
strictly true, *must place you in a light* much inferior
to that *in which you have* long been fixed *by the love*
and esteem *of your fellow-citizens,* whose choice of
you for *one of their* representatives in parliament,
has sufficiently declared their sense of your merit.
Nor hath the knowledge of your worth been confined
to the city: the proprietors in the South-Sea Company, in which are included numbers of persons as
considerable for their rank, fortune, and understanding, as any in the kingdom, **gave** the greatest proof
of their **confidence** in your capacity and probity, by
choosing you Sub-Governor of their Company, at a
time when their affairs were in the utmost confusion,
and their properties in **the greatest** danger. Neither is
the court insensible **of your** importance. I shall not,
therefore, attempt a character so well known, nor
pretend to add any thing **to a** reputation so well esta-
blished.

Whatever others may think of a Dedication, wherein
there is so much said of other things, and so little of
the person to whom it is addressed, I have reason to
believe that you will the more easily pardon it upon
that very account.

I am, Sir,

Your most obedient, humble servant,

GEORGE LILLO.

GEORGE BARNWELL.

T<small>HIS</small> Play affects the middle or mercantile part of life as it once was, but the application of it now must be among the lowest occupations of society.—The snares of *Millwood* would now be nearly ineffectual to the London Merchant's seduction; general dissipation has taken away our constancy even in our vices.

There is, however, a merit in this play that does not fall to the share of many.—The sentiments are easy and natural, and the interest such as will be acknowledged powerful by all, although the polish of modern manners should not eagerly desire its performance upon the stage. Indeed, from the nature of the principal female character, it is not possible that it should ever be among the current amusements of the season. Knowing this, the Managers perform it now and then as an hereditary obligation from past times, but then in so vile a way, that nothing but the powerful pathos of the writing could make it bearable:—yet badly as we have always seen it acted, we have never been able to refrain from tears.

The best of Mr. L<small>ILLO</small>'s dramatic productions is the F<small>ATAL</small> C<small>URIOSITY</small>, a play that comes closer to the sublime horrors of Shakspere's M<small>ACBETH</small> than any one produced this century.

PROLOGUE.

THE tragic muse, sublime, delights to show
Princes distress'd, and scenes of royal wo;
In awful pomp, majestic, to relate
The fall of nations, or some hero's fate;
That scepter'd chiefs may, by example, know
The strange vicissitudes of things below;
What dangers on security attend;
How pride and cruelty in ruin end:
Hence Providence supreme, to know, and own
Humanity adds glory to a throne.
In 'ev'ry former age, and foreign tongue,
With native grandeur thus the goddess sung.
Upon our stage, indeed, with wish'd success,
You've sometimes seen her in an humbler dress;
Great only in distress, when she complains
In Southern's, Rowe's, or Otway's moving strains,
The brilliant drops that fall from each bright eye,
The absent pomp, with brighter gems supply.
Forgive us, then, if we attempt to show,
In artless strains, a tale of private wo.
A London 'Prentice ruin'd is our theme,
Drawn from the fam'd old song that bears his name.
We hope your taste is not so high to scorn
A moral tale esteem'd ere you were born;

Which, for a century of rolling years,
Has fill'd a thousand thousand eyes with tears.
If thoughtless youth to warn, and shame the age
From vice destructive, well becomes the stage;
If this example innocence insure,
Prevent our guilt, or by reflection cure,
If Millwood's dreadful crimes, and sad despair,
Commend the virtue of the good and fair;
Tho' art be wanting, and our numbers fail,
Indulge th' attempt, in justice to the tale.

Dramatis Personae.

COVENT-GARDEN.

Men.

THOROWGOOD,	Mr. Hull.
BARNWELL, *uncle to* George,	Mr. Booth.
GEORGE BARNWELL,	Mr. Farren.
TRUEMAN,	Mr. Davies.
BLUNT,	Mr. Thompson.
Gaoler,	Mr. Ledger.

Women.

MARIA,	Mrs. T. Kennedy.
MILLWOOD,	Mrs. Bates.
LUCY,	Mrs. Wilson.

Officers with their Attendants, and Footmen.

SCENE, *London, and an adjacent Village.*

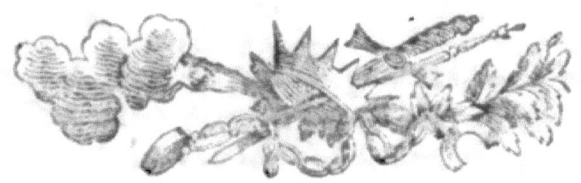

GEORGE BARNWELL.

ACT I. SCENE I.

A Room in THOROWGOOD'S *House.* *Enter* THOROW-
GOOD *and* TRUEMAN.

Trueman.

SIR, the packet from Genoa is arrived. [*Gives letters.*

Thor. Heaven be prais'd! The storm that threatened our royal mistress, pure religion, liberty, and
laws, is for a time diverted. The haughty and re-
vengeful Spaniard, disappointed of the loan on which
he depended from Genoa, must now attend the slow
returns of wealth from his new world, to supply his
empty coffers, ere he can execute his proposed inva-
sion of our happy island. By this means, time is
gained to make such preparations on our part, as may,
Heaven concurring, prevent his malice, or turn the
meditated mischief on himself.

True. He must be insensible indeed, who is not affected when the safety of his country is concerned.

B

Sir, may I know by what means?——If I am not too
bold——

Thor. Your curiosity is laudable; and I gratify it
with the greater pleasure, because from thence you
may learn, how honest merchants, as such, may sometimes contribute to the safety of their country, as they
do at all times to its happiness; that if hereafter you
should be tempted to any action that has the appearance of vice or meanness in it, upon reflecting on the
dignity of our profession, you may, with honest scorn,
reject whatever is unworthy of it.

True. Should Barnwell, or I, who have the benefit
of your example, by our ill conduct bring any imputation on that honourable name, we must be left without excuse.

Thor. You compliment, young man. [*Trueman
bows respectfully.*] Nay, I am not offended. As the
name of merchant never degrades the gentleman, so
by no means does it exclude him; only take heed not
to purchase the character of complaisant at the expence of your sincerity.——But to answer your question: The bank of Genoa had agreed, at an excessive
interest, and on good security, to advance the King
of Spain a sum of money sufficient to equip his vast
Armada; of which our peerless Elizabeth (more than
in name the mother of her people) being well informed, sent Walsingham, her wise and faithful se-
cretary, to consult the merchants of this loyal city
who all agreed to direct their several agents to influence, if possible, the Genoese to break their contract

with the Spanish court. 'Tis done: the state and bank of Genoa having maturely weighed, and rightly judged of their true interest, prefer the friendship of the merchants of London to that of the monarch, who proudly stiles himself king of both Indies.

True. Happy success of prudent counsels! What an expence of blood and treasure is here saved! " Ex- " cellent queen; O how unlike those princes, who " make the danger of foreign enemies a pretence to " oppress their subjects by taxes great, and grievous " to be borne!

" *Thor.* Not so our gracious queen! whose richest " exchequer is her people's love, as their happiness " her greatest glory.

" *True.* On these terms to defend us, is to make " our protection a benefit worthy her who confers it, " and well worth our acceptance." **Sir, have you** any commands for me at this time?

Thor. Only look carefully over the files, to see whe- ther there are any tradesmen's bills unpaid; if there are, send and discharge 'em. We must not let arti- ficers lose their time, so useful to the public and their families, in unnecessary attendance. [*Exit* Trueman.

Enter MARIA.

Well, Maria, have you given orders for the enter- tainment? I would have it in some measure worthy the guests. Let there be plenty, and of the best, that the courtiers may at least commend our hospita- lity.

Mar. **Sir,** I have endeavoured not to wrong your well-known generosity by an ill-timed parsimony.

Thor. Nay, 'twas a needless caution: I have no cause to doubt your prudence.

Mar. Sir, I find myself unfit for conversation; I should but increase the number of the company, without adding to their satisfaction.

Thor. Nay, my child, this melancholy must not be indulged.

Mar. Company will but increase it: I wish you would dispense with my absence. Solitude best suits my present temper.

Thor. You are not insensible, that it is chiefly on your account these noble lords do me the honour so frequently to grace my board. Should you be absent, the disappointment may make them repent of their condescension, and think their labour lost.

Mar. He that shall think his time or honour lost in visiting you, can set no real value on your daughter's company, whose only merit is, that she is yours. The man of quality who chooses to converse with a gentleman and merchant of your worth and character, may confer honour by so doing, but he loses none.

Thor. Come, come, Maria, I need not tell you, that a young gentleman may prefer your conversation to mine, and yet intend me no disrespect at all; for though he may lose no honour in my company, 'tis very natural for him to expect more pleasure in yours. I remember the time when the company of the greatest and wisest men in the kingdom would have been insipid and tiresome to me, if it had deprived me of an opportunity of enjoying your mother's.

Mar. Yours, no doubt, was as agreeable to her; for generous minds know no pleasure in society but where 'tis mutual.

Thor. Thou knowest I have no heir, no child, but thee; the fruits of many years successful industry must all be thine. Now it would give me pleasure, great as my love, to see on whom you will bestow it. I am daily solicited by men of the greatest rank and merit for leave to address you: but I have hitherto declined it, in hopes that, by observation, I should learn which way your inclination tends; for, as I know love to be essential to happiness in the married state, I had rather my approbation should confirm your choice than direct it.

Mar. What can I say? How shall I answer, as I ought, this tenderness, so uncommon even in the best of parents? But you are without example: yet, had you been less indulgent, I had been most wretched. That I look on the crowd of courtiers that visit here, with equal esteem, but equal indifference, you have observed, and I must needs confess; yet, had you asserted your authority, and insisted on a parent's right to be obey'd, I had submitted, and to my duty sacrificed my peace.

Thor. From your perfect obedience in every other instance, I feared as much; and therefore would leave you without a bias in an affair wherein your happiness is so immediately concerned.

Mar. Whether from a want of that just ambition that would become your daughter, **or** from some other cause, I know not; but I find high birth and titles don't recommend the man who owns them, to my affections.

Thor. I would not that they should, unless his merit recommends him more. A noble birth and fortune, though they make not a bad man good, yet they are a real advantage to a worthy one, and place his virtues in the fairest light.

Mar. I cannot answer for my inclinations; but they shall ever be submitted to your wisdom and authority. And as you will not compel me to marry where I cannot love, love shall never make me act contrary to my duty. Sir, have I your permission to retire?

Thor. I'll see you to your chamber.   [*Exeunt.*

SCENE II.

A Room in MILLWOOD's *House. Enter* MILLWOOD *and* LUCY.

Mill. How do I look to-day, Lucy?

Lucy. Oh, killingly, madam! A little more red, and you'll be irresistible.——But why this more than ordinary care of your dress and complexion? What new conquest are you aiming at?

Mill. A conquest would be new indeed.

Lucy. Not to you, who make 'em every day——but

to me——Well, 'tis what I'm never to expect—unfortunate as I am——But your wit and beauty——

Mill. First made me a wretch, and still continue me so. Men, however generous or sincere to one another, are all selfish hypocrites in their affairs with us; we are no otherwise esteemed or regarded by them, but as we contribute to their satisfaction.

Lucy. You are certainly, madam, on the wrong side in this argument. Is not the expence all theirs? And I am sure it is our own fault if we have not our share of the pleasure.

Mill. We are but slaves to men.

Lucy. Nay, 'tis they that are slaves most certainly, for we lay them under contribution.

Mill. Slaves have no property; no, not even in themselves: all is the victor's.

Lucy. You are strangely arbitrary in your principles, madam.

Mill. I would have my conquest complete, like those of the Spaniards in the New World; who first plundered the natives of all the wealth they had, and then condemned the wretches to the mines for life, to work for more.

Lucy. Well, I shall never approve of your scheme of government: I should think it much more politic, as well as just, to find my subjects an easier employment.

Mill. It is a general maxim among the knowing part of mankind, that a woman without virtue, like a man without honour or honesty, is capable of any

action, though never so vile: and yet what pains will
they not take, what arts not use, to seduce us from
our innocence, and make us contemptible and wicked,
even in their own opinion? Then is it not just, the
villains, to their cost, should find us so? But guilt
makes them suspicious, and keeps them on their guard;
therefore we can take advantage only of the young
and innocent part of the sex, who having never injured women, apprehend no injury from them.

Lucy. Ay, they must be young indeed.

Mill. Such a one, I think, I have found. As I
have passed through the city, I have often observed
him receiving and paying considerable sums of money; from thence I conclude he is employed in affairs of consequence.

Lucy. Is he handsome?

Mill. Ay, ay, the stripling is well made, and has a
good face.

Lucy. About——

Mill. Eighteen.

Lucy. Innocent, handsome, and about eighteen!—
You'll be vastly happy. Why, if you manage well,
you may keep him to yourself these two or three years.

Mill. If I manage well, I shall have done with him
much sooner. Having long had a design on him, and
meeting him yesterday, I made a full stop, and gazing
wishfully in his face, ask'd his name. He blush'd, and
bowing very low, answer'd, George Barnwell. I
begged his pardon for the freedom I had taken, and
told him, that he was the person I had long wished to

see, and to whom I had an affair of importance to
communicate at a proper time and place. He named
a tavern; I talked of honour and reputation, and invited him to my house. He swallowed the bait, promised to come; and this is the time I expect him.
[*Knocking at the door.*] Somebody knocks——D'ye
hear; I am at home to nobody to-day but him. [*Exit
Lucy.*] Less affairs must give way to those of more
consequence; and I am strangely mistaken if this
does not prove of great importance to me, and him
too, before I have done with him. Now, after what
manner shall I receive him? Let me consider——
What manner of person am I to receive? He is
young, innocent, and bashful; therefore I must take
care not to put him out of countenance at first. " But
" then, if I have any skill in physiognomy, he is amo-
" rous; and, with a little assistance, will soon get
" the better of his modesty." I'll e'en trust to nature, who does wonders in these matters. " If to
" seem what one is not, in order to be the better
" liked for what one really is; if to speak one thing,
" and mean the direct contrary, be art in a woman——
" I know nothing of nature."

Enter BARNWELL, *bowing very low.* LUCY *at a
distance.*

Mill. Sir, the surprise and joy——
Barn. Madam!
Mill. This is such a favour——   [*Advancing.*
Barn. Pardon me, madam.

Mill. So unhop'd for! 　　　　　*[Still advances.*

　　　　[Barnwell *salutes her, and retires in confusion.*
To see you here——Excuse the confusion——

　Barn. I fear I am too bold——

　Mill. Alas, sir, I may justly apprehend you think me so. Please, sir, to sit. I am as much at a loss how to receive this honour as I ought, as I am surprised at your goodness in conferring it.

　Barn. I thought you had expected me: I promised to come.

　Mill. That is the more surprising; few men are such religious observers of their word.

　Barn. All who are honest are.

　Mill. To one another; but we simple women are seldom thought of consequence enough to gain a place in their remembrance.

　　　　　　[*Laying her hand on his, as by accident.*
　Barn. Her disorder is so great, she don't perceive she has laid her hand on mine. Heav'ns! How she trembles!—What can this mean? 　　　[*Aside.*

　Mill. The interest I have in all that relates to you, (the reason of which you shall know hereafter) excites my curiosity; and were I sure you would pardon my presumption, I should desire to know your real sentiments on a very particular subject.

　Barn. Madam, you may command my poor thoughts on any subject, I have none that I would conceal.

　Mill. You'll think me bold.

　Barn. No, indeed.

　Mill. What then are your thoughts of love?

Barn. If you mean the love of women, I have not thought of it at all. My youth and circumstances make such thoughts improper in me yet. But if you mean the general love we owe to mankind, I think no one has more of it in his temper than myself. I don't know that person in the world, whose happiness I don't wish, and would not promote, were it in my power. In an especial manner I love my uncle, and my master; but above all, my friend.

Mill. You have a friend, then, whom you love?

Barn. As he does me, sincerely.

Mill. He is, no doubt, often bless'd with your company and conversation?

Barn. We live in one house, and both serve the same worthy merchant.

Mill. Happy, happy youth! Whoe'er thou art, I envy thee, " and so must all, who see and know this " youth." What have I lost, by being form'd a woman! I hate my sex, myself. Had I been a man, I might, perhaps, have been as happy in your friendship, as he who now enjoys it is: but as it is——— Oh!———

Barn. I never observed woman before; or this is, sure, the most beautiful of her sex. [*Aside.*] You seem disordered, madam—May I know the cause?

Mill. Do not ask me——I can never speak it, whatever is the cause. I wish for things impossible. I would be a servant, bound to the same master, to live in one house with you.

Barn. How strange, and yet how kind, her words

and actions are! And the effect they have on me is as strange. I feel desires I never knew before. I must be gone, while I have power to go. [*Aside.*] Madam, I humbly take my leave.

Mill. You will not, sure, leave me so soon!

Barn. Indeed I must.

Mill. You cannot be so cruel! I have prepared a poor supper, at which I promised myself your company.

Barn. I am sorry I must refuse the honour you designed me: but my duty to my master calls me hence. I never yet neglected his service. He is so gentle, and so good a master, that should I wrong him, though he might forgive me, I should never forgive myself.

Mill. Am I refused, by the first man, the second favour I ever stooped to ask? Go then, thou proud hard-hearted youth; but know, you are the only man that could be found, who would let me sue twice for greater favours.

Barn. What shall I do? How shall I go, or stay?

Mill. Yet do not, do not leave me. I with my sex's pride would meet your scorn; but when I look upon you, when I behold those eyes—Oh! spare my tongue, and let my blushes—this flood of tears too, that will force its way, declare—what woman's modesty should hide.

Barn. Oh, Heavens! she loves me, worthless as I am. Her looks, her words, her flowing tears confess **it.** And can I leave her then? Oh, never, never!

Madam, dry up your tears: you shall command me always; I will stay here for ever, if you would have me.

Lucy. So: she has wheedled him out of his virtue of obedience already, and will strip him of all the rest, one after another, till she has left him as few as her ladyship, or myself.

Mill. Now you are kind, indeed: but I mean not to detain you always: I would have you shake off all slavish obedience to your master; but you may serve him still.

Lucy. Serve him still! Ay, or he'll have no opportunity of fingering his cash; and then he'll not serve your end, I'll be sworn.   [*Aside.*

Enter BLUNT.

Blunt. Madam, supper's on the table.

Mill. Come, sir, you'll excuse all defects. My thoughts were too much employed on my guest to observe the entertainment.

     [*Exeunt* Barnwell *and* Millwood.

Blunt. What! is all this preparation, this elegant supper, variety of wines, and music, for the entertainment of that young fellow?

Lucy. So it seems.

Blunt. How! is our mistress turned fool at last? She's in love with him, I suppose.

Lucy. I suppose not. But she designs to make him in love with her, if she can.

C

Blunt. What will she get by that ? He seems under age, and cann't be supposed to have much money.

Lucy. But **his master** has, **and that's** the same thing, as she'll manage it.

Blunt. I don't like this fooling with a handsome young **fellow** : while she's endeavouring to ensnare him, she may be caught herself.

Lucy. Nay, were she like me, that would certainly be the consequence; for, I confess, there is something in youth and innocence that moves me mightily.

Blunt. Yes; so does the smoothness and plumpness of a partridge move a mighty desire in the hawk to be the destruction of it.

Lucy. Why, birds are their prey, and men are ours; though, as you observed, we are sometimes caught ourselves. But that, I dare say, will never be the case of our mistress.

Blunt. I wish it may prove so; for you know we all depend upon her. Should she trifle away her time with a young fellow that there's nothing to be got by, we must all starve.

Lucy. There's no danger of that; for I am sure she has no view in this affair but interest.

Blunt. Well, and what hopes are there of success in that ?

Lucy. The most promising that can be. 'Tis true the youth has his scruples ; but she'll soon teach him to answer them, by stifling his conscience. Oh, the lad is in a hopeful way, depend upon't.   [*Exeunt.*

SCENE III.

Draws, and discovers BARNWELL *and* MILLWOOD *at Supper. An Entertainment of Music and Singing. After which they come forward.*

Barn. What can I answer? All that I know is, that you are fair, and I am miserable.

Mill. We are both so, and yet the fault is in ourselves.

Barn. To ease our present anguish by plunging into guilt, is to buy a moment's pleasure with an age of pain.

Mill. I should have thought the joys of love as lasting as they are great: if ours prove otherwise, 'tis your inconstancy must make them so.

Barn. The law of Heaven will not be reversed, and that requires us to govern our passions.

Mill. To give us sense of beauty and desires, and yet forbid us to taste and be happy, is a cruelty to nature. Have we passions only to torment us?

Barn. To hear you talk, though in the cause of vice; to gaze upon your beauty, press your hand, " and see your snow-white bosom heave and fall," inflames my wishes; my pulse beats high, " my " senses all are in a hurry," and I am on the rack of wild desire.——Yet, for a moment's guilty pleasure, shall I lose my innocence, my peace of mind, and hopes of solid happiness?

Mill. Chimeras all!

Barn. I would not——yet must on——

    " *Reluctant thus the merchant quits his ease,*

    " *And trusts to rocks and sands, and stormy seas;*

    " *In hopes some unknown golden coast to find,*

    " *Commits himself, though doubtful, to the wind,*

    " *Longs much for joys to come—yet mourns those left*

      " *behind.*"

Mill. *Along with me, and prove*

No joys like woman-kind, no heaven like love.

                       [*Exeunt.*

ACT II. SCENE I.

A Room in THOROWGOOD'*s House. Enter* BARN-
WELL.

Barnwell.

How strange are all things round me! Like some
thief who treads forbidden ground, and fain would
lurk unseen, fearful I enter each apartment of this
well-known house. To guilty love, as if that were
too little, already have I added breach of trust——
A thief!——Can I know myself that wretched thing,
and look my honest friend and injured master in the
face? Though hypocrisy may a while conceal my
guilt, at length it will be known, and public shame
and ruin must ensue. In the mean time, what must

be my life? Ever to speak a language foreign to my
heart; hourly to add to the number of my crimes, in
order to conceal 'em.   Sure such was the condition
of the grand apostate, when first he lost his purity.
Like me, disconsolate, he wandered; and while yet
in heaven, bore all his future hell about him.

Enter TRUEMAN.

True. Barnwell, Oh, how I rejoice to see you safe!
So will our master and his gentle daughter; who,
during your absence, often inquired after you.

Barn. Would he were gone! His officious love will
pry into the secrets of my soul.   [*Aside.*

True. Unless you knew the pain the whole family
has felt on your account, you cann't conceive how
much you are beloved.   But why thus cold and silent? When my heart is full of joy for your return,
why do you turn away? why thus avoid me? What
have I done? How am I altered since you saw me
last? Or rather, what have you done? and why **are**
you thus changed? for I am still the same?

Barn. What have I done, indeed!   [*Aside.*

True. Not speak!——nor look **upon me!**——

Barn. By my face he will discover all I would conceal; methinks already I begin to hate him. [*Aside.*

True. I cannot bear this usage from a friend; one
whom till now I ever found so loving; whom yet I
love; though this unkindness strikes at the root of
friendship, and might destroy it in any breast but
mine.

C iij

Barn. I am not well. [*Turning to him.*] Sleep has been a stranger to these eyes since you beheld them last.

True. Heavy they look indeed, and swoln with tears ;——now they overflow. Rightly did my sympathising heart forebode last night, when thou wast absent, something fatal to our peace.

Barn. Your friendship engages you too far. My troubles, whate'er they are, are mine alone : you have no interest in them, nor ought your concern for me give you a moment's pain.

True. You speak as if you knew of friendship nothing but the name. Before I saw your grief, I felt it. " Since we parted last I have slept no more than " you, but pensive in my chamber sat alone, and " spent the tedious night in wishes for your safety " and return :" e'en now, though ignorant of the cause, your sorrow wounds me to the heart.

Barn. 'Twill not be always thus. Friendship and all engagements cease, as circumstances and occasions vary; and since you once may hate me, perhaps it might be better for us both that now you loved me less.

True. Sure I but dream ! Without a cause would Barnwell use me thus ? Ungenerous and ungrateful youth, farewell; I shall endeavour to follow your advice. [*Going.*] Yet stay, perhaps, I am too rash, and angry when the cause demands compassion. Some unforeseen calamity may have befallen him too great to bear.

Barn. What part am I reduced to act? 'Tis vile and base to move his temper thus, the best of friends and men.

True. I am to blame; pr'ythee, forgive me, Barnwell. Try to compose your ruffled mind; and let me know the cause that thus transports you from yourself; my friendly counsel may restore your peace.

Barn. All that is possible for man to do for man, your generous friendship may effect; but here even that's in vain.

True. Something dreadful is labouring in your breast; oh, give it vent, and let me share your grief; 'twill ease your pain, should it admit no cure, and make it lighter by the part I bear.

Barn. Vain supposition! my woes increase by being observed; should the cause be known, they would exceed all bounds.

True. So well I know thy honest heart, guilt cannot harbour there.

Barn. Oh, torture insupportable!　　　　*[Aside.*

True. Then why am I excluded? Have **I a** thought I would conceal from you?

Barn. If still you urge me on this hated subject, I'll never enter more beneath this roof, nor see your face again.

True. 'Tis strange——but I have done, say but you hate me not.

Barn. Hate you! I am not that monster yet.

True. Shall our friendship still continue?

Barn. It's a blessing I never was worthy of, yet now must stand on terms; and but upon conditions can confirm it.

True. What are they?

Barn. Never hereafter, though you should wonder at my conduct, desire to know more than I am willing to reveal.

True. 'Tis hard; but upon any conditions I must be your friend.

Barn. Then, as much as one lost to himself can be another's, I am yours.   [*Embracing.*

True. Be ever so, and may Heaven restore your peace!

" *Barn.* Will yesterday return? We have heard
" the glorious sun, that till then incessant roll'd,
" once stopp'd his rapid course, and once went back.
" The dead have risen, and parched rocks pour'd
" forth a liquid stream to quench a people's thirst.
" The sea divided, and form'd walls of water, while
" a whole nation pass'd in safety through its sandy
" bosom. Hungry lions have refus'd their prey;
" and men unhurt have walk'd amidst consuming
" flames; but never yet did time, once past, return."

True. " Though the continued chain of time has
" never once been broke, nor ever will, but unin-
" terrupted must keep on its course, till lost in eter-
" nity, it ends where it first began; yet as Heaven
" can repair whatever evils time can bring upon us,
" we ought never to despair." But business requires
our attendance; business, the youth's best preserva-

tive from ill, as idleness his worst of snares. Will
you go with me?

Barn. I'll take a little **time to** reflect on what has
past, and follow you. [*Exit* Trueman.] I might have
trusted Trueman, and engaged him to apply **to** my
uncle to repair the wrong I have done my master;
but what of Millwood? " Must I expose her **too**? Un-
" generous and base! Then Heaven requires **it not.**
" But Heaven requires that I forsake her. What!
" never to see her more? Does Heaven require that?
" I hope I may see her, and Heaven not be offended.
" Presumptuous hope! Dearly already have I proved
" my frailty. Should I once more tempt Heaven, I
" may be left to fall, never to rise again. Yet," shall
I leave her, for ever leave her, and not let her **know**
the cause? She who loves me with such a boundless
passion! Can cruelty be duty? I judge of what she
then must feel, by what I now endure. The love of
life, and fear of shame, opposed by inclination strong
as death or shame, like wind and tide in raging conflict meet, when neither can prevail, keep me in
doubt. How then can I determine? '

Enter THOROWGOOD.

Thor. Without a cause assign'd, or notice given, to
absent yourself last night was a fault, young man,
and I came to chide your for it, but hope I am prevented. That modest blush, the confusion so visible
in your face, speak grief and shame. When we have
offended Heaven, it requires no more; and shall

man, who needs himself to be forgiven, be harder to
appease? If my pardon or love be of moment to your
peace, look up secure of both.

Barn. This goodness has o'ercome me. [*Aside.*]
Oh, sir, you know not the nature and extent of my
offence; and I should abuse your mistaken bounty to
receive it.   Though I had rather die than speak my
shame; though racks could not have forced the
guilty secret from my breast, your kindness has.

Thor. Enough, enough, whate'er it be; this concern shews you're convinced, and I am satisfied.
How painful is the sense of guilt to an ingenuous
mind? Some youthful folly, which it were prudent
not to inquire into.   " When we consider the frail
" condition of humanity, it may raise our pity, not
" our wonder, that youth should go astray; when
" reason, weak at the best, opposed to inclination,
" scarce formed, and wholly unassisted by experi-
" ence, faintly contends, or willingly becomes the
" slave of sense. The state of youth is much to be
" deplored, and the more so, because they see it not;
" being then to danger most exposed, when they are
" least **prepared** for their defence."   [*Aside.*

Barn. It will be known, and you'll recall your
pardon and abhor me.

Thor. I never will. Yet be upon your guard in
this gay thoughtless season of your life; " when the
" sense of pleasure's quick, and passions high, the
" voluptuous appetites, raging and fierce, demand
" the strongest curb; take heed of a relapse:" when

vice becomes habitual, the **very** power of leaving it is lost.

Barn. Hear me, on my knees, confess——

Thor. Not a syllable more upon this subject; it were not mercy, but cruelty, to hear what must give you such torment to reveal.

Barn. This generosity amazes and distracts me.

Thor. This remorse makes thee dearer to me than if thou hadst never offended. Whatever is your fault, of this I am certain, 'twas harder for you to offend, than me to pardon.   [*Exit* Thorowgood.

Barn. Villain, villain, villain! basely to wrong so excellent a man. Should I again return to folly?— Detested thought!—But what of Millwood then?— Why, I renounce her;—I give her up——The struggle's over, and virtue **has** prevailed. Reason may convince, **but** gratitude compels. This unlooked-for generosity has sav'd me from destruction. [*Going.*

Enter a Footman.

Foot. Sir, two ladies from your uncle in the country desire to see you.

Barn. Who should they be. [*Aside.*] Tell them I'll wait upon 'em. Methinks I dread to see 'em.— Now every thing alarms me.——Guilt, what a coward hast thou made me!

SCENE II.

Another Room in THOROWGOOD's *House.* ENTER MILLWOOD, LUCY, *and a Footman.*

Foot. Ladies, he'll wait upon you immediately.

Mill. 'Tis very well.——I thank you. [*Exit Foot.*

Enter BARNWELL.

Barn. Confusion! Millwood!

Mill. That angry look tells me that here I am an unwelcome guest; I feared as much; the unhappy are so every where.

Barn. Will nothing but my utter ruin content you?

Mill. Unkind and cruel! Lost myself, your happiness is now my only care.

Barn. How did you gain admission?

Mill. Saying we were desired by your uncle to visit, and deliver a message to you, we were received by the family without suspicion, and with much respect conducted here.

Barn. Why did you come at all?

Mill. I never shall trouble you more. I'm come to take my leave for ever. Such is the malice of my fate: I go hopeless, despairing ever to return. This hour is all I have left: one **short** hour is all I have to bestow on love and you, **for** whom I thought the longest life too short.

Barn. Then we are met to part for ever?

Mill. It must be so. Yet think not that time or absence shall ever put a period to my grief, or make me love you less. Tho' I must leave you, yet condemn me not.

Barn. Condemn you! No, I approve your resolution, and rejoice to hear it; 'tis just——'tis necessary,——I have well weigh'd and found it so.

Lucy. I am afraid the young man has more sense than she thought he had.   [*Aside.*

Barn. Before you came, I had determin'd never to see you more.

Mill. Confusion!   [*Aside.*

Lucy. Ay, we are all out; this is a turn so unexpected, that I shall make nothing of my part; they must e'en play the scene betwixt themselves. [*Aside.*

Mill. 'Twas some relief to think, tho' absent, you would love me still; but to find, " tho' fortune had " been indulgent, that you, more cruel and incon- " stant," *you* had resolved to cast me off——This, as I never could expect, I have not learnt to bear.

Barn. I am sorry to hear you blame me in a resolution that so well becomes us both.

Mill. I have reason for what I do, but you have none.

Barn. Can we want a reason for parting, **who** have so many to wish we never had met ?

Mill. Look on me, Barnwell. Am I deform'd or old, that satiety so soon succeeds enjoyment ? Nay, look again; am I not she whom yesterday you thought the fairest and the kindest of her sex; whose

hand, trembling with ecstasy, you press'd and mould-
ed thus, while on my eyes you gazed with such delight, as if desire increased by being fed ?

Barn. No more ; let me repent my former follies,
if possible, without remembering what they were.

Mill. Why ?

Barn. Such is my frailty, that 'tis dangerous.

Mill. Where is the danger, since we are to part ?

Barn. The thought of that already is too painful.

Mill. If it be painful to part, then I may hope, at
least, you do not hate me ?

Barn. No——no——I never said I did———Oh,
my heart !

Mill. Perhaps you pity me ?

Barn. I do——I do—— Indeed I do.

Mill. You'll think upon me ?

Barn. Doubt it not, while I can think at all.

Mill. You may judge an embrace at parting too
great a favour—though it would be the last. [*He
draws back.*] A look shall then suffice——Farewell—
for ever.   [*Exeunt* Millwood *and* Lucy.

Barn. If to resolve to suffer be to conquer,——I
have conquer'd———Painful victory !

Re-enter MILLWOOD *and* LUCY.

Mill. One thing I had forgot ;——I never must return to my own house again. This I thought proper
to let you know, lest your mind should change, and
you should seek in vain to find me there. Forgive

2

me this second intrusion ; I only came to give you this caution, and that, perhaps, was needless.

Barn. I hope it was ; yet it is kind, and I must thank you for it.

Mill. My friend, your arm. [*To* Lucy.] Now, I am gone for ever.   [*Going.*

Barn. One thing more—Sure there's no danger in my knowing where you go ? If you think otherwise—

Mill. Alas !   [*Weeping.*

Lucy. We are right, I find ; that's my cue. [*Aside.*] Ah, dear sir ! she's going she knows not whither ; but go she must.

Barn. Humanity obliges me to wish you well : why will you thus expose yourself to needless troubles ?

Lucy. Nay, there's no help for it : she must quit the town immediately; and the kingdom as soon as possible. It was no small matter, you may be sure, that could make her resolve to leave you.

Mill. No more, my friend ; since he for whose dear sake alone I suffer, and am content to suffer, is kind and pities me ; where'er I wander, thro' wilds and deserts benighted and forlorn, that thought shall give me comfort.

Barn. For my sake !—Oh, tell me how, which way am I so curs'd to bring such ruin on thee ?

Mill. No matter ; I am contented with my lot.

Barn. Leave me not in this uncertainty.

Mill. I have said too much.

Barn. How, how am I the cause of your undoing ?

Mill. To know it will but increase your troubles.

Barn. My troubles cann't be greater than they are.

Lucy. Well, well, sir, if she won't satisfy you, I will.

Barn. I am bound to you beyond expression.

Mill. Remember, sir, that I desired you not to hear it.

Barn. Begin, and ease my racking expectation.

Lucy. Why, you must know, my lady here was an only child, and her parents dying while she was young, left her and her fortune (no inconsiderable one, I assure you) to the care of a gentleman who has a good estate of his own.

Mill. Ay, ay, the barbarous man is rich enough; but what are riches when compar'd to love?

Lucy. For a while he perform'd the office of a faithful guardian, settled her in a house, hir'd her servants.——But you have seen in what manner she liv'd, so I need say no more of that.

Mill. How I shall live hereafter, Heaven knows!

Lucy. All things went on as one could wish; till some time ago, his wife dying, he fell violently in love with his charge, and would fain have marry'd her. Now the man is neither old nor ugly, but a good personable sort of a man, but I don't know how it was, she could never endure him. In short, her ill usage so provoked him, that he brought in an account of his executorship, wherein he makes her debtor to him.——

Mill. A trifle in itself, but more than enough to

ruin me, whom, by this unjust account, he had stripp'd of all before.

Lucy. Now, she having neither money nor friend, except me, who am as unfortunate as herself, he compell'd her to pass his account, and give bond for the sum he demanded ; but still provided handsomely for her, and continued his courtship, till being inform'd by his spies (truly I suspect some in her own family), that you were entertain'd at her house, and staid with her all night, he came this morning raving and storming like a madman, talks no more of marriage (so there's no hope of making up matters that way), but vows her ruin, unless she'll allow him the same favour that he supposes she granted you.

Barn. Must she be ruin'd, or find her refuge in another's arms ?

Mill. He gave me but an hour to resolve in ; that's happily spent with you——And now I go——

Barn. To be expos'd to all the rigours of the various seasons ; the summer's parching heat, and winter's cold ; unhoused, to wander, friendless, thro' the unhospitable world, in misery and want ; attended with fear and danger, and pursued by malice and revenge. Wouldst thou endure all this for me, and can I do nothing, nothing, to prevent it ?

Lucy. 'Tis really a pity there can be no way found out.

Barn. Oh, where are all my resolutions now ?
" Like early vapours, or the morning dew, chas'd by

" the sun's warm beams, they're vanish'd and lost,
" as tho' they had never been."

Lucy. Now I advised her, sir, to comply with the
gentleman ; "that would not only put an end to her
" troubles, but make her fortune at once."

Barn. Tormenting fiend, away! I had rather perish, nay, see her perish, than have her saved by him.
I will, myself, prevent her ruin, though with my
own. A moment's patience ; I'll return immediately.   [*Exit* Barnwell.

Lucy. 'Twas well you came, or, by what I can perceive, you had lost him.

Mill. That, I must confess, was a danger I did not
foresee ; I was only afraid he should have come without money. You know, a house of entertainment,
like mine, is not kept without expence.

Lucy. That's very true; but then you should be
reasonable in your demands; 'tis pity to discourage
a young man.

Mill. Leave that to me.

Re-enter BARNWELL, *with a Bag of Money.*

Barn. What am I about to do?——Now you, who
boast your reason all-sufficient, suppose yourselves
in my condition, and determine for me ; whether 'tis
right to let her suffer for my faults, or, by this small
addition to my guilt, prevent **the** ill effects of what
is past.

Lucy. These young sinners think every thing in
the ways of wickedness so strange!——But I could

tell him, that this is nothing but what's very common; for one vice as naturally begets another, as a father a son. But he'll find out that himself, if he lives long enough. [*Aside.*

Barn. Here, take this, and with it purchase your deliverance; return to your house, and live in peace and safety.

Mill. So, I may hope to see you there again?

Barn. Answer me not, but fly, lest, in the agonies of my remorse, I take again what is not mine to give, and abandon thee to want and misery.

Mill. Say but you'll come.

Barn. You are my fate, my Heaven or my hell; only leave me now, dispose of me hereafter as you please. [*Exeunt* Millwood *and* Lucy.

What have I done? Were my resolutions founded on reason, and sincerely made? Why then has Heaven suffer'd me to fall? I sought not the occasion; and if my heart deceives me not, compassion and generosity were my motives. "Is virtue inconsistent "with itself, or are vice and virtue only empty names; "or do they depend on accidents, beyond our power "to produce, or to prevent; wherein we have no "part, and yet must be determined by the event?" But why should I attempt to reason? All is confusion, horror, and remorse. I find I am lost, cast down from all my late-erected hope, and plunged again in guilt, yet scarce know how or why:

Such undistinguish'd horrors make my brain,
Like hell, the seat of darkness and of pain. [*Exit.*

ACT III.   SCENE I.

A Room in THOROWGOOD's *House.* THOROWGOOD
and TRUEMAN *discovered (with Account Books) sitting at a Table.*

" *Thorowgood.*

" METHINKS I would not have you only learn the
" method of merchandise, and practise it hereafter,
" merely as a means of getting wealth : it will be
" well worth your pains to study it as a science, to
" see how it is founded in reason and the nature of
" things ; how it promotes humanity, as it has open'd,
" and yet keeps up an intercourse between nations,
" far remote from one another in situation, customs,
" and religion ; promoting arts, industry, peace, and
" plenty ; by mutual benefits diffusing mutual love
" from pole to pole.

" *True.* Something of this I have consider'd, and
" hope, by your assistance, to extend my thoughts
" much farther. I have observ'd those countries
" where trade is promoted and encouraged, do not
" make discoveries to destroy, but to improve man-
" kind by love and friendship ; to tame the fierce,
" and polish the most savage ; to teach them the ad-
" vantage of honest traffic, by taking from them,
" with their own consent, their useless superfluities,
" and giving them, in return, what, from their ig-

" norance in manual arts, their situation, or some
" other accident, they stand in need of.

" *Thor.* 'Tis justly observ'd : the populous east,
" luxuriant, abounds with glittering gems, bright
" pearls, aromatic spices, and health-restoring drugs :
" the late-found western world's rich earth glows
" with unnumber'd veins of gold and silver ore. On
" every climate, and on every country, Heaven has
" bestow'd some good peculiar to itself. It is the in-
" dustrious merchant's business to colleƈt the various
" blessings of each soil and climate; and, with the
" produƈt of the whole, to enrich his native coun-
" try."——Well, I have examin'd your accounts ;
they are not only just, as I have always found them,
but regularly kept, and fairly enter'd. I commend
your diligence. Method in business is the surest
guide : " he who negleƈts it, frequently stumbles,
" and always wanders perplex'd, uncertain, and in
" danger." Are Barnwell's accounts ready for my
inspeƈtion ? He does not use to be the last on these
occasions.

True. Upon receiving your orders he retir'd, I
thought in some confusion. If you please, I'll go and
hasten him. I hope he has not been guilty of any
negleƈt.

Thor. I'm now going to the Exchange; let him know
at my return I expeƈt to find him ready.   [*Exeunt.*

Enter MARIA *with a book. Sits and reads.*

Mar. How forcible is truth! The weakest mind,

inspired with love of that, fixed and collected in itself, with indifference beholds the united force of earth and hell opposing. Such souls are raised above the sense of pain, or so supported that they regard it not. The martyr cheaply purchases his Heaven; small are his sufferings, great is his reward. Not so the wretch who combats love with duty; whose mind, weakened and dissolved by the soft passion, feeble and hopeless, opposes his own desires——What is an hour, a day, a year of pain, to a whole life of tortures such as these?

Enter TRUEMAN.

True. Oh, Barnwell! Oh, my friend! how art thou fallen!

Mar. Ha! Barnwell! What of him? Speak, say, what of Barnwell?

True. 'Tis not to be conceal'd: I've news to tell of him, that will afflict your generous father, yourself, and all who know him.

Mar. Defend us, Heaven!

True. I cannot speak it. See there. [*Gives a letter.*

Mar. [*Reads.*] ' I know my absence will surprise my honoured master and yourself; and the more, when you shall understand that the reason of my withdrawing, is my having embezzled part of the cash with which I was entrusted. After this, 'tis needless to inform you, that I intend never to return again. Though this might have been known, by examining my accounts, yet to prevent that unnecessary trouble, and to cut off all fruitless expectations of my return, I have left this from the lost

GEORGE BARNWELL.'

True. Lost indeed! Yet how he should be guilty of what he there charges himself withal, raises my wonder equal to my grief. Never had youth a higher sense of virtue. Justly he thought, and as he thought he practised; never was life more regular than his.— An understanding uncommon at his years, an open, generous manliness of temper, his manners easy, unaffected, and engaging.

Mar. This, and much more you might have said with truth. He was the delight of every eye, and joy of every heart that knew him.

True. Since such he was, and was my friend, can I support his loss? See, the fairest, happiest maid this wealthy city boasts, kindly condescends to weep for thy unhappy fate, poor, ruined Barnwell!

Mar. Trueman, do you think a soul so delicate as his, so sensible of shame, can e'er submit to live a slave to vice?

True. Never, never. So well I know him, I'm sure this act of his, so contrary to his nature, must have been caused by some unavoidable necessity.

Mar. Is there no means yet to preserve him?

True. Oh, that there were! but few men recover their reputation lost, a merchant never. Nor would he, I fear, though I should find him, ever be brought to look his injured master in the face.

Mar. I fear as much, and therefore would never **have** my father know it.

True. That's impossible.

Mar. What's the sum?

True. 'Tis considerable ; I've marked it here, to shew it, with the letter, to your father, at his return.

Mar. If I should supply the money, could you so dispose of that and the account, as to conceal this unhappy mismanagement from my father ?

True. Nothing more easy. But can you intend it ? —Will you save a helpless wretch from ruin?—Oh, 'twere an act worthy such exalted virtue as Maria's! Sure Heaven, in mercy to my friend, inspired the generous thought.

Mar. Doubt not but I would purchase so great a happiness at a much dearer price. But how shall he be found?

True. Trust to my diligence for that. In the mean time, I'll conceal his absence from your father, or find such excuses for it, that the real cause shall never be suspected.

Mar. In attempting to save from shame, one whom we hope may yet return to virtue, to Heaven, and you, the only witnesses of this action, I appeal, whether I do any thing misbecoming my sex and character.

True. Earth must approve the deed, and Heaven, I doubt not, will reward it.

Mar. If Heaven succeeds it, I am well rewarded.

A virgin's fame is sullied by suspicion's lightest breath: and, therefore, as this must be a secret from my father and the world, for Barnwell's sake, for mine, let it be so to him.   [*Exeunt.*

SCENE II.

A Room in MILLWOOD's *House. Enter* LUCY *and* BLUNT.

Lucy. Well, what do you think of Millwood's conduct now?

Blunt. I own it is surprising: I don't know which to admire most, her feigned, or his real passion; tho' I have sometimes been afraid that her avarice would discover her. But his youth and want of experience make it the easier to impose on him.

Lucy. No, it is his love. To do him justice, notwithstanding his youth, he don't want understanding. But you men are much easier imposed on in these affairs, than your vanity will allow you to believe. Let me see the wisest of you all as much in love with me as Barnwell is with Millwood, and I'll engage to make as great a fool of him.

Blunt. And, all circumstances considered, to make as much money of him too?

Lucy. I cann't answer for that. Her artifice, in making him rob his master at first, and the various stratagems by which she has obliged him to conti-

E

nue that course, astonish even me, who know her so
well.

Blunt. But then you are to consider that the money
was his master's.

Lucy. There was the difficulty of it.   **Had** it been
his own, it had been nothing.   Were the world his,
she might have it for a smile.   But those golden days
are done: he's ruined, and Millwood's hopes of farther profits there, are **at** an end.

Blunt. That's no more than we all expected.

Lucy. **Being** called by his master to make up his
accounts, he was forced to quit his house and service, and wisely flies to Millwood for relief and entertainment.

Blunt. I have not heard of this before: how did
she receive him?

Lucy. As you would expect.   She wondered what
he meant, was astonished at his impudence, and, with
an air of modesty peculiar to herself, swore so heartily that she never saw him before, that she put me
out of countenance.

Blunt. That's much indeed! But how did Barnwell
behave?

Lucy. He grieved; and at length, enraged at this
barbarous treatment, was preparing to be gone; and
making towards the door, shewed a sum of money,
which he had brought from his master's, the last he
is ever likely to have from thence.

Blunt. But then, Millwood——

Lucy. Ay, she, with her usual address, returned to

her old arts of lying, swearing, and dissembling; hung on his neck, wept, and swore 'twas meant in jest.— The amorous youth melted into tears, threw the money into her lap, and swore he had rather die than think her false.

Blunt. Strange infatuation!

Lucy. But what ensued was stranger still. As doubts and fears, followed by reconcilement, [ever increase love where the passion is sincere; so in him it caused so wild a transport of excessive fondness, such joy, such grief, such pleasure, and such anguish, that nature seemed sinking with the weight, and his charmed soul disposed to quit his breast for hers. Just then, when every passion with lawless anarchy prevailed, and reason was in the raging tempest lost, the cruel, artful Millwood prevailed upon the wretched youth to promise——what I tremble but to think of.

Blunt. I am amazed! What can it be?

Lucy. You will be more so, to hear it is to attempt the life of his nearest relation, and best benefactor.

Blunt. His uncle! whom we have often heard him speak of as a gentleman of a large estate, and fair character, in the country where he lives!

Lucy. The same. She was no sooner possessed of the last dear purchase of his ruin; but her avarice, insatiate as the grave, demanded this horrid sacrifice. Barnwell's near relation, " and unsuspected virtue, " must give too easy means to seize this good man's " treasure;" whose blood must seal the dreadful secret, and prevent the terrors of her guilty fears.

Blunt. Is it possible she could persuade him to do an act like that? He is by nature honest, grateful, compassionate, and generous; "and though his love, "and her artful persuasions, have wrought him to "practise what he most abhors; yet we all can wit- "ness for him, with what reluctance he has still com- "plied: so many tears he shed o'er each offence, as "might, if possible, sanctify theft, and make a merit "of a crime."

Lucy. 'Tis true, at the naming of the murder of his uncle he started into rage; and, breaking from her arms (where she till then had held him with well-dis- sembled love, and false endearments), called her cruel, monster, devil, and told her she was born for his destruction. She thought it not for her purpose to meet his rage with her rage, but affected a most passionate fit of grief, railed at her fate, and cursed her wayward stars, that still her wants should force her to press him to act such deeds, as she must needs abhor as well as he. She told him necessity had no law, and love no bounds; that therefore he never truly loved, but meant, in her necessity, to for- sake her. Then she kneeled, and swore, that since by his refusal he had given her cause to doubt his love, she never would see him more, unless, to prove it true, he robbed his uncle to supply her wants, and murdered him to keep it from discovery.

Blunt. I am astonished. What said he?

Lucy. Speechless he stood; but in his face you might have read, that various passions tore his very

soul. Oft he in anguish threw his eyes towards heaven, " and then as often bent their beams on her;"
then wept and groaned, and beat his troubled breast:
at length, with horror not to be express'd, he cried,
—' Thou cursed fair, have I not given dreadful
proofs of love? What drew me from my youthful
innocence, and stained my then unspotted soul, but
love? What caused me to rob my worthy, gentle
master, but cursed love? What makes me now a fu-
gitive from his service, loathed by myself, and
scorned by all the world, but love? What fills my
eyes with tears, my soul with torture never felt on this
side death before? Why love, love, love! And why,
above all, do I resolve (for, tearing his hair, he cried,
I do resolve) to kill my uncle?'

Blunt. Was she not moved? It makes me weep to
hear the sad relation.

Lucy. Yes—with joy, that she had gained her point.
She gave him no time to cool, but urged him to attempt it instantly. He's now gone. If he performs
it, and escapes, there's more money for her; if not,
he'll ne'er return, and then she's fairly rid of him.

Blunt. 'Tis time the world were rid of such a
monster.

Lucy. If we don't use our endeavours to prevent
the murder, we are as bad as she.

Blunt. I am afraid it is too late.

Lucy. Perhaps not. Her barbarity to Barnwell
makes me hate her. We have run too great a length

with her already. I did not think her or myself so wicked, as I find, upon reflection, we are.

Blunt. 'Tis true, we have been all too much so. But there is something so horrid in murder, that all other crimes seem nothing when compared to that: I would not be involved in the guilt of it for all the world.

Lucy. Nor I, Heaven knows. Therefore let us clear ourselves, by doing all that is in our power to prevent it. I have just thought of a way that to me seems probable. Will you join with me to detect this cursed design?

Blunt. With all my heart. He who knows of a murder intended to be committed, and does not discover it, in the eye of the law and reason, is a murderer.

Lucy. Let us lose no time; I'll acquaint you with the particulars as we go.   [*Exeunt.*

SCENE III.

A Walk at some Distance from a Country Seat. Enter
BARNWELL.

Barn. A dismal gloom obscures the face of day. Either the sun has slipped behind a cloud, or journeys down the west of heaven with more than common speed, to avoid the sight of what I am doomed to act. Since I set forth on this accurs'd design,

where'er I tread, methinks, the solid earth trembles
beneath my feet. *Murder my uncle !*——" Yonder
" limpid stream, whose hoary fall has made a natu-
" ral cascade, as I passed by, in doleful accents
" seem'd to murmur——Murder ! The earth, the
" air, and water seem'd concern'd. But that's not
" strange : the world is punish'd, and nature feels a
" shock, when Providence permits a good man's fall.
" Just Heaven ! then what should I feel for him that
" was" my father's only brother, and since his death
has been to me a father ; that took me up an infant
and an orphan, reared me with tenderest care, and
still indulged me with most paternal fondness ? Yet
here I stand his destined murderer——I stiffen with
horror at my own impiety——'Tis yet unperformed—
What if I quit my bloody purpose, and fly the place ?
[*Going, then stops.*]——But whither, oh, whither shall
I fly ? My master's once friendly doors are ever shut
against me ; and without money Millwood will never
see me more ; and she has got such firm possession
of my heart, and governs there with such despotic
sway, that life is not to be endured without her.
Ay, there's the cause of all my sin and sorrow : 'tis
more than love ; it is the fever of the soul, and madness of desire. In vain does nature, reason, conscience, all oppose it ; the impetuous passion bears
down all before it, and drives me on to lust, to theft,
and murder. Oh, conscience ! feeble guide to virtue, thou only shew'st us when we go astray, but
wantest power to stop us in our course !——Ha ! in

yonder shady walk I see my uncle——He's alone——
Now for my disguise. [*Plucks out a vizor.*]——This is
his hour of private meditation. Thus daily he prepares his soul for Heaven; while I——But what
have I to do with Heaven? Ha! no struggles, conscience——

Hence, hence remorse, and every thought that's good;
The storm that lust began, must end in blood. _

      [Puts on the vizor, draws a pistol, and exit.

SCENE IV.

A close Walk in a Wood. *Enter* Uncle.

Unc. If I were superstitious, I should fear some
danger lurked unseen, or death were nigh. A heavy
melancholy clouds my spirits. My imagination is
filled with ghastly forms of dreary graves, and bodies
changed by death; when the pale lengthened vi-
sage attracts each weeping eye, and fills the musing
soul at once with grief and horror, pity and aversion.
—I will indulge the thought. The wise man prepares himself for death, by making it familiar to his
mind. When strong reflections hold the mirror near,
and the living in the dead behold their future self,
how does each inordinate passion and desire cease, or
sicken at the view! The mind scarce moves; the
blood, curdling and chilled, creeps slowly through
the veins: fixed, still, and motionless we stand, so

like the solemn object of our thoughts, we are almost at present what we must be hereafter; till curiosity awakes the soul, and sets it on enquiry.

Enter BARNWELL, *at a distance.*

Oh, death! thou strange, mysterious power, seen every day, yet never understood, but by the incommunicative dead, what art thou? The extensive mind of man, that with a thought circles the earth's vast globe, sinks to the centre, or ascends above the stars; that worlds exotic finds, or thinks it finds, thy thick clouds attempts to pass in vain; lost and bewildered in the horrid gloom, defeated, she returns more doubtful than before, of nothing certain but of labour lost.

[*During this speech,* Barnwell *sometimes presents the pistol, and draws it back again.*

Barn. Oh! 'tis impossible.

[*Throwing down the pistol.*
[*Uncle starts, and attempts to draw his sword.*]
Unc. A man so near me! armed and masked——
Barn. Nay then, there's no retreat.

[*Plucks a poignard from his bosom, and stabs him.*
Unc. Oh! I am slain. All gracious Heaven, regard the prayer of thy dying servant; bless, with the choicest blessings, my dearest nephew; forgive my murderer, and take my fleeting soul to endless mercy.

[Barnwell *throws off his mask, runs to him, and, kneeling by him, raises and chafes him.*
Barn. Expiring saint! Oh, murdered, martyred

uncle! lift up your dying eyes, and view your nephew in your murderer———Oh, do not look so tenderly upon me!———Let indignation lighten from your eyes, and blast me ere you die.———By Heaven, he weeps, in pity of my woes.———Tears, tears, for blood!———The murdered, in the agonies of death, weeps for his murderer.———Oh, speak your pious purpose ; pronounce my pardon then, and take me with you———He would, but cannot———Oh, why, with such fond affection, do you press my murdering hand ?———[*Uncle sighs and dies.*]——— " What, will " you kiss me ?"———Life, that hovered on his lips but till he had sealed my pardon, in that sigh expired.— He's gone for ever, " and, oh! I follow———[*Swoons* " *away upon his uncle's dead body.*]"———Do I still breathe, and taint with my infectious breath the wholesome air?———Let Heaven from its high throne, in justice or in mercy now look down on that dear murdered saint, and me the murderer, and if his vengeance spares, let pity strike and end my wretched being.———Murder the worst of crimes, and parricide the worst of murders, and this the worst of parricides.——— " Cain, who stands on record " from the birth of time, and must to its last final " period, as accursed, slew a brother favoured above " him : detested Nero, by another's hand, dispatched " a mother that he feared and hated : but I, with my " own hand, have murdered a brother, mother, fa- " ther, and a friend most loving and beloved.——— " This execrable act of mine is without a parallel.—

" Oh, may it ever stand alone, the last of murders, as
" it is the worst!

" The rich man thus, in torment and despair,
" Preferr'd his vain, his charitable pray'r.
" The fool, his own soul lost, would fain be wise
" For others' good, but Heav'n his suit denies.
" By laws and means well-known we stand or fall;
" And one eternal rule remains for all."

Oh, may it ever stand alone accurst,
The last of murders, as it is the worst.   [*Exit.*

ACT IV. SCENE I.

A Room in THOROWGOOD'*s House.*   *Enter* MARIA,
meeting TRUEMAN.

Maria.

" How falsely do they judge, who censure or ap-
" plaud, as we are afflicted or rewarded here. I know
" I am unhappy; yet cannot charge myself with any
" crime, more than the common frailties of our kind,
" that should provoke just Heaven to mark me out
" for sufferings so uncommon and severe. Falsely
" to accuse ourselves, Heaven must abhor. Then it
" is just and right that innocence should suffer; for
" Heaven must be just in all its ways. Perhaps by
" that we are kept from moral evils, much worse
" than penal, or more improved in virtue. Or may
" not the lesser ills that we sustain be made the means

" of greater good to others?   Might all the joyless
" days and sleepless nights that I have passed, but
" purchase peace for thee.

    " *Thou dear, dear cause of all my grief and pain ;*
    " *Small were the loss, and infinite the gain,*
    " *Though to the grave in secret love I pine,*
    " *So life and fame, and happiness were thine.*"

What news of Barnwell?

True. None; I have sought him with the greatest
diligence, but all in vain.

Mar. Does my father yet suspect the cause of his
absence?

True. All appeared so just and fair to him, it is not
possible he ever should. But his absence will no longer
be concealed. Your father is wise; and though he
seems to hearken to the friendly excuses I would make
for Barnwell, yet I am afraid he regards them only
as such, without suffering them to influence his
judgment.

" *Mar.* How does the unhappy youth defeat all
" our designs to serve him? yet I can never repent
" what we have done. Should he return, 'twill make
" his reconciliation with my father easier, and pre-
" serve him from future reproach of a malicious un-
" forgiving world."

      Enter THOROWGOOD *and* LUCY.

Thor. This woman here has given me a sad, and,
'bating some circumstances, too probable an account
of Barnwell's defection.

Lucy. I am sorry, sir, that my frank confession of

my former unhappy course of life, should cause you
to suspect my truth on this occasion.   •

Thor. It is not that; your confession has in it all
the appearance of truth. Among many other particulars, she informs me, that Barnwell has been influenced to break his trust, and wrong me at several
times of considerable sums of money. Now, as I
know this to be false, I would fain doubt the whole
of her relation, too dreadful to be willingly believed.

Mar. Sir, your pardon; I find myself on a sudden
so indisposed that I must retire. " Providence op-
" poses all attempts to save him." Poor ruined Barnwell! Wretched, lost Maria! [*Aside. Exit.*

Thor. How am I distressed on every side! Pity for
that unhappy youth, fear for the life of a much valued
friend——and then my child—the only joy and hope
of my declining life!——Her melancholy increases
hourly, and gives me painful apprehensions of her
loss——Oh, Trueman, this person informs me that
your friend, at the instigation of an impious woman,
is gone to rob and murder his venerable uncle.

True. Oh, execrable deed! I am blasted with the
horror of the thought.

Lucy. This delay may ruin all.

Thor. What to do or think, I know not. That he
ever wronged me, I know is false; the rest may be
so too; there's all my hope.

True. Trust not to that; rather suppose all true,
than lose a moment's time. Even now the horrid

F

deed may be doing—dreadful imagination!——or it may be done, and we be vainly debating on the means to prevent what is already past.

Thor. This earnestness convinces me, that he knows more than he has yet discovered. What, ho! without there! who waits?

Enter a Servant.

Order the groom to saddle the swiftest horse, and prepare to set out with speed; an affair of life and death demands his diligence. [*Exit Servant.*] For you, whose behaviour on this occasion I have no time to commend as it deserves, I must engage your further assistance. Return, and observe this Millwood till I come. I have your directions, and will follow you as soon as possible. [*Exit* Lucy.] Trueman, you, I am sure, will not be idle on this occasion.

[*Exit* Thorowgood.

True. He only who is a friend can judge of my distress. [*Exit.*

SCENE II.

MILLWOOD's *House.* Enter MILLWOOD.

Mill. I wish I knew the event of his design. The attempt without success would ruin him. Well; what have I to apprehend from that? I fear too much. The mischief being only intended, his friends,

through pity of his youth, turn all their rage on me.
I should have thought of that before. Suppose the
deed done; then, and then only, I shall be secure.—
Or what if he returns without attempting it at all!—

Enter BARNWELL *bloody.*

But he is here, and I have done him wrong. His
bloody hands shew he has done the deed, but shew
he wants the prudence to conceal it.

Barn. Where shall I hide me? Whither shall I
fly, to avoid the swift unerring hand of justice?

Mill. Dismiss your fears: though thousands had
pursued you to the door, yet being entered here, you
are as safe as innocence. I have a cavern, by art so
cunningly contrived, that the piercing eyes of jealousy
and revenge may search in vain, nor find the entrance
to the safe retreat. There will I hide you, if any
danger's near.

Barn. Oh, hide me——from myself, if it be possible; for while I bear my conscience in my bosom,
though I were hid where man's eye never saw, nor
light e'er dawned, 'twere all in vain. For, oh, that
inmate, that impartial judge, will try, convict, and
sentence me for murder, and execute me with never-
ending torments. Behold these hands, all crimsoned
o'er with my dear uncle's blood. Here's a sight to
make a statue start with horror, or turn a living man
into a statue!

Mill. Ridiculous! Then it seems you are afraid of

F ij

your own shadow, or, what's less than a shadow,
your conscience.

Barn. Though to man unknown I did the accursed
act, what can we hide from Heaven's all-seeing eye?

Mill. No more of this stuff, What advantage have
you made of his death? or what advantage may yet
be made of it? Did you secure the keys of his treasure, which, no doubt, were about him? What gold,
what jewels, or what else of value have you brought
me?

Barn. Think you I added sacrilege to murder?—
Oh, had you seen him as his life flowed from him in
a crimson flood, and heard him praying for me by
the double name of nephew and of murderer—(alas,
alas, he knew not then, that his nephew was his murderer!)—how would you have wished, as I did,
though you had a thousand years of life to come, to
have given them all to have lengthened his one hour!
But being dead, I fled the sight of what my hands
had done; nor could I, to have gained the empire of
the world, have violated, by theft, his sacred corpse.

Mill. Whining, preposterous, canting villain! to
murder your uncle, rob him of life, nature's first,
last, dear prerogative, after which there's no injury,
then fear to take what he no longer wanted, and
bring to me your penury and guilt. Do you think
I'll hazard my reputation, nay, my life, to entertain
you?

Barn. Oh, Millwood!——this from thee?——But
I have done. If you hate me, if you wish me dead,

then are you happy ; for, oh, 'tis sure my grief will
quickly end me.

Mill. In his madness he will discover all, and involve me in his ruin. We are on a precipice from
whence there's no retreat for both——Then to preserve myself——[*Pauses.*]——There is no other way.
——'Tis dreadful, but reflection comes too late when
danger's pressing, and there's no room for choice.
——It must be done. [*Aside. Rings a bell, enter a
Servant.*] Fetch me an officer, and seize this villain.
He has confessed himself a murderer. Should I let
him escape, I might justly be thought as bad as he.

                         [*Exit Servant.*

Barn. Oh, Millwood! sure you do not, you cannot
mean it. Stop the messenger ; upon my knees, I beg
you'd call him back. 'Tis fit I die indeed, but not
by you. I will this instant deliver myself into the
hands of justice, indeed I will ; for death is all I
wish. But thy ingratitude so tears my wounded
soul, 'tis worse ten thousand times than death with
torture.

Mill. Call it what you will ; I am willing to live,
and live secure, which nothing but your death can
warrant.

Barn. If there be a pitch of wickedness that sets
the author beyond the reach of vengeance, you must
be secure. But what remains for me, but a dismal
dungeon, hard galling fetters, an awful trial, and an
ignominious death, justly to fall unpitied and ab-

horred : " After death to be suspended between
" heaven and earth, a dreadful spectacle, the warn-
" ing and horror of a gaping crowd!" This I could
bear, nay, wish not to avoid, had it but come from
any hand but thine.

Enter BLUNT, *Officer, and Attendants.*

Mill. Heaven defend me! Conceal a murderer!
Here, sir, take this youth into your custody. I accuse him of murder, and will appear to make good
my charge.   [*They seize him.*

Barn. To whom, of what, or how shall I complain?
I'll not accuse her. The hand of Heaven is in it, and
this the punishment of lust and parricide. " Yet
" Heaven, that justly cuts me off, still suffers her to
" live ; perhaps to punish others. Tremendous
" mercy! So fiends are cursed with immortality to
" be the executioners of Heaven."
Be warn'd, ye youths, who see my sad despair :
Avoid lewd women, false as they are fair.
" *By reason guided, honest joys pursue :*
" *The fair, to honour and to virtue true,*
" *Just to herself, will ne'er be false to you.*"
By my example learn to shun my fate :
(How wretched is the man who's wise too late!)
Ere innocence, and fame, and life be lost,
Here purchase wisdom cheaply, at my cost.

          [*Exeunt Barnwell,* Officer, and Attendants.

Mill. Where's Lucy? Why is she absent at such a
time?

Blunt. Would I had been so too! Lucy will soon be here; and I hope to thy confusion, thou devil!

Mill. Insolent!—This to me?

Blunt. The worst that we know of the devil is, that he first seduces to sin, and then betrays to punishment. [*Exit.*

Mill. They disapprove of my conduct then, " and " mean to take this opportunity to set up for them-" selves."——My ruin is resolved.——I see my danger, but scorn both it and them. I was not born to fall by such weak instruments. [*Going.*

Enter THOROWGOOD.

Thor. Where is the scandal of her own sex, and curse of ours?

Mill. What means this insolence? Whom do you seek?

Thor. Millwood.

Mill. Well, you have found her then. I am Millwood.

Thor. Then you are the most impious wretch that e'er the sun beheld.

Mill. From your appearance I should have expected wisdom and moderation, but your manners belie your aspect. What is your business here? I know you not.

Thor. Hereafter you may know me better; I am Barnwell's master.

Mill. Then you are master to a villain, which, I think, is not much to your credit.

Thor. Had he been as much above thy arts, as my credit is superior to thy malice, I need not have blushed to own him.

Mill. My arts! I don't understand you, sir; if he has done amiss, what's that to me? Was he my servant, or yours? you should have taught him better.

Thor. Why should I wonder to find such uncommon impudence in one arrived to such a height of wickedness? " When innocence is banished, mo-" desty soon follows." Know, sorceress, I'm not ignorant of any of the arts by which you first deceived the unwary youth. I know how, step by step, you've led him on, reluctant and unwilling, from crime to crime, to this last horrid act, which you contrived, and by your cursed wiles even forced him to commit.

Mill. Ha! Lucy has got the advantage, and accused me first. Unless I can turn the accusation, and fix it upon her and Blunt, I am lost.   [*Aside.*

Thor. Had I known your cruel design sooner, it had been prevented. To see you punished, as the law directs, is all that now remains. " Poor satisfaction! for he, innocent as he is, compared to you, must suffer too. " But Heaven, who knows our " frame, and graciously distinguishes between frailty " and presumption, will make a difference, though " man cannot, who sees not the heart, but only " judges by the outward action."

Mill. I find, sir, we are both unhappy in our servants. I was surprised at such ill treatment without

cause from a gentleman of your appearance, and
therefore too hastily returned it; for which I ask
your pardon. I now perceive you have been so far
imposed on, as to think me engaged in a former corre-
spondence with your servant, and some way or other
accessary to his undoing.

Thor. I charge you as the cause, the sole cause of
all his guilt, and all his suffering, of all he now en-
dures, and must endure, till a violent and shameful
death shall put a dreadful period to his life and miseries together.

Mill. 'Tis very strange. But who's secure from
scandal and detraction? So far from contributing to
his ruin, I never spoke to him till since this fatal accident, which I lament as much as you. 'Tis true, I
have a servant, on whose account he hath of late fre-
quented my house. If she has abused my good opinion of her, am I to blame? Has not Barnwell done
the same by you?

Thor. I hear you; pray go on.

Mill. I have been informed he had a violent passion
for her, and she for him: but till now I always
thought it innocent. I know her poor, and given to
expensive pleasures. Now, who can tell but she may
have influenced the amorous youth to commit this
murder to supply her extravagancies?——It must be
so. I now recollect a thousand circumstances that
confirm it. I'll have her, and a man-servant whom
I suspect as an accomplice, secured immediately. I
hope, sir, you will lay aside your ill-grounded suspi-

cions of me, and join to punish the real contrivers of
this bloody deed.   [*Offers to go.*

Thor. Madam, you pass not this way : I see your
design, but shall protect them from your malice.

Mill. I hope you will not use your influence, and
the credit of your name, to screen such guilty
wretches. Consider, sir, the wickedness of persuading a thoughtless youth to such a crime.

Thor. I do——and of betraying him when it was
done.

Mill. That which you call betraying him may convince you of my innocence. She who loves him,
though she contrived the murder, would never have
delivered him into the hands of justice, as I, struck
with horror at his crimes, have done.

Thor. How should an unexperienced youth escape
her snares ? " The powerful magic of her wit and
" form might betray the wisest to simple dotage, and
" fire the blood that age had froze long since." Even
I, that with just prejudice came prepared, had by her
artful story been deceived, but that my strong conviction of her guilt makes even a doubt impossible.
[*Aside.*] Those whom subtilly you would accuse, you
know are your accusers ; and, which proves unan-
swerably their innocence and your guilt, they accused
you before the deed was done, and did all that was
in their power to prevent it.

Mill. Sir, you are very hard to be convinced ; but
I have a proof, which, when produced, will silence
all objections.   [*Exit* Millwood.

Enter LUCY, TRUEMAN, BLUNT, *Officers, &c.*

Lucy. Gentlemen, pray place yourselves, some on one side of that door, and some on the other; watch her entrance, and act as your prudence shall direct you. This way, [*To* Thorowgood.] and note her behaviour. I have observed her; she's driven to the last extremity, and is forming some desperate resolution. I guess at her design.

Re-enter MILLWOOD *with a Pistol*; TRUEMAN *secures her.*

True. Here thy power of doing mischief ends, deceitful, cruel, bloody woman!

Mill. Fool, hypocrite, villain, man! thou canst not call me that.

True. To call thee woman were to wrong thy sex, thou devil!

Mill. That imaginary being is an emblem of thy cursed sex collected. A mirror, wherein each particular man may see his own likeness, and that of all mankind.

Thor. Think not, by aggravating the faults of others, to extenuate thy own, of which the abuse of such uncommon perfections of mind and body is not the least.

Mill. If such I had, well may I curse your barbarous sex, who robbed me of 'em ere I knew their worth; then left me, too late, to count their value by their loss. Another and another spoiler came, and all my gain was poverty and reproach. My soul disdain'd, and yet disdains, dependance and contempt. Riches, no matter by what means obtained, I saw secured the worst of men from both. I found it therefore necessary to be rich, and to that end I summoned all my arts. You call 'em wicked, be it so, they were such as my conversation with your sex had furnished me withal.

Thor. Sure none but the **worst of** men conversed with thee.

Mill. Men of all degrees, and all professions, I have known, yet found no difference, but in their several capacities; all were alike wicked to the utmost of their power. " In pride, contention, avarice,
" cruelty, and revenge, the reverend priesthood were
" my unerring guides. From suburb magistrates,
" who live by ruined reputations, as the unhospitable
" natives of Cornwall do by shipwrecks, I learned,
" that to charge my innocent neighbours with my
" crimes, was to merit their protection: for to screen
" the guilty is the less scandalous, when many are
" suspected; and detraction, like darkness and death,
" blackens all objects, and levels all distinction.—
" Such are your venal magistrates, who favour none
" but such as by their office they are sworn to pu-
" nish. With them, not to be guilty is the worst of
" crimes, and large fees, privately paid, are every
" needful virtue.
" *Thor.* Your practice has sufficiently discovered
" your contempt of laws, both human and divine;

" no wonder then that you should hate the officers of
" both.

" *Mill.*" I know you, and I hate you all ; I expect no mercy, and I ask for none ; I followed my
inclinations, and that the best of you do every day.
" All actions seem alike natural and indifferent to
" man and beast, who devour, or are devoured, as
" they meet with others weaker or stronger than
" themselves.

" *Thor.* What pity it is a mind so comprehensive,
" daring, and inquisitive, should be a stranger to
" religion's sweet and powerful charms !

" *Mill.* I am not fool enough to be an atheist,
" though I have known enough of men's hypocrisy
" to make a thousand simple women so. Whatever
" religion is in itself, as practis'd by mankind, it has
" caused the evils you say it was designed to cure.
" War, plague, and famine have not destroyed so
" many of the human race, as this pretended piety
" has done ; and with such barbarous cruelty, as if
" the only way to honour Heaven were to turn the
" present world into hell.

" *Thor.* Truth is truth, though from an enemy,
" and spoken in malice. You bloody, blind, and
" superstitious bigots, how will you answer this ?

" *Mill.*" What are your laws, of which you make
your boast, but the fool's wisdom, and the coward's
valour, the instrument and screen of all your vil-
anies ? By them you punish in others what you act
yourselves, or would have acted, had you been in

G

their circumstances. The judge, who condemns the
poor man for being a thief, had been a thief himself had he been poor. Thus you go on deceiving
and being deceived, harassing, plaguing, and de-
stroying one another. But women are your univer-
sal prey.

Women, by whom you are, the source of joy,
With cruel arts you labour to destroy:
A thousand ways our ruin you pursue,
Yet blame in us those arts first taught by you.
Oh, may from hence each violated maid,
By flattering, faithless, barb'rous man betray'd,
When robb'd of innocence, and virgin fame,
From your destruction raise a nobler name,
T' avenge their sex's wrongs devote their mind,
And future Millwoods prove to plague mankind.

         [Exeunt.

ACT V. " SCENE I.

" *A Room in a Prison.* Enter THOROWGOOD,
BLUNT, *and* LUCY.

" *Thorowgood.*

" I HAVE recommended to Barnwell a reverend di-
" vine, whose judgment and integrity I am well ac-
" quainted with. Nor has Millwood been neglected ;
" but she, unhappy woman, still obstinate, refuses
" his assistance.

" *Lucy.* This pious charity to the afflicted well be-
" comes your character; yet pardon me, sir, if I
" wonder you were not at their trial.

" *Thor.* I knew it was impossible to save him; and
" I and my family bear so great a part in his distress,
" that to have been present would but have aggra-
" vated our sorrows without relieving his.

" *Blunt.* It was mournful indeed. Barnwell's
" youth and modest deportment, as he passed, drew
" tears from every eye. When placed at the bar,
" and arraigned before the reverend judges, with
" many tears and interrupting sobs, he confessed and
" aggravated his offences, without accusing, or once
" reflecting on Millwood, the shameless author of
" his ruin. But she, dauntless and unconcerned,
" stood by his side, viewing with visible pride and
" contempt the vast assembly, who, all with sym-
" pathizing sorrow, wept for the wretched youth.
" Millwood, when called upon to answer, loudly in-
" sisted upon her innocence, and made an artful and
" a bold defence; but finding all in vain, the impar-
" tial jury and the learned bench concurring to find
" her guilty, how did she curse herself, poor Barn-
" well, us, her judges, all mankind. But what
" could that avail? She was condemned, and is this
" day to suffer with him.

" *Thor.* The time draws on. I am going to visit
" Barnwell, as you are Millwood.

" *Lucy.* We have not wronged her, yet I dread
" this interview. She's proud, impatient, wrathful,

" and unforgiving. To be the branded instruments
" of vengeance, to suffer in her shame, and sympa-
" thize with her in all she suffers, is the tribute we
" must pay for our former ill-spent lives, and long
" confederacy with her in wickedness.

" *Thor.* Happy for you it ended when it did. What
" you have done against Millwood I know proceeded
" from a just abhorrence of her crimes, free from in-
" terest, malice, or revenge. Proselytes to virtue
" should be encouraged ; pursue your proposed
" reformation, and know me hereafter for your
" friend.

" *Lucy.* This is a blessing as unhoped for as un-
" merited. But Heaven, that snatched us from im-
" pending ruin, sure intends you as its instrument
" to secure us from apostacy.

" *Thor.* With gratitude to impute your deliverance
" to Heaven is just. Many less virtuously disposed
" than Barnwell was, have never fallen in the man-
" ner he has done. May not such owe their safety
" rather to Providence than to themselves ? With
" pity and compassion let us judge him. Great were
" his faults, but strong was the temptation. Let his
" ruin teach us diffidence, humanity, and circum-
" spection : for if we, who wonder at his fate, had
" like him been tried, like him perhaps we had
" fallen." 　　　　　　　　　　　　[*Exeunt.*

SCENE II.

A Dungeon, a Table, and a Lamp. BARNWELL *reading.* Enter THOROWGOOD *at a distance.*

Thor. There see the bitter fruits of passion's detested reign, and sensual appetite indulged; severe reflections, penitence, and tears.

Barn. My honoured, injured master, whose goodness has covered me a thousand times with shame, forgive this last unwilling disrespect. Indeed I saw you not.

Thor. 'Tis well; I hope you are better employed in viewing of yourself; " your journey's long, your " time for preparation almost spent." I sent a reverend divine to teach you to improve it, and should be glad to hear of his success.

Barn. The word of truth, which he recommended for my constant companion in this my sad retirement, has at length removed the doubts I laboured under. From thence I've learned the infinite extent of heavenly mercy; that my offences, though great, are not unpardonable; and that 'tis not my interest only, but my duty, to believe and to rejoice in my hope. So shall Heaven receive the glory, and future penitents the profit of my example.

Thor. Proceed.

Barn. 'Tis wonderful that words should charm despair, speak peace and pardon to a murderer's conscience; but truth and mercy flow in every sentence, attended with force and energy divine. How shall I describe my present state of mind ? I hope in doubt, and trembling I rejoice ; I feel my grief increase, even as my fears give way. Joy and gratitude now supply more tears than the horror and anguish of despair before.

Thor. These are the genuine signs of true repentance ; the only preparatory, the certain way to everlasting peace. "Oh, the joy it gives to see a soul "formed and prepared for Heaven ! For this the "faithful minister devotes himself to meditation, ab- "stinence, and prayer, shunning the vain delights "of sensual joys, and daily dies, that others may live "for ever. For this he turns the sacred volumes "o'er, and spends his life in painful search of truth. "The love of riches and the lust of power, he looks "upon with just contempt and detestation ; he only "counts for wealth the souls he wins, and his high- "est ambition is to serve mankind. If the reward "of all his pains be to preserve one soul from wan- "dering, or turn one from the error of his ways, "how does he then rejoice, and own his little labours "overpaid."

Barn. What do I owe for all your generous kindness ? But though I cannot, Heaven can and will reward you.

Thor. To see thee thus, is joy too great for words. Farewell.—Heaven strengthen thee :—Farewell.

Barn. Oh, sir, there's something I would say, if my sad swelling heart would give me leave.

Thor. Give it vent awhile, and try.

Barn. I had a friend—'tis true I am unworthy—yet methinks your generous example might persuade——Could not I see him once, before I go from whence there's no return?

Thor. He's coming, and as much thy friend as ever. I will not anticipate his sorrow; too soon he'll see the sad effect of this contagious ruin. This torrent of domestic misery bears too hard upon me. I must retire to indulge a weakness I find impossible to overcome. [*Aside.*] Much loved—and much lamented youth!—Farewell.—Heaven strengthen thee,——Eternally farewell.

Barn. The best of masters and of men—Farewell. While I live let me not want your prayers.

Thor. Thou shalt not. Thy peace being made with Heaven, death is already vanquished. Bear a little longer the pains that attend this transitory life, and cease from pain for ever. [*Exit* Thorowgood.

Barn. Perhaps I shall. I find a power within, that bears my soul above the fears of death, and, spite of conscious shame and guilt, gives me a taste of pleasure more than mortal.

Enter TRUEMAN *and* Keeper.

Keep. Sir, there's the prisoner. [*Exit Keeper.*

Barn. Trueman!—My friend, whom I so wished to see, yet now he's here, I dare not look upon him.
  [*Weeps.*

True. Oh, Barnwell! Barnwell!

Barn. Mercy! Mercy! gracious Heaven! For death, but not for this, I was prepared.

True. What have I suffered since I saw thee last! What pain has absence given me!—But, oh, to see thee thus!——

Barn. I know it is dreadful! I feel the anguish of thy generous soul—But I was born to murder all who **love** me!   [*Both weep.*

True. I came not to reproach you; I thought to bring you comfort; but I'm deceiv'd, for I have none to give. I came to share thy sorrow, but cannot bear my own.

Barn. My sense of guilt indeed you cannot know; 'tis what the good and innocent, like you, can ne'er conceive: but other griefs at present I have none, but what I feel for you. In your sorrow I read you love me still; but yet, methinks, 'tis strange, when I consider what I am.

True. No more of that; I can remember nothing but thy virtues, thy honest, tender friendship, our former happy state, and present misery. Oh, had you trusted me when first the fair seducer tempted you, all might **have been** prevented.

Barn. Alas, thou knowest not what a wretch I've been. Breach of friendship was my first **and** least offence. So far **was** I lost to goodness, so devoted to the author of my ruin, that had she insisted on my murdering thee,——I think——I should have done it.

True. Pr'ythee, aggravate thy faults no more.

Barn. I think I should ? Thus good and generous
as you are, I should have murdered you !

True. We have not yet embraced, and may be interrupted. Come to my arms.

Barn. Never, never will I taste such joys on earth ;
never will I so soothe my just remorse. / Are those
honest arms and faithful bosom fit to embrace and to
support a murderer ? These iron fetters only shall
clasp, and flinty pavement bear me ; [*throwing himself on the ground.*] even these too good for such a
bloody monster.

True. Shall fortune sever those whom friendship
joined ? Thy miseries cannot lay thee so low, but
love will find thee. Here will we offer to stern calamity ; this place the altar, and ourselves the sacrifice. Our mutual groans shall echo to each other
through the dreary vault ; our sighs shall number
the moments as they pass, and mingling tears communicate such anguish, as words were never made
to express.

Barn. Then be it so. [*Rising.*] Since you propose
an intercourse of wo, pour all your griefs into my
breast, and in exchange take mine. [*Embracing.*]
Where's now the anguish that you promised ? You've
taken mine, and make me no return. Sure peace and
comfort dwell within these arms, and sorrow cann't
approach me while I am here. " This too is the
" work of Heaven ; which having before spoke peace
" and pardon to me, now sends thee to confirm it."

Oh, take, take some of the joy that overflows my breast!

True. I do, I do. Almighty power! how hast thou made us capable to bear at once the extremes of pleasure and of pain.

Enter Keeper.

Keep. Sir.

True. I come.   [*Exit Keeper.*

Barn. Must you leave me? Death would soon have parted us for ever.

True. Oh, my Barnwell! there's yet another task behind. Again your heart must bleed for others' woes.

Barn. To meet and part with you I thought was all I had to do on earth. What is there more for me to do or suffer?

True. I dread to tell thee, yet it must be known! Maria——

Barn. Our master's fair and virtuous daughter?——

True. The same.

Barn. No misfortune, I hope, has reached that maid! Preserve her, Heaven, from every ill, to shew mankind that goodness is your care!

True. Thy, thy misfortunes, my unhappy friend, have reached her. Whatever you and I have felt, and more, if more be possible, she feels for you.

Barn. " I know he doth abhor a lie, and would

" not trifle with his dying friend." This is indeed
the bitterness of death.   '[*Aside.*

True. You must remember (for we all observed it)
for some time past, a heavy melancholy weighed her
down. Disconsolate she seemed, and pined and lan-
guished from a cause unknown; till, hearing of your
dreadful fate, the long-stifled flame blazed out;
" she wept, and wrung her hands, and tore her hair,"
and in the transport of her grief discovered her own
lost state, while she lamented yours.

Barn. " Will all the pain I feel restore thy ease,
" lovely unhappy maid! [*Weeping.*]" Why did you
not let me die, and never know it?

True. It was impossible. She makes no secret of
her passion for you; she is determined to see you ere
you die, and waits for me to introduce her.

[*Exit* Trueman.

Barn. Vain, busy thoughts, be still! What avails
it to think on what I might have been! I now am——
——what I've made myself.

Enter TRUEMAN *and* MARIA.

True. Madam, reluctant I lead you to this dismal
scene. This is the seat of misery and guilt. Here
awful justice reserves her public victims. This is the
entrance to a shameful death.

Mar. To this sad place then no improper guest,
the abandoned lost Maria brings despair, and sees the
subject and the cause of all this world of wo. Silent
and motionless he stands, as if his soul had quitted

her abode, and the lifeless form alone was left behind, " yet that so perfect, that beauty and death, " ever at enmity, now seem united there."

Barn. " I groan, but murmur not." Just Heaven! I am your own ; do with me what you please.

Mar. Why are your streaming eyes still fix'd below, as though thou'dst give the greedy earth thy sorrows, and rob me of my due ? Were happiness within your power, you should bestow it where you pleased ; but in your misery I must and will partake.

Barn. Oh, say not so, but fly, abhor, and leave me to my fate! Consider what you are, " how vast your " fortune, and how bright your fame. Have pity on " your youth, your beauty, and unequalled virtue ; " for which so many noble peers have sighed in " vain." Bless with your charms some honourable lord. " Adorn with your beauty, and by your ex- " ample improve, the English court, that justly " claims such merit ;" so shall I quickly be to you— as though I had never been.

Mar. When I forget **you, I** must be so indeed. Reason, choice, virtue, all forbid it. Let women, like Millwood, if there are more such women, smile in prosperity, and in adversity forsake. Be it the pride of virtue to repair, or to partake, the ruin such have made.

True. Lovely, ill-fated maid! " Was there ever " such generous distress before ? How must this " pierce his grateful heart, and aggravate his woes!"

Barn. Ere I knew guilt or shame, when fortune

smiled, and when my youthful hopes were at the highest ; if then to have raised my thoughts to you, had been presumption in me never to have been pardoned, think how much beneath yourself you condescend to regard me now !

" *Mar.* Let her blush, who proffering love, invades
" the freedom of your sex's choice, and meanly sues
" in hopes of a return. Your inevitable fate hath
" rendered hope impossible as vain. Then why
" should I fear to avow a passion so just and so dis-
" interested ?

" *True.* If any should take occasion from Mill-
" wood's crimes to libel the best and fairest part of
" the creation, here let them see their error. The
" most distant hopes of such a tender passion from so
" bright a maid, might add to the happiness of the
" most happy, and make the greatest proud : yet
" here 'tis lavished in vain. Though by the rich pre-
" sent the generous donor is undone, he on whom it
" is bestowed receives no benefit.

" *Barn.* So the aromatic spices of the east, which
" all the living covet and esteem, are with unavailing
" kindness wasted on the dead."

Mar. Yes, fruitless is my love, and unavailing all my sighs and tears. Can they save thee from approaching death ?—from such a death ?——*Oh sorrow insupportable!*——" Oh, terrible idea ! What is her
" misery and distress, who sees the first, last object
" of her love, for whom alone she'd live, for whom

H

" she'd die a thousand thousand deaths, if it were
" possible, expiring in her arms! Yet she is happy
" when compared to me. Were millions of worlds
" mine, I'd gladly give them in exchange for her
" condition. The most consummate wo is light to
" mine. The last of curses to other miserable maids,
" is all I ask for my relief, and that's denied me.

" *True.* Time and reflection cure all ills.

" *Mar.* All but this. His dreadful catastrophe
" virtue herself abhors. To give a holiday to suburb
" slaves, and passing entertain the savage herd, who
" elbowing each other for a sight, pursue and press
" upon him like his fate !——A mind with piety and
" resolution armed may smile on death :——But pub-
" lic ignominy, everlasting shame, shame the death
" of souls, to die a thousand times, and yet survive
" even death itself in never-dying infamy—Is this to
" be endured ?—— Can I who live in him, and must
" each hour of my devoted life feel all these woes re-
" newed—— Can I endure this?

" *True.* Grief has so impaired her spirits, she pants
" as in the agonies of death."

Barn. **Preserve** her, Heaven, and restore her
peace, nor let her death be added to my crimes. [*Bell
tolls.*] I am summoned to my fate.

Enter Keeper.

Keep. Sir, the officers attend you. Millwood is already summoned.

Barn. Tell 'em, I'm ready. And now, my friend, farewell. [*Embracing.*] Support and comfort, the best you can, this mourning fair.—No more—Forget not to pray for me. [*Turning to* Maria.] Would you, bright excellence, permit me the honour of a chaste embrace, the last happiness this world could give were mine. [*She inclines towards him, they embrace.*] Exalted goodness! Oh, turn your eyes from earth and me to Heaven, where virtue, like yours, is ever heard! Pray for the peace of my departing soul. Early my race of wickedness began, and soon I reached the summit. " Ere nature has finished her work, and stamped me " man, just at the time when others begin to stray, " my course is finished. Though short my span of " life, and few my days; yet count my crimes for " years, and I have lived whole ages." Thus justice, in compassion to mankind, cuts off a wretch like me; by one such example to secure thousands from future ruin. " Justice and mercy are in Heaven the same : " its utmost severity is mercy to the whole; thereby " to cure man's folly and presumption, which else " would render even infinite mercy vain and inef- " fectual."

If any youth, like you, in future times
Shall mourn my fate, tho' he abhors my crimes ;
Or tender maid, like you, my tale shall hear,
And to my sorrows give a pitying tear ;
To each such melting eye and throbbing heart,
Would gracious Heaven this benefit impart,

Never to know my guilt, nor feel my pain,
Then must you own, you ought not to complain,
Since you nor weep, nor shall I die in vain.

[Exeunt *Barnwell* and Officers.

" *SCENE III.*

" *The Place of Execution. The Gallows and Ladder at*
" *the farther End of the Stage. A Crowd of Specta-*
" *tors,* BLUNT *and* LUCY.

" *Lucy.* Heavens! what a throng!

" *Blunt.* How terrible is death when thus pre-
" pared!

" *Lucy.* Support them, Heaven! Thou only canst
" support them; all other help is vain.

" *Officer.* [*Within.*] Make way there; make way,
" and give the prisoners room.

" *Lucy.* They are here: observe them well. How
" humble and composed young Barnwell seems! but
" Millwood looks wild, ruffled with passion, con-
" founded, and amazed.

" *Enter* BARNWELL, MILLWOOD, *Officers, and Exe-*
" *cutioners.*

" *Barn.* See, Millwood, see, our journey's at an
" end! Life, like a tale that's told, is passed away.
" That short, but dark and unknown passage, death,
" is all the space between us and endless joys, or
" woes eternal.

" *Mill.* Is this the end of all my flattering hopes ?
" Were youth and beauty given me for a curse, and
" wisdom only to ensure my ruin ? They were, they
" were. Heaven, thou hast done thy worst. Or, if
" thou hast in store some untried plague, somewhat
" that's worse than shame, despair, and death, unpi-
" tied death, confirmed despair, and soul-confound-
" ing shame; something that men and angels cann't
" describe, and only fiends, who bear it, can con-
" ceive; now, pour it now on this devoted head, that
" I may feel the worst thou canst inflict, and bid de-.
" fiance to thy utmost power.

" *Barn.* Yet ere we pass the dreadful gulf of death,
" yet ere you're plunged in everlasting wo, Oh,
" bend your stubborn knees, and harder heart, hum-
" bly to deprecate the wrath divine! Who knows,
" but Heaven, in your dying moments, may bestow
" that grace and mercy which your life despised ?

" *Mill.* Why name you mercy to a wretch like me ?
" Mercy is beyond my hope, almost beyond my wish.
" I cann't repent, nor ask to be forgiven.

" *Barn.* Oh, think what 'tis to be for ever, ever
" miserable, nor with vain pride oppose a power that
" is able to destroy you !

" *Mill.* That will destroy me ; I feel it will. A
" deluge of wrath is pouring on my soul. Chains,
" darkness, wheels, racks, sharp-stinged scorpions,
" molten lead, and whole seas of sulphur, are light to
" what I feel.

." Barn. Oh, add not to your vast account despair;
" a sin more injurious to Heaven, than all you've yet
" committed.

" Mill. Oh, I have sinned beyond the reach of
" mercy!

" Barn. Oh, say not so; 'tis blasphemy to think
" it. As yon bright roof is higher than the earth,
" so, and much more, does Heaven's goodness pass
" our apprehension. Oh, what created being shall
" presume to circumscribe mercy that knows no
" bounds!

" Mill. This yields no hope. Though pity may
" be boundless, yet 'tis free. I was doomed before
" the world began to endless pains, and thou to joys
" eternal.

" Barn. Oh, gracious Heaven! extend thy pity to
" her; let thy rich mercy flow in plenteous streams
" to chase her fears, and heal her wounded soul.

" Mill. It will not be: your prayers are lost in air,
" or else returned perhaps with double blessings to
" your bosom: they help not me.

" Barn. Yet hear me, Millwood:

" Mill. Away, I will not hear thee: I tell thee,
" youth, I am by Heaven devoted a dreadful instance
" of its power to punish. [Barnwell *seems to pray.*] If
" thou wilt pray, pray for thyself, not me. How
" doth his fervent soul mount with his words, and
" both ascend to heaven! that heaven, whose gates
" are shut with adamantine bars against my prayers,

" had I the will **to pray. I** cannot bear it. Sure 'tis
" the worst of torments to behold others enjoy that
" bliss which we must never taste.

" *Officer.* The utmost limit of your time's expired.

" *Mill.* Encompassed with horror, whither must I
" go? I would not live—nor die——That I could
" cease to be——or ne'er had been!

" *Barn.* Since peace and comfort are denied her
" here, may she find mercy where she least expects
" it, and this be all her hell! From our example
" may all be taught to fly the first approach of vice:
" but if o'ertaken,

> " *By strong temptation, weakness, or surprise,*
> " *Lament their guilt, and by repentance rise.*
> " *Th'impenitent alone die unforgiven:*
> " *To sin's like man, and to forgive like Heaven.*

" Enter T R U E M A N.

" *Lucy.* Heart-breaking sight!——Oh, wretched,
" wretched Millwood!

" *True.* How is she disposed to meet **her** fate?

" *Blunt.* Who can describe unutterable wo?

" *Lucy.* She goes to death encompassed with hor-
" ror, loathing life, and yet afraid **to die.** No tongue
" can tell her anguish and despair.

" *True.* Heaven be better to her than her fears.—
" May she prove a warning to others, a monument
" of mercy in herself.

" *Lucy.* Oh, sorrow insupportable! Break, break,
" my heart!"

True. In vain,
  With bleeding hearts, and weeping eyes, we show,
  A humane, gen'rous sense of others' wo;
  Unless we mark what drew their ruin on,
  And, by avoiding that——prevent our own.

                              [*Exeunt omnes.*

EPILOGUE.

WRITTEN BY COLLEY CIBBER, ESQ.

Spoken by MARIA.

SINCE fate has robb'd me of the hapless youth,
For whom my heart had hoarded up its truth;
By all the laws of love and honour, now,
I'm free again to choose——and one of you.

But soft——With caution first I'll round me peep :
Maids, in my case, should look before they leap.
Here's choice enough, of various sorts and hue,
The cit, the wit, the rake cock'd up in cue,
The fair spruce mercer, and the tawny Jew.

Suppose I search the sober gallery?——No;
There's none but 'prentices, and cuckolds all-a-row ;
And these, I doubt, are those that make them so.

                                [Pointing to the Boxes.

'Tis very well, enjoy the jest :——But you,
Fine powder'd sparks,——nay, I am told 'tis true,——
Your happy spouses——can make cuckolds too.

'Twixt you and them the diff'rence this, perhaps:
The cit's ashamed whene'er his duck he traps;
But you, when Madam's tripping, let her fall,
Cock *up* your hats, and take no shame at all.

What if some favour'd poet I could meet,
Whose love would lay his laurels at my feet.
No————Painted passions real love abhors————
His flame would prove the suit of creditors.

Not to detain you then with longer pause,
In short, my heart to this conclusion draws;
I yield it to the hand that's loudest in applause.

THE END.

THE

CLANDESTINE MARRIAGE.

A

COMEDY,

BY G. COLMAN AND D. GARRICK, ESQRS.

ADAPTED FOR

THEATRICAL REPRESENTATION,

AS PERFORMED AT THE

THEATRES-ROYAL,

DRURY-LANE AND COVENT-GARDEN.

REGULATED FROM THE **PROMPT-BOOKS,**

By Permission of the Managers.

" The Lines distinguished by inverted Commas, are omitted in the Representation."

LONDON:

Printed for the Proprietors, under the Direction of
JOHN BELL, British-Library, STRAND,
Bookseller to His Royal Highness the PRINCE of WALES.

MDCCXCII.

PROLOGUE.

WRITTEN BY MR. GARRICK.

Spoken by Mr. HOLLAND.

POETS and Painters, who from Nature draw
Their best and richest stores, have made this law:
That each should neighbourly assist his brother,
And steal with decency from one another.
To-night, your matchless Hogarth **gives** *the thought,*
Which from his canvas to the stage is brought.
And who so fit to warm the poet's mind,
As he who pictur'd morals and mankind?
But not the same their characters and scenes;
Both labour for **one** *end, by different means;*
Each, as it suits him, takes a separate road,
Their one great object, MARRIAGE-A-LA-MODE!
Where titles deign with cits to have and hold,
And change rich blood for more substantial gold!
And honour'd trade from interest turns aside,
To hazard happiness for titled pride.
The Painter dead, yet still he charms the eye;
While England lives, his fame can never die:
But **he,** *who struts his hour upon the stage,*
Can scarce extend his fame for half an age;
Nor pen nor pencil can the actor save,
The art and artist share one common grave.

O let me drop one tributary tear,
On poor Jack Falstaff's grave and Juliet's bier!
You to their worth must testimony give ;
'Tis in your hearts alone their fame can live.
Still as the scenes of **life** *will shift away,*
The strong impressions of their art decay.
Your children cannot feel what you have known ;
They'll boast of QUINS *and* CIBBERS *of their own :*
The greatest glory of our happy few,
Is *to be felt, and be approv'd by* YOU.

COVENT-GARDEN.

		Men.
Lord OGLEBY,	- - -	- Mr. King.
Sir JOHN MELVIL,	- - -	- Mr. Farren.
STERLING,	- - - -	- Mr. Quick.
LOVEWELL,	- - - -	- Mr. Holman.
CANTON,	- - - -	- Mr. C. Powell.
BRUSH,	- - - - -	- Mr. Bernard.
Serjeant FLOWER,	- - -	- Mr. Powel.
TRAVERSE,	- - - -	- Mr. Thompson.
TRUEMAN,	- - -	- Mr. Evatt.

		Women.
Mrs. HEIDELBERG,	- -	- Mrs. Webb.
Miss STERLING,	- - -	- Mrs. Mattocks.
FANNY,	- - - - -	- Mrs. Merry.
BETTY,	- - -	- Mrs. Wells.
Chambermaid,	- - -	- Mrs. Rock.
TRUSTY,	- - -	- Mrs. Platt.

THE
CLANDESTINE MARRIAGE.

ACT I. SCENE I.

A Room in STERLING's *House. Miss* FANNY *and* BETTY
meeting.

Betty running in.

MA'AM! Miss Fanny! ma'am!

Fanny. What's the matter! Betty!

Betty. Oh la! ma'am! as sure as I am alive, here
is your husband—

Fanny. Hush! my dear Betty! if any body in the
house should hear you, I am ruined.

Betty. Mercy on me! it has frightened me to such a
degree that my heart is come up to my mouth.—But
as I was saying, ma'am, here's that dear, sweet—

Fanny. Have a care! Betty.

Betty. Lord! I am bewitched, I think.—But as I
was a saying, ma'am, here's Mr. Lovewell just come
from London.

Fanny. Indeed!

Betty. Yes, indeed and indeed, ma'am, he is. I saw him crossing the court-yard in his boots.

Fanny. I am glad to hear it.—But pray now, my dear Betty, be cautious. Don't mention that word again, on any account. You know, we have agreed never to drop any expressions of that sort, for fear of an accident.

Betty. Dear ma'am, you may depend upon me. There is not a more trustier creature on the face of the earth, than I am. Though I say it, I am as secret as the grave—and if it is never told till I tell it, it may remain untold till doom's-day for Betty.

Fanny. I know you are faithful—but in our circumstances we cannot be too careful.

Betty. Very true, ma'am! and yet I vow and protest, there's more plague than pleasure with a secret; especially if a body mayn't mention it to four or five of one's particular acquaintance.

Fanny. Do but keep this secret a little while longer, and then, I hope, you may mention it to any body.— Mr. Lovewell will acquaint the family with the nature of our situation as soon as possible.

Betty. The sooner the better, I believe: for if he does not tell it, there's a little tell-tale, I know of, will come and tell it for him.

Fanny. Fie, Betty. [*Blushing.*

Betty. Ah! you may well blush. But you're not so sick, and so pale, and so wan, and so many qualms—

Fanny. Have done! I shall be quite angry with you.

Betty. Angry!—Bless the dear puppet! I am sure

I shall love it, as much as if it was my own.—I meant no harm, Heaven knows.

Fanny. Well, say no more of this—It makes me uneasy—All I have to ask of you, is to be faithful and secret, and not to reveal this matter, till we disclose it to the family **ourselves.**

Betty. Me reveal it!—If I say a word, I wish I may be burned. I would not do you any harm for the world—And as for Mr. Lovewell, I am sure I have loved the dear gentleman ever since he got a tide-waiter's place for my brother—But let me tell you both, you must leave off your soft looks to each other, and your whispers, and your glances, and your always sitting next to one another at dinner, and your long walks together in the evening.—For my part, if I had not been in the secret, I should have known you were a pair of lovers at least, if not man and wife, as——

Fanny. See there now! again. Pray be careful.

Betty. Well—well—nobody hears me.—Man and wife.—I'll say no more—what I tell you is very true for all that——

Lovewell. [*Calling within.*] William!

Betty. Hark! I hear your husband——

Fanny. What!

Betty. I say, here comes Mr. Lovewell—Mind the caution I give you—I'll be whipped now, if you are not the first person he sees or speaks to in the family. However, if you choose it, it's nothing at all to me—as you sow, so you must reap—as you brew, so you must bake.—I'll e'en slip down the back-stairs and leave you together.   [*Exit.*

Fanny. I see, I see I shall never have a moment's ease till our marriage is made public. New distresses crowd in upon me every day. The solicitude of my mind sinks my spirits, preys upon my health, and destroys every comfort of my life. It shall be revealed, let what will be the consequence.

Enter LOVEWELL.

Lov. My love!—How's this ?—In tears?—Indeed this is too much. You promised me to support your spirits, and to wait the determination of our fortune with patience. For my sake, for your own, be comforted! Why will you study to add to our uneasiness and perplexity ?

Fanny. Oh, Mr. Lovewell; the indelicacy of a secret marriage grows every day more and more shocking to me. I walk about the house like a guilty wretch: I imagine myself the object of the suspicion of the whole family; and am under the perpetual terrors of a shameful detection.

Lov. Indeed, indeed, you are to blame. The amiable delicacy of your temper, and your quick sensibility, only serve to make you unhappy.—To clear up this affair properly to Mr. Sterling, is the continual employment of my thoughts. Every thing now is in a fair train. It begins to grow ripe for a discovery ; and I have no doubt of its concluding to the satisfaction of ourselves, of your father, and the whole family.

Fanny. End how it will, I am resolved it shall end soon—very soon. I would not live another week in this agony of mind to be mistress of the universe.

Lov. Do not be too violent neither. Do not let us disturb the joy of your sister's marriage with the tumult this matter may occasion!—I have brought letters from Lord Ogleby and Sir John Melvil to Mr. Sterling. They will be here this evening—and I dare say, within this hour.

Fanny. I am sorry for it.

Lov. Why so?

Fanny. No matter—Only let us disclose our marriage immediately!

Lov. As soon as possible.

Fanny. But directly.

Lov. In a few days, you may depend on it.

Fanny. To-night—or to-morrow morning.

Lov. That, I fear, will be impracticable.

Fanny. Nay, but you must.

Lov. Must! Why?

Fanny. Indeed you must.—I have the most alarming reasons for it.

Lov. Alarming, indeed! for they alarm me, even before I am acquainted with them—What are they?

Fanny. I cannot tell you.

Lov. Not tell me?

Fanny. Not at present. When all is settled, you shall be acquainted with every thing.

Lov. Sorry they are coming!—Must be discovered!

—What can this mean! Is it possible you can have any reasons that need be concealed from me?

Fanny. Do not disturb yourself with conjectures—but rest assured, that though you are unable to divine the cause, the consequence of a discovery, be it what it will, cannot be attended with half the miseries of the present interval.

Lov. You put me upon the rack.—I would do any thing to make you easy.——But you know your father's temper.—Money (you will excuse my frankness) is the spring of all his actions, which nothing but the idea of acquiring nobility or magnificence, can ever make him forego—and these he thinks his money will purchase.—You know too your aunt's, Mrs. Heidelberg's, notions of the splendor of high life; her contempt for every thing that does not relish of what she calls quality; and that from the vast fortune in her hands; by her late husband, she absolutely governs Mr. Sterling and the whole family: now if they should come to the knowledge of this affair too abruptly, they might, perhaps, be incensed beyond all hopes of reconciliation.

Fanny. But if they are made acquainted with it otherwise than by ourselves, it will be ten times worse: and a discovery grows every day more probable. **The** whole family have long suspected our affection. We are also in the power of a foolish maid-servant; and if we may even depend on her fidelity, we cannot answer for her discretion.—Discover it therefore, immediately, **lest** some accident should bring it to light, and involve us in additional disgrace.

Lov. Well—well—I mean to discover it soon, but would not do it too precipitately. I have more than once sounded Mr. Sterling about it, and will attempt him more seriously the next opportunity. But my principal hopes are these.—My relationship to Lord Ogleby, and his having placed me with your father, have been, you know, the first links in the chain of this connection between the two families; in consequence of which, I am at present in high favour with all parties: while they all remain thus well affected to me, I propose to lay our case before the old lord; and if I can prevail on him to mediate in this affair, I make no doubt but he will be able to appease your father; and, being a lord and a man of quality, I am sure he may bring Mrs. Heidelberg into good humour at any time.——Let me beg you, therefore, to have but a little patience, as, you see, we are upon the very eve of a discovery, that must probably be to our advantage.

Fanny. Manage it your own way. I am persuaded.

Lov. But in the mean time make yourself easy.

Fanny. As easy as I can, I will.—We had better not remain together any longer at present.—Think of this business, and let me know how you proceed.

Lov. Depend on my care! But, pray, be cheerful, *Fanny.* I will.

As she is going out, enter STERLING.

Sterl. Hey day! who have we got here ?

Fanny. [*Confused*] Mr. Lovewell, sir !

Sterl And where are you going, hussy ?

Fanny To my sister's chamber, sir !   [*Exit.*

Sterl. Ah, Lovewell ! What ! always getting my foolish girl yonder into a corner ?—Well—well—let us but once see her eldest sister fast married to Sir John Melvil, we'll soon provide a good husband for Fanny, I warrant you.

Lov. Would to Heaven, sir, you would provide her one of my recommendation !

Sterl Yourself ! eh, Lovewell ?

Lov. With your pleasure, sir !

Sterl. Mighty well !

Lov. And I flatter myself, that such a proposal would not be very disagreeable to Miss Fanny.

Sterl. Better and better !

Lov. And if I could but obtain your consent, sir——

Sterl. What ! you marry Fanny !—no—no—that will never do, Lovewell !——You're a good boy, to be sure—I have a great value for you——but cann't think of you for a son in-law.——There's no stuff in the case; no money, Lovewell !

Lov. My pretensions to fortune, indeed, are but moderate ; but though not equal to splendor, sufficient to keep us above distress.—Add to which, that

I hope by diligence to increase it—and have love, honour——

Sterl. But not the stuff, Lovewell!—Add one little round o to the sum total of your fortune, and that will be the finest thing you can say to me.—You know I've a regard for you—would do any thing to serve you—any thing on the footing of friendship—but——

Lov. If you think me worthy of your friendship, sir, be assured, that there is no instance in which I should rate your friendship so highly.

Sterl. Psha! psha! that's another thing, you know. —Where money or interest is concerned, friendship is quite out of the question.

Lov. But where the happiness of a daughter is at stake, you would not scruple, sure, to sacrifice a little to her inclinations.

Sterl. Inclinations! why, you would not persuade me that the girl is in love with you—eh, Lovewell?

Lov. I cannot absolutely answer for Miss Fanny, sir; but am sure that the chief happiness or misery of my life depends intirely upon her.

Sterl. Why, indeed, now if your kinsman, Lord Ogleby, would come down handsomely for you—but that's impossible—No, no—'twill never do—I must hear no more of this—Come, Lovewell, promise me that I shall hear no more of this.

Lov. [*Hesitating.*] I am afraid, sir, I should not be able to keep my word with you, if I did promise you

Sterl. Why you would not offer to marry her without my consent I would you, Lovewell ?

Lov. Marry her, sir !   [*Confused.*

Sterl. Ay, marry her, sir I—I know very well that a warm speech or two from such a dangerous young spark as you are, would go much farther towards persuading a silly girl to do what she has more than a month's mind to do, than twenty grave lectures from fathers or mothers, or uncles or aunts, to prevent her. But you would not, sure, be such a base fellow, such a treacherous young rogue, as to seduce my daughter's affections, and destroy the peace of my family in that manner.—I must insist on it, that you give me your word not to marry her without my consent.

Lov. Sir—I—I—as to that—I—I—beg, sir—— Pray, sir, excuse me on this subject at present.

Sterl. Promise then, that you will carry this matter no farther without my approbation.

Lov. You may depend on it, sir, that it shall go no further.

Sterl. Well—well—that's enough—I'll take care of the rest, I warrant you.—Come, come, let's have done with this nonsense I—What's doing in town ? Any news upon 'Change.?

Lov. Nothing material.

Sterl. Have you seen the currants, the soap, and Madeira safe in the warehouses? Have you compared the goods with the invoice and bills of lading, and are they all right ?

Lov. They are, sir!

Sterl. And how are stocks?

Lov. Fell one and a half this morning.

Sterl. Well, well,—some good news from America, and they'll be up again.——But how are Lord Ogleby and Sir John Melvil? When are we to expect them?

Lov. Very soon, sir. I came on purpose to bring you their commands. Here are letters from both of them. [*Giving letters.*

Sterl. Let me see—let me see—'Slife, how his lordship's letter is perfumed!—It takes my breath away. [*Opening it.*] And French paper too! with a fine border of flowers and flourishes—and a slippery gloss on it that dazzles one's eyes. ' My dear Mr. Sterling.' [*Reading.*] Mercy on me! his lordship writes a worse hand than a boy at his exercise.——But how's this? —Eh!—' with you to night'—[*Reading.*]—' Lawyers to morrow morning'—To night!——that's sudden, indeed——Where's my sister Heidelberg? she should know of this immediately.—Here, John! Harry! Thomas! [*Calling the servants.*] Hark ye, Lovewell!

Lov. Sir.

Sterl. Mind now, how I'll entertain his lordship and Sir John—We'll shew your fellows at the other end of the town how we live in the city——They shall eat gold—and drink gold—and lie in gold.——Here, cook! butler! [*Calling.*] What signifies your birth, and education, and titles!——Money, money!— that's the stuff that makes the great man in this country.

Lov. Very true, sir.

Sterl. True, sir!——Why then, have done with your nonsense of love and matrimony. You're not rich enough to think of a wife yet. A man of business should mind nothing but his business.——Where are these fellow?—John! Thomas! [*Calling.*]—— Get an estate, and a wife will follow of course.—— Ah, Lovewell! an English merchant is the most respectable character in the universe.——'Slife, man, a rich English merchant may make himself a match for the daughter of a nabob.——Where are all my rascals? Here, William!   [*Exit, calling.*

Lov. So—as I suspected.——Quite averse to the match, and likely to receive the news of it with great displeasure.——What's best to be done?——Let me see!—Suppose I get Sir John Melvil to interest himself in this affair. He may mention it to Lord Ogleby with a better grace than I can, and more probably prevail on him to interfere in it. I can open my mind also more freely to Sir John. He told me, when I left him in town, that he had something of consequence to communicate, and that I could be of use to him. I am glad of it : for the confidence he reposes in me, and the service I may do him, will ensure me his good offices.——Poor Fanny! It hurts me to see her so uneasy, and her making a mystery of the cause adds to my anxiety.——Something must be done upon her account; for, at all events, her solicitude shall be removed.   [*Exit.*

SCENE II.

Changes to another Apartment. Enter Miss STERLING, *and Miss* FANNY.

Miss Sterl. Oh, my dear sister, say no more!—This is downright hypocrisy.—You shall never convince me that **you** don't envy me beyond measure.—Well, after all, **it is** extremely natural—It is impossible **to** be angry with you.

Fanny. Indeed, sister, you have no cause.

Miss **Sterl.** And you really pretend not to envy me?

Fanny. Not in the least.

Miss Sterl. **And** you don't **in** the least wish that you was just in my situation?

Fanny. No, indeed, **I** don't. Why should I?

Miss **Sterl.** Why should you? What! on the **brink** of marriage, fortune, title—But I had forgot—There's that **dear** sweet creature Mr. Lovewell **in** the case.—You would not break your faith with your true love now for the world, I warrant you.

Fanny. Mr. Lovewell!—always **Mr.** Lovewell!—Lord, what signifies Mr. **Lovewell,** sister?

Miss Sterl. Pretty peevish soul!—Oh, my dear grave, romantic sister!—a perfect philosopher in petticoats!—Love and a cottage!—Eh, Fanny—Ah, give me indifference and **a** coach and six!——

Fanny. And why not the coach and six without the indifference?—But, pray, when is this **happy mar-**

riage of yours to be celebrated? I long to give you joy.

Miss Sterl. In a day or two—I cannot tell exactly—Oh, my dear sister!—I must mortify her a little. [*Aside.*] I know you have a pretty taste. Pray, give me your opinion of my jewels.—How do you like the stile of this esclavage? [*Shewing jewels.*

Fanny. Extremely handsome, indeed, and well fancied.

Miss Sterl. What d'ye think of these bracelets? I shall have a miniature of my father set round with diamonds, to one, and Sir John's to the other.—And this pair of ear-rings! set transparent! here, the tops, you see, will take off to wear in a morning, or in an undress—how d'ye like them? [*Shews jewels.*

Fanny. Very much, I assure you—Bless me, sister, you have a prodigious quantity of jewels—you'll be the very queen of diamonds.

Miss Sterl. Ha, ha, ha! very well, my dear!—I shall be as fine as a little queen, indeed.—I have a bouquet to come home to-morrow—made up of diamonds, and rubies, and emeralds, and topazes, and amethysts—jewels of all colours, green, red, blue, yellow, intermixt—the prettiest thing you ever saw in your life!—The jeweller, says, I shall set out with as many diamonds as any body in town, except Lady Brilliant, and Polly What d'ye call it, Lord Squander's kept mistress.

Fanny. But what are your wedding clothes, sister?

Miss Sterl. Oh, white and silver to be sure, you

know.—I bought them at Sir Joseph Lutestring's, and sat above an hour in the parlour behind the shop, consulting Lady Lutestring about gold and silver stuffs, on purpose to mortify her.

Fanny. Fie, sister! how could you be so abominably provoking.

Miss Sterl. Oh, I have no patience with the pride of your city-knights' ladies.—Did you ever observe the airs of Lady Lutestring, drest in the richest brocade out of her husband's shop, playing crown whist at Haberdasher's Hall—Whilst the civil smirking Sir Joseph, with a snug wig trimmed round his broad face as close as a new-cut yew-hedge, and his shoes so black that they shine again, stands all day in his shop, fastened to his counter like a bad shilling?

Fanny. Indeed, indeed, sister, this is too much—If you talk at this rate, you will be absolutely a byeword in the city—You must never venture on the inside of Temple Bar again.

Miss Sterl. Never do I desire it—never, my dear Fanny, I promise you. Oh, how I long to be transported to the dear regions of Grosvenor-square—far —far from the dull districts of Aldersgate, Cheap, Candlewick, and Farringdon Without and Within! —my heart goes pit-a-pat at the very idea of being introduced at Court!—gilt chariot!—pyeballed horses!—laced liveries!—and then the whispers buzzing round the circle—'Who is that young lady! Who is she?'—'Lady Melvil, ma'am!'——Lady

C

Melvill. My ears tingle at the sound.—And then at dinner, instead of my father perpetually asking—' Any news upon 'Change?'—to cry, Well, Sir John! any thing new from Arthur's?—or—to say to some other woman of quality, Was your Ladyship at the Dutchess of Rubber's last night?—Did you call in at Lady Thunder's? In the immensity of crowd I swear I did not see you—scarce a soul at the opera last Saturday—shall I see you at Carlisle House next Thursday!—Oh, the dear Beau Monde! I was born to move in the sphere of the great world.

Fanny. And so, in the midst of all this happiness, you have no compassion for me—no pity for us poor mortals in common life.

Miss Sterl. [*Affectedly.*] You?—You're above pity. —You would not change conditions with me.— You're over head and ears in love, you know.—Nay, for that matter, if Mr. Lovewell and you come together, as I doubt not you will, you will live very comfortably, I dare say.—He will mind his business —you'll employ yourself in the delightful care of your family—and once in a season perhaps you'll sit together in a front box at a benefit play, as we used to do at our dancing-master's, you know—and perhaps I may meet you in the summer with some other citizens at Tunbridge. For my part, I shall always entertain a proper regard for my relations.—You sha'n't want my countenance, I assure you.

Fanny. Oh, you're too kind, sister!

Enter Mrs. HEIDELBERG.

Mrs. Heidel. [*At entering.*] Here this evening!—I vow and pertest we shall scarce have time to provide for them—Oh, my dear! [*to Miss* Sterl.] I am glad to see you're not quite in a dish-abille. Lord Ogleby and Sir John Melvil will be here to-night.

Miss Sterl. To-night, ma'am?

Mrs. Heidel. Yes, my dear, to-night.—Oh, put on a smarter cap, and change those ordinary ruffles!—Lord, I have such a deal to do, I shall scarce have time to slip on my Italian lutestring.—Where is this dawdle of a housekeeper? [*Enter Mrs.* Trusty.] Oh, here, Trusty! do you know that people of qualaty are expected here this evening?

Trusty. Yes, ma'am.

Mrs. Heidel. Well—Do you be sure now that every thing is done in the most genteelest manner—and to the honour of the famaly.

Trusty. Yes, ma'am.

Mrs. Heidel. Well—but mind what I say to you.

Trusty. Yes, ma'am.

Mrs. Heidel. His lordship is to lie in the chintz bed-chamber—d'ye hear?—and Sir John in the blue damask room—his lordship's valet-de-shamb in the opposite————

Trusty. But Mr. Lovewell is come down—and you know that's his room, ma'am.

Mrs. Heidel. Well—well—Mr. Lovewell may make

C ij

shift—or get a bed at the George.——But hark ye, Trusty !

Trusty. Ma'am !

Mrs. Heidel. Get the great dining room in order as soon as possable. Unpaper the curtains, take the civers off the couch and the chairs, and put the china figures on the mantle piece immediately.

Trusty. Yes, ma'am.

Mrs. Heidel. Be gonë then ! fly, this instant !—— Where's my brother Sterling ?

Trusty. Talking to the butler, ma'am.

Mrs. Heidel. Very well. [*Exit* Trusty.] Miss Fanny! ! pertest I did not see you before——Lord, child, what's the matter with you ?

Fanny. With me ! Nothing, ma'am.

Mrs. Heidel. Bless me ! Why your face is as pale, and black, and yellow—of fifty colours, I pertest.—— And then you have drest yourself as loose and as big ——I declare there is not such a thing to be seen now, as a young woman with a fine waist——You all make yourselves as round as Mrs. Deputy Barter. Go, child!——You know the qualaty will be here by and by.—Go, and make yourself a little more fit to be seen. [*Exit* Fanny.] She is gone away in tears— absolutely crying, I vow and pertest.——This ridi-calous love ! we must put a stop to it. It makes a perfect nataral of the girl.

Miss Sterl. Poor soul ! she cann't help it. [*Affectedly.*

Mrs. Heidel. Well, my dear ! Now I shall have an opportoonity of convincing you of the absurdity of what you was telling me concerning Sir John Melvil's behaviour to you.

Miss Sterl. Oh, it gives me no manner of uneasiness. But, indeed, ma'am I cannot be persuaded but that Sir John is an extremely cold lover. Such distant civility, grave looks, and lukewarm professions of esteem for me and the whole family! I have heard of flames and darts, but Sir John's is a passion of mere ice and snow.

Mrs. Heidel. Oh fie, my dear! I am perfectly ashamed of you. That's so like the notions of your poor sister! What you complain of as coldness and indiffarence, is nothing but the extreme gentilaty of his address, an exact pictur of the manners of qualaty.

Miss Sterl. Oh, he is the very mirror of complaisance! full of formal bows and set speeches!——I declare, if there was any violent passion on my side, I should be quite jealous of him.

Mrs. Heidel. I say jealus indeed——Jealus of who, pray?

Miss Sterl. My sister Fanny. She seems a much greater favourite than I am, and he pays her infinitely more attention, I assure you.

Mrs. Heidel Lord! d'ye think a man of fashion, as he is, cannot distinguish between the genteel and the wulgar part of the famaly?——Between you and your sister, for instance—or me and my brother?——. Be advised by me, child! It is all puliteness and good-breeding. Nobody knows the qualaty better than I do.

Miss Sterl. In my mind the old lord, his uncle, has ten times more gallantry about him than Sir John. He is full of attentions to the ladies, and smiles, and grins, and leers, and ogles, and fills every wrinkle of his old wizen face with comical expressions of tenderness. I think he would make an admirable sweetheart.

Enter STERLING.

Sterl. [*At entering.*] No fish?—Why the pond was dragged but yesterday morning——There's carp and tench in the boat.——Pox on't, if that dog Lovewell had any thought, he wou'd have brought down a turbot, or some of the land-carriage mackrell.

Mrs. Heidel. Lord, brother, I am afraid his lordship and Sir John will not arrive while it is light.

Sterl. I warrant you.——But, pray, sister Heidelberg, let the turtle be drest to-morrow, and some venison—and let the gardiner cut some pine-apples—and get out some ice.——I'll answer for wine, I warrant you——I'll give them such a glass of Champagne as they never drank in their lives—no, not at a duke's table.

Mrs. Heidel. Pray now, brother, mind how you behave. I am always in a fright about you with people of qualaty. Take care that you don't fall asleep directly after supper, as you commonly do. Take a good deal of snuff; and that will keep you awake—And don't burst out with your horrible loud horse-laughs. It is monstrous wulgar.

Sterl. Never fear, sister!——Who have we here?

Mrs. Heidel. It is Mons. Cantoon, the Swish gentleman, that lives with his lordship, I vow and pertest.

Enter CANTON.

Sterl. Ah, mounseer! your servant.——I am very glad to see you, mounseer.

Can. Mosh oblige to Mons. Sterling.—Ma'am, I am yours——Matemoiselle, I am yours. [*Bowing round.*

Mrs. Heidel. Your humble servant, Mr. Cantoon!

Can. I kiss your hands, matam!

Sterl. Well, mounseer!—and what news of your good family!——when are we to see his lordship and Sir John?

Can. Mons. Sterling! Milor Ogleby and Sir Jean Melville will be here in one quarter-hour.

Sterl. I am glad to hear it.

Mrs. Heidel. O, I am perdigious glad to hear it. Being so late, I was afeard of some accident.——Will you please to have any thing, Mr. Cantoon, after your journey?

Can. No, I tank you, ma'am.

Mrs. Heidel. Shall I go and shew you the apartments, sir?

Can. You do me great honeur, ma'am.

Mrs. Heidel. Come then!—come, my dear!

[*To Miss* Sterling. *Exeunt.*

Sterl. Pox on't, it's almost dark—It will be too late to go round the garden this evening.——However, I will carry them to take a peep at my fine canal at least, I am determined.

ACT II. SCENE I.

An Anti-chamber to Lord OGLEBY's *Bed-chamber. Table with Chocolate, and small Case for Medicines. Enter* BRUSH, *my Lord's Valet-de-chambre, and* STERLING's *Chambermaid.*

Brush.

YOU shall stay, my dear, I insist upon it.

Cham. Nay, pray, sir, don't be so positive; I cannot stay indeed.

Brush. You shall drink one cup to our better acquaintance.

Cham. I seldom drinks chocolate; and, if I did, one has no satisfaction with such apprehensions about one—if my lord should wake, or the Swish gentleman should see one, or Madam Heidelberg should know of it, I should be frighted to death—besides, I have had my tea already this morning——I'm sure I hear my lord.   [*In a fright.*

Brush. No, no, madam, don't flutter yourself—— the moment my lord wakes, he rings his bell, which I answer sooner or later, as it suits my convenience.

Cham. But should he come upon us without ring-
ing———

Brush. I'll forgive him if he does—This key [*Takes
a phial out of the case.*] locks him up till I please to let
him out.

Cham. Law! Sir, that's potecary's stuff.

Brush. It is so—but without this he can no more
get out of bed—than he can read without spectacles—
[*Sips.*] What with qualms, age, rheumatisms, and a
few surfeits in his youth, he must have a great deal of
brushing, oiling, screwing, and winding-up, to set
him a-going for the day.

Cham. [*Sips.*] That's prodigious indeed—[*Sips.*]
My lord seems quite in a decay.

Brush. Yes, he's quite a spectacle, [*Sips.*] a mere
corpse, till he is reviv'd and refresh'd from our little
magazine here——When the restorative pills, and
cordial waters warm his stomach, and get into his
head, vanity frisks in his heart, and then he sets up
for the lover, the rake, and the fine gentleman.

Cham. [*Sips.*] Poor gentleman! but should the
Swish gentleman come upon us.   [*Frightened.*

Brush. Why then the English gentleman would be
very angry.——No foreigner must break in upon my
privacy. [*Sips.*] But I can assure you Monsieur Canton is otherwise employed—He is obliged to skim the
cream of half a score newspapers for my lord's breakfast—ha, ha, ha! Pray, madam, drink your cup
peaceably—My lord's chocolate is remarkably good,
he won't touch a drop, but what comes from Italy.

Cham. [*Sipping.*] 'Tis very fine indeed ! [*Sips.*] and charmingly perfum'd—it smells for all the world like our young ladies' dressing-boxes.

Brush. You have an excellent taste, madam; and I must beg of you to accept of a few cakes for your own drinking, [*Takes them out of a drawer in the table,*] and, in return, I desire nothing but to taste the perfume of your lips. [*Kisses her.*]—A small return of favours, madam, will make, I hope, this country and retirement agreeable to us both. [*He bows, she curtsies.*] ——Your young ladies are fine girls, faith : [*Sips.*] though, upon my soul, I am quite of my old lord's mind about them; and were I inclin'd to matrimony, I should take the youngest.   [*Sips.*

Cham. Miss Fanny's the most affablest, and the most best natur'd creter !——

Brush. And the eldest a little haughty or so——

Cham. More haughtier and prouder than Saturn himself—but this I say quite confidential to you ; for one would not hurt a young lady's marriage, you know.   [*Sips.*

Brush. By no means; but you cannot hurt it with us —we don't consider tempers—we want money, Mrs. Nancy. Give us plenty of that, we'll abate you a great deal in other particulars, ha, ha, ha !

Cham. Bless me, here's somebody !—[*Bell rings.*]— Oh, 'tis my lord !——Well, your servant, Mr. Brush ——I'll clean the cups in the next room.

Brush. Do so—but never mind the bell—I sha'n't

go this half hour.——Will you drink tea with me in
the afternoon ?

Cham. Not for the world, Mr. Brush—I'll be here
to set all things to rights—But I must not drink tea
indeed——and so your servant.

[Exit with tea-board. Bell rings again.

Brush. It is impossible to stupify one's self in the
country for a week, without some little flirting with
the Abigails :—this is much the handsomest wench in
the house, except the old citizen's youngest daughter,
and I have not time enough to lay a plan for her.—— .
[Bell rings.]—And now I'll go to my lord, for I have
nothing else to do. *[Going.*

Enter CANTON, *with Newspapers in his Hand.*

Can. Monsieur Brush !———Maistre Brush !———my
lor stirra yet ?

Brush. He has just rung his bell—I am going to
him. *[Exit.*

Can. Depechez vous donc. *[Puts on his spectacles.]*
—I wish de deveil had all dese papiers—I forget as
fast as I read—de Advertise put out of my head de
Gazette, de Chronique, and so dey all go l'un aprés
l'autre—I must get some nouvelle for my lor, or he'll
be enragé contre moi.——Voyons ! *[Reads the paper.]*
Here is nothing but Anti-sejanus & advertise——

Enter Maid with Chocolate things.

Vat you want, child?——

Maid. Only the chocolate things, sir.

Can. O, ver well—dat is good girl—and very prit too.   [*Exit maid.*

Lord Og. [*Within.*] Canton ! he, he !—[*Coughs.*]—Canton !——

Can. I come, my lor !——vat shall I do ?—I have no news---he will make great tintamarre !——

Lord Og. [*Within.*] Canton ! I say, Canton ! Where are you ?

Enter Lord OGLEBY, *leaning on* BRUSH.

Can. Here, my lor ;---I ask pardon, my lor, I have not finish de papiers.——

Lord Og. Damn your pardon, and your papiers ---I want you here, Canton.

Can. Den I run, dat is all. [*Shuffles along. Lord Ogleby leans upon Canton too, and comes forward.*]

Lord Og. You Swiss are the most unaccountable mixture---you have the language and the impertinence of the French, with the laziness of Dutchmen.

Can. 'Tis very true, my lor—I cann't help——

Lord Og. [*Cries out.*] O Diavolo !

Can. You are not in pain, I hope, my lor.

Lord Og. Indeed but I am, my lor.——That vulgar fellow, Sterling, with his city politeness, would force me down his slope last night to see a clay-colour'd ditch, which he calls a canal; and what with the dew, and the east wind, my hips and shoulders are absolutely screw'd to my body.

Can. A littel veritable eau d'arquibusade vil set all to right again.——

　　　[*Lord* Og. *sits down, and* Brush *gives chocolate.*

Lord Og. Where are the palsy drops, Brush?

Brush. Here, my lord!　　　　　　[*Pouring out.*

Lord Og. Quelle nouvelle avez vous, Canton.

Can. A great deal of papier, but no news at all.

Lord Og. What! nothing at all, you stupid fellow?

Can. Yes, my lor, I have little advertise here vil give you more plaisir den all de lies about nothing at all. La viola!　　　　　　　[*Puts on his spectacles.*

Lord Og. Come, read it, Canton, with good emphasis, and good discretion.

Can. I vil, my lor.——[*Can. reads.*] ' Dere is no question, but that the Cosmetique Royale vil utterly take away all heats, pimps, frecks, oder eruptions of de skin, and likewise de wrinque of old age, &c. &c.' ---A great deal more, my lor.---' Be sure to ask for de Cosmetique Royale, signed by the Docteur own hand---Dere is more raison for dis caution dan good men vil tink.'---Eh bien, my lor!

Lord Og. Eh bien, Canton!——Will you purchase any?

Can. For you, my lor?

Lord Og. For me, you old puppy! for what?

Can. My lor!

Lord Og. Do I want cosmeticks?

Can. My lor!

Lord Og. Look in my face---come, be sincere.—— Does it want the assistance of art?

Can. [*With his spectacles.*] En verité non——'Tis very smoose and brillian——but tote dat you might take a little by way of prevention.

Lord Og. You thought like an old fool, monsieur, as you generally do.——The surfeit water, Brush ! [*Brush pours out.*]——What do you think, Brush, of this family we are going to be connected with ? ——Eh !

Brush. Very well to marry in, my lord; but it would never do to live with.

Lord Og. You are right, Brush——There is no washing the blackmoor white——Mr. Sterling will never get rid of Blackfriars——always taste of the Borachio——and the poor woman his sister, is so busy, and so notable, to make one welcome, that I have not yet got over her first reception; it almost amounted to suffocation !——I think the daughters are tolerable——Where's my cephalic snuff ? [*Brush gives him a box.*]

Can. Dey tink so of you, my lor, for dey look at no ting else, ma foi.

Lord Og. Did they ? Why, I think they did a little ——Where's my glass ? [*Brush puts one on the table.*] The youngest is delectable.   [*Takes snuff.*

Can. O oui, my lor, vey delect, inteed; she made doux yeux at you, my lor.

Lord Og. She was particular.——The eldest, my nephew's lady, will be a most valuable wife; she has all the vulgar spirits of her father and aunt, happily blended with the termagant qualities of her deceased mother.———Some peppermint water, Brush ———How happy is it, Canton, for young ladies in general, that people of quality overlook every thing in a marriage contract but their fortune.

Can. C'est bien heureux, et commode aussi.

Lord Og. Brush, give me that pamphlet by my bed side.———[*Brush goes for it.*] Canton, do you wait in the anti-chamber, and let nobody interrupt me till I call you.

Can. Mush good may do your lordship.

Lord Og. [*To* Brush, *who brings the pamphlet.*] And now, Brush, leave me a little to my studies. [*Exit* Brush.]———What can I possibly do among these wo-men here, with this confounded rheumatism? It is a most grievous enemy to gallantry and address. [*Gets off his chair.*] He! courage, my lor! by Heavens, I'm another creature. [*Hums and dances a little.*] It will do, faith.———Bravo, my lor! these girls have absolutely inspir'd me———If they are for a game of romps——— Me viola pret! [*Sing and dances.*]———Oh!---that's an ugly twinge—but its gone.———I have rather too much of the lily this morning in my complexion; a faint tincture of the rose will give a delicate spirit to my eyes for the day. [*Unlocks a drawer at the bottom of the glass, and takes out rouge; while he's painting himself, a knocking at the door.*] Who's there? I won't be dis-turb'd.

Can. [*Without.*] My lor! my lor! here is Monsieur Sterling to pay his devoir to you this morn in your chambre.

Lord Og. [*Softly.*] What a fellow!——[*Aloud.*] I am extremely honour'd by Mr. Sterling.----Why don't you see him in, monsieur!——I wish he was at the bottom of his stinking canal. [*Door opens.*] Oh, my dear Mr. Sterling, you **do** me a great deal of honour.

Enter STERLING *and* LOVEWELL.

Ster. I hope, my lord, that your lordship slept well in the night——I believe there are no better beds in Europe than I have—I spare no pains to get them, nor money to buy them.——His majesty, God bless him, don't sleep upon a better out of his palace ; and if I had said in too, I hope no treason, my lord.

Lord Og. Your beds are like every thing else about you---incomparable!——They not only make one rest well, but give one spirits, Mr. Sterling.

Ster. What say you then, my lord, to another walk in the garden. You must see my water by day-light, and my walks, and my slopes, and my clumps, and my bridge, and my flow'ring trees, and my bed of Dutch tulips —Matters look'd but dim last night, my lord. I feel the dew in my great toe---but I would put on a cut shoe, that I might be able to walk you about---I may be laid up to-morrow.

Lord Og. I pray Heaven you may!   [*Aside.*

Ster. What say you, my lord?

Lord Og. I was saying, sir, that I was in hopes of seeing the young ladies at breakfast: Mr. Sterling, they are, in my mind, the finest tulips in this part of the world, he, he, he!

Can. Bravissimo, my lor! ha, ha, he!

Sterl. They shall meet your lordship in the garden ---we don't lose our walk for them; I'll take you a little round before breakfast, and a larger before dinner, and in the evening you shall go the grand tour, as I call it, ha, ha, ha!

Lord Og. Not a foot, I hope, Mr. Sterling; consider your gout, my good friend---you'll certainly be laid by the heels for your politeness, he, he, he!

Can. Ha, ha, ha! 'tis admirable, en verité!

[Laughing very heartily.

Sterl. If my young man [*To Lov.*] here would but laugh at my jokes, which he ought to do, as mounseer does at yours, my lord, we should be all life and mirth.

Lord Og. What say you, Canton, will you take my kinsman into your tuition? You have certainly the most companionable laugh I ever met with, and never out of tune.

Can. But when your lordship is out of spirits.

Lord Og. Well said, Canton! But here comes my nephew, to play his part.

Enter Sir JOHN MELVIL.

Well, Sir John, what news from the island of love? Have you been sighing and serenading this morning?

Sir John. I am glad to see your lordship in such spirits this morning.

Lord Og. I'm sorry to see you so dull, sir—What poor things, Mr. Sterling, these very young fellows are! they make love with faces, as if they were burying the dead—though, indeed, a marriage sometimes may be properly called a burying of the living —eh, Mr. Sterling?

Sterl. Not if they have enough to live upon, my lord—Ha, ha, ha!

Can. Dat is all Monsieur Sterling tink of.

Sir John. [*Apart.*] Pr'ythee, Lovewell, come with me into the garden; I have something of consequence for you, and I must communicate it directly.

Lov. [*Apart.*] We'll go together.——If your lordship and Mr. Sterling please, we'll prepare the ladies to attend you in the garden.

[*Exeunt Sir* John *and* Lovewell.

Sterl. My girls are always ready, I make them rise soon and to bed early; their husbands shall have them with good constitutions, and good fortunes, if they have nothing else, my lord.

Lord Og. Fine things, Mr. Sterling!

Sterl. Fine things, indeed, my lord!—Ah, my lord, had not you run off your speed in your youth, you had not been so crippled in your age, my lord.

Lord Og. Very pleasant, he, he, he.——

[*Half laughing.*

Sterl. Here's mounseer now, I suppose, is pretty near your lordship's standing; but having little to eat, and little to spend in his own country, he'll wear three of your lordship out—eating and drinking kills us all.

Lord Og. Very pleasant, I protest—What a vulgar dog! [*Aside.*

Can. My lor so old as me !—He is chicken to me— and look like a boy to pauvre me.

Sterl. Ha, ha, ha ! Well said, mounseer—keep to that, and you'll live in any country of the world—— Ha, ha, ha !—But, my lord, I will wait upon you in the garden : we have but a little time to breakfast— I'll go for my hat and cane, fetch a little walk with you, my lord, and then for the hot rolls and butter ! [*Exit.*

Lord Og. I shall attend you with pleasure——Hot rolls and butter in July ! I sweat with the thoughts of it—What a strange beast it is !

Can. C'est un barbare.

Lord Og. He is a vulgar dog, and if there was not so much money in the family, which I cann't do without, I would leave him and his hot rolls and butter directly——Come along, monsieur !

[*Exeunt Lord* Ogleby *and* Canton.

SCENE II.

Changes to the Garden. Enter Sir JOHN MELVIL, *and* LOVEWELL.

Love. In my room this morning ? Impossible.

Sir John. Before five this morning, I promise you.

Lov. On what occasion?

Sir John. I was so anxious to disclose my mind to you, that I could not sleep in my bed—but I found that you could not sleep neither—The bird was flown, and the nest long since cold.——Where was you, Lovewell?

Lov. Pooh! pr'ythee! ridiculous!

Sir John. Come now, which was it? Miss Sterling's maid? a pretty little rogue! or Miss Fanny's Abigail? a sweet soul too—or—

Lov. Nay, nay, leave trifling, and tell me your business.

Sir John. Well, but where was you, Lovewell?

Lov. Walking—writing—what signifies where I was?

Sir John. Walking, yes, I dare say. It rained as hard as it could pour. Sweet refreshing showers to walk in! No, no, Lovewell.—Now would I give twenty pounds to know which of the maids——

Lov. But your business! your business, Sir John!

Sir John. Let me a little into the secrets of the family.

Lov. Psha!

Sir John. Poor Lovewell, he can't bear it, I see. She charged you not to kiss and tell.—Eh, Lovewell! However, though you will not honour me with your confidence, I'll venture to trust you with mine.——What do you think of Miss Sterling?

Lov. What do I think of Miss Sterling?

Sir John. Ay; what d'ye think of her?

Lov. An odd question !—but I think her a smart, lively girl, full of mirth and sprightliness.

Sir John. All mischief and malice, I doubt.

Lov. How ?

Sir John. But her person—what d'ye think of that ?

Lov. Pretty and agreeable.

Sir John. A little grisette thing.

Lov. What is the meaning of all this ?

Sir John. I'll tell you. You must know, Love-well, that notwithstanding all appearances. [*Seeing Lord* Ogleby, *&c.*] We are interrupted—When they are gone, I'll explain.

Enter Lord OGLEBY, STERLING, *Mrs.* HEIDELBERG, *Miss* STERLING, *and* FANNY.

Lord Ogl. Great improvements indeed, Mr. Ster-ling! wonderful improvements! The four seasons in lead, the flying Mercury, and the bason with Nep-tune in the middle, are all in the very extreme of fine taste. You have as many rich figures as the man at Hyde-Park Corner.

Sterl. The chief pleasure of a country-house is to make improvements, you know, my lord. I spare no expence, not I.——This is quite another-guess sort of a place than it was when I first took it, my lord. We were surrounded with trees. I cut down above fifty to make the lawn before the house, and let in the wind and the sun—smack-smooth—as you see.——Then I made a green-house out of the old laundry, and turned the brewhouse into a pinery.—

The high octagon summer-house, you see yonder, is
raised on the mast of a ship, given me by an East-
India captain, who has turned many a thousand of
my money. It commands the whole road. All the
coaches and chariots, and chaises, pass and repass
under your eye. I'll mount you up there in the afternoon, my lord. 'Tis the pleasantest place in the
world to take a pipe and a bottle, and so you shall
say, my lord.

Lord Og. Ay, or a bowl of punch, or a can of
flip, Mr. Sterling! for it looks like a cabin in the air.
——If flying chairs were in use, the captain might
make a voyage to the Indies in it still, if he had but
a fair wind.

Can. Ha, ha, ha, ha!

Mrs. Heidel. My brother's a little comical in his
ideas, my lord!—But you'll excuse him.—I have a
little Gothic dairy, fitted up entirely in my own
taste.—In the evening I shall hope for the honour of
your lordship's company to take a dish of tea there,
or a sullabub warm from the cow.

Lord Og. I have every moment a fresh opportunity of admiring the elegance of Mrs. Heidelberg—
the very flower of delicacy, and cream of politeness.

Mrs. Heidel. O, my lord!   [*Leering at Lord Og.*
Lord Og. O, madam!   [*Leering at Mrs. Heidel.*
Sterl. How d'ye like these close walks, my lord?

Lord Og. A most excellent serpentine! It forms
a perfect maze, and winds like a true lover's knot.

Sterl. Ay, here's none of your straight lines here

——but all taste—zig-zag—crinkum-crankum—in and out—right and left—to and again—twisting and turning like a worm, my lord!

Lord Og. Admirably laid out indeed, Mr. Sterling! one can hardly see an inch beyond one's nose any where in these walks.——You are a most excellent œconomist of your land, and make a little go a great way.——It lies together in as small parcels as if it was placed in pots out at your window in Grace-church-street.

Can. Ha, ha, ha, ha!

Lord Og. What d'ye laugh at, Canton?

Can. Ah! que cette similitude est drole! So clever what you say, mi lor!——

Lord Og. [*To* Fanny.] You seem mightily engaged, madam. What are those pretty hands so busily employed about?

Fanny. Only making up a nosegay, my lord!—— Will your lordship do me the honour of accepting it?   [*Presenting it.*

Lord Og. I'll wear it next my heart, madam!—— I see the young creature dotes on me!   [*Apart.*

Miss Sterl. Lord, sister! you've loaded his lordship with a bunch of flowers as big as the cook or the nurse carry to town, on a Monday morning, for a beau-pot. ——Will your lordship give me leave to present you with this rose and a sprig of sweet-briar?

Lord Og. The truest emblems of yourself, madam! all sweetness and poignancy.——A little jealous, poor soul!   [*Apart.*

Sterl. Now, my lord, if you please, I'll carry you to see my ruins.

Mrs. Heidel. You'll absolutely fatigue his lordship with over-walking, brother!

Lord Og. Not at all, madam! We're in the garden of Eden, you know; in the region of perpetual spring, youth, and beauty.   [*Leering at the women.*

Mrs. Heidel. Quite the man of qualaty, I pertest.

                                        ‾ [*Apart.*

Can. Take a my arm, my lor!

                        [*Lord* Ogleby *leans on him.*

Sterl. I'll only shew his lordship my ruins, and the cascade, and the Chinese bridge, and then we'll go in to breakfast.

Lord Og. Ruins, did you say, Mr. Sterling?

Sterl. Ay, ruins, my lord! and they are reckoned very fine ones too. You would think them ready to tumble on your head. It has just cost me a hundred and fifty pounds to put my ruins in thorough repair. This way, if your lordship pleases.

Lord Og. [*Going, stops.*] What steeple's that we see yonder?—the parish church, I suppose.

Sterl. Ha, ha, ha! that's admirable. It is no church at all, my lord! it is a spire that I have built against a tree, a field or two off, to terminate the prospect. One must always have a church, or an obelisk, or something to terminate the prospect, you know. That's a rule in taste, my lord!

Lord Og. Very ingenious, indeed! For my part, I desire no finer prospect than this I see before me.

[*Leering 'at the women.*]—Simple, yet varied; bounded, yet extensive.——Get away, Canton! [*Pushing away Canton.*] I want no assistance—I'll walk with the ladies.

Sterl. This way, my lord!

Lord Og. Lead on, sir!——We young folks here, will follow you.——Madam!——Miss Sterling!—— Miss Fanny! I attend you.

[*Exit after* Sterling, *gallanting the ladies.*

Can. [*Following.*] He is cock o'de game, ma foy!

[*Exit.*

Sir John. At length, thank Heaven, I have an opportunity to unbosom.——I know you are faithful, Lovewell, and flatter myself you would rejoice to serve me.

Lov. Be assured you may depend upon me.

Sir John. You must know, then, notwithstanding all appearances, that this treaty of marriage between Miss Sterling and me will come to nothing.

Lov. How!

Sir John. It will be no match, Lovewell.

Lov. No match?

Sir John. No.

Lov. You amaze me. What should prevent it?

Sir John. I.

Lov. You! wherefore?

Sir John. I don't like her.

Lov. Very plain, indeed! I never supposed that you was extremely devoted to her from inclination,

E

but thought you always considered it as a matter of convenience, rather than affection.

Sir John. Very true. I came into the family without any impressions on my mind—with an unimpassioned indifference ready to receive one woman as soon as another. I looked upon love, serious, sober love, as a chimæra, and marriage as a thing of course, as you know most people do. But I who was lately so great an infidel in love, am now one of its sincerest votaries.——In short, my defection from Miss Sterling proceeds from the violence of my attachment to another.

Lov. Another! So, so! here will be fine work. And pray, who is she?

Sir John. Who is she! who can she be? but Fanny, the tender, amiable, engaging Fanny.

Lov. Fanny! What Fanny?

Sir John. Fanny Sterling. Her sister—Is not she an angel, Lovewell?

Lov. Her sister? Confusion!—You must not think of it, Sir John.

Sir John. Not think of it? I can think of nothing else Nay tell me, **Lovewell!** was it possible for me to be indulged in a perpetual intercourse with two such objects as Fanny and her sister, and not find my heart led by insensible attraction towards her?—You **seem** confounded—Why don't you answer me?

Lov. Indeed, Sir John, this event gives me infinite concern.

Sir John. Why so ?——Is she not an angel, Love-well ?

Lov. I foresee that it must produce the worst con-sequences. Consider the confusion it must unavoid-ably create. Let me persuade you to drop these thoughts in time.

Sir John. Never——never, Lovewell ?

Lov. You have gone too far to recede. A negoci-ation, so nearly concluded, cannot be broken off with any grace. The lawyers, you know, are hourly ex-pected ; the preliminaries almost finally settled be-tween Lord Ogleby and Mr. Sterling ; and Miss Ster-ling herself ready to receive you as a husband.

Sir John. Why, the banns have been published, and nobody has forbidden them, 'tis true. But you know either of the parties may change their minds even after they enter the church.

Lov. You think too lightly of this matter. To carry your addresses so far—and then to desert her— and for her sister too !——It will be such an affront to the family, that they can never put up with it.

Sir John. I don't think so : for as to my transfer-ring my passion from her to her sister, so much the better ! for then you know, I don't carry my affec-tion out of the family.

Lov. Nay, but pr'ythee be serious, and think better of it.

Sir John. I have thought better of it already, you see. Tell me honestly, Lovewell ? Can you blame me ? Is there any comparison between them ?

E ij

Lov. As to that now—why that—is just—just as it may strike different people. There are many admirers of Miss Sterling's vivacity.

Sir John. Vivacity! a medley of Cheapside pertness, and Whitechapel pride.—No—no, if I do go so far into the city for a wedding dinner, it shall be upon turtle at least.

Lov. But I see no probability of success; for granting that Mr. Sterling would have consented to it at first, he cannot listen to it now. Why did not you break this affair to the family before?

Sir John. Under such embarrassed circumstances as I have been, can you wonder at my irresolution or perplexity? nothing but despair, the fear of losing my dear Fanny, could bring me to a declaration even now; and yet, I think I know Mr. Sterling so well, that, strange as my proposal may appear, if I can make it advantageous to him as a money transaction, as I am sure I can, he will certainly come into it.

Lov. But even suppose he should, which I very much doubt, I don't think Fanny herself would listen to your addresses.

Sir John. You are deceived a little in that particular.

Lov. You'll find I am in the right.

Sir John. I have some little reason to think otherwise.

Lov. You have not declared your passion to her already.

Sir John. Yes, I have.

Lov. Indeed!—And—and—and how did she receive it?

Sir John. I think it is not very easy for me to make
my addresses to any woman, without receiving some
little encouragement.

Lov. Encouragement! did she give you any encouragement?

Sir John. I don't know what you call encouragement—but she blushed—and cried—and desired me
not to think of it any more :——upon which I prest
her hand—kissed it—swore she was an angel——and
I could see it tickled her to the soul.

Lov. And did she express no surprise at your declaration?

Sir John. Why, faith, to say the truth, she was a
little surprised——and she got away from me too, before I could thoroughly explain myself. If I should
not meet with an opportunity of speaking to her, I
must get you to deliver a letter for me.

Lov. I I—a letter !—I had rather have nothing——

Sir John. Nay, you promised me your assistance—
and I am sure you cannot scruple to make yourself
useful on such an occasion.——You may, without
suspicion, acquaint her verbally of my determined affection for her, and that I am resolved to ask her father's consent.

Lov. As to that, I—your commands, you know
——that is, if she——Indeed, Sir John, I think you
are in the wrong.

Sir John. Well—well—that's my concern——Ha! there she goes, by heaven! along that walk yonder, d'ye see! I'll go to her immediately.

Lov. You are too precipitate. Consider what you are doing.

Sir John. I would not lose this opportunity for the universe.

Lov. Nay, pray don't go! Your violence and eagerness may overcome her spirits.——The shock will be too much for her.   [*Detaining him.*

Sir John. Nothing shall prevent me.——Ha! now she turns into another walk——Let me go! [*Breaks from him.*] I shall lose her. [*Going, turns back.*] Be sure now to keep out of the way! If you interrupt us, I shall never forgive you.   [*Exit hastily.*

Lov. 'Sdeath! I cann't bear this. In love with my wife! acquaint me with his passion for her! make his addresses before my face!—I shall break out before my time.——This was the meaning of Fanny's uneasiness. She could not encourage him——I am sure she could not.——Ha! they are turning into the walk, and coming this way. Shall I leave the place?——Leave him to solicit my wife! I cann't submit to it.——They come nearer and nearer——If I stay, it will look suspicious—It may betray us, and incense him——They are here——I must go——I am the most unfortunate fellow in the world.   [*Exit.*

Enter FANNY *and Sir* JOHN.

Fanny. Leave me, Sir John, I beseech you leave me! nay, why will you persist to follow me with idle solicitations, which are an affront to my character, and an injury to your own honour.

Sir John. I know your delicacy, and tremble to offend it : but let the urgency of the occasion be my excuse! Consider, madam, that the future happiness of my life depends on my present application to you! consider that this day must determine my fate ; and these are perhaps the only moments left me to incline you to warrant my passion, and to intreat you not to oppose the proposals I mean to open to your father.

Fanny. For shame, for shame, Sir John! Think of your previous engagements! Think of your own situation, and think of mine! What have you discovered in my conduct that might encourage you to so bold a declaration? I am shocked that you should venture to say so much, and blush that I should even dare to give it a hearing.—— Let me begone!

Sir John. Nay, stay, madam, but one moment—— Your sensibility is too great.——Engagements! what engagements have been pretended on either side more than those of family convenience? I went on in the trammels of matrimonial negociation with a blind submission to your father and Lord Ogleby ; but my heart soon claimed a right to be consulted. It has devoted itself to you, and obliges me to plead earnestly for the same tender interest in yours.

Fanny. **Have a care,** Sir John! do not mistake a depraved will for a virtuous inclination. By these common pretences **of the** heart, half our sex are

made fools, and a greater part of yours despise them
for it.

Sir John. Affection, you will allow, is involuntary.
We cannot always direct it to the object on which it
should fix—— But when it is once inviolably attached
—inviolably as mine is to you, it often creates reci-
procal affection.——When I last urged you on this
subject, you heard me with more temper, and I hoped
with some compassion.

Fanny. You deceived yourself. If I forbore to exert a proper spirit; nay, if I did not even express the
quickest resentment of your behaviour, it was only
in consideration of that respect I wish to pay you, in
honour to my sister : and be assured, sir, woman as
I am, that my vanity could reap no pleasure from a
triumph that must result from the blackest treachery
to her.   [*Going.*

Sir John. One word, and I have done. [*Stopping
her.*] Your impatience and anxiety, and the urgency
of the occasion, oblige me to be brief and explicit
with you.——I appeal therefore from your delicacy
to your justice.——Your sister, I verily believe, neither entertains any real affection for me, or tenderness for you. Your father, I am inclined to think, is
not much concerned by means of which of his daughters the families are united.——Now, as they cannot,
shall not be connected, otherwise than by my union
with you, why will you, from a false delicacy, oppose
a measure so conducive to my happiness, and, I hope,
your own? I love you, most passionately and sin-

cerely love you—and hope to propose terms agreeable to Mr. Sterling:——If then you don't absolutely
loath, abhor, and scorn me—if there is no other happier man——

Fanny. Hear me, sir, hear my final determination.
——Were my father and sister as insensible as you
are pleased to represent them;——were my heart for
ever to remain disengaged to any other, I could not
listen to your proposals.——What! you on the **very**
eve of a marriage with my sister; I living under **the**
same roof with her, bound not only by the laws **of**
friendship and hospitality, but even the ties of blood,
to contribute **to** her happiness, and not to conspire
against her peace; the peace of a whole family; and
that of my own too!—Away, away, Sir John!——At
such a time, and in such circumstances, your addresses
only inspire me with horror.——Nay, you must detain me **no** longer——I will **go.**

Sir John. **Do** not leave me in absolute despair!—
Give me a glimpse of hope!   [*Falling **on** his knees.*

Fanny. I cannot.——Pray, Sir John!

                          [*Struggling to go.*

Sir John. Shall this hand be given to another?
[*Kissing her hand.*] No, I cannot endure it.——My
whole soul is yours, and the whole happiness of my
life is in your power.

Enter Miss STERLING.

Fanny. Ha! my sister is here. Rise, for shame,
Sir John.

Sir John. Miss Sterling !   [*Rising.*

Miss Sterl. I beg pardon, sir;—You'll excuse me, madam!—I have broke in upon you a little unopportunely, I believe—but I did not mean to interrupt you——I only came, sir, to let you know that breakfast waits, if you have finished your morning's devotions.

Sir John. I am very sensible, Miss Sterling, that this may appear particular, but——

Miss Sterl. O dear, Sir John, don't put yourself to the trouble of an apology——The thing explains itself.

Sir John. It will soon, madam.——In the mean time, I can only assure you of my profound respect and esteem for you, and make no doubt of convincing Mr. Sterling of the honour and integrity of my intentions.——And—and—your humble servant, madam!   [*Exit in confusion.*

Miss Sterl. Respect!—Insolence!—Esteem!—Very fine, truly!——And you, madam! my sweet, delicate, innocent, sentimental sister! will you convince my papa too of the integrity of your intentions?

Fanny. Do not upbraid me, my dear sister! Indeed I don't deserve it. Believe me, you can't be more offended at his behaviour than I am, and I am sure it cannot make you half so miserable.

Miss Sterl. Make me miserable! You are mightily deceived, madam; it gives me no sort of uneasiness, I assure you.—A base fellow!—As for you, miss! the pretended softness of your disposition, your artful good-

nature, never imposed upon me. I always knew you
to be sly, and envious, and deceitful.

Fanny Indeed you wrong me.

Miss Sterl. Oh, you are all goodness, to be sure!—
Did not I find him on his knees before you? Did not
I see him kiss your sweet hand? Did not I hear his
protestations? Was not I a witness of your dissembled
modesty?——No, no, my dear! don't imagine that
you can make a fool of your elder sister so easily.

Fanny. Sir John, I own, is to blame; but I am
above the thoughts of doing you the least injury.

Miss Sterl. We shall try that, madam.——I hope,
miss, you'll be able to give a better account to my
papa and my aunt, for they shall both know of this
matter, I promise you. [*Exit.*

Fanny. How unhappy I am! my distresses multiply
upon me.——Mr. Lovewell must now become acquainted with Sir John's behaviour to me, and in a
manner that may add to his uneasiness. My father,
instead of being disposed by fortunate circumstances
to forgive any transgression, will be previously incensed against me. My sister and my aunt will become
irreconcilably my enemies, and rejoice in my disgrace.
——Yet, on all events, I am determined on a discovery. I dread it, and am resolved to hasten it. It
is surrounded with more horrors every instant, as it
appears every instant more necessary. [*Exit.*

ACT III. SCENE I.

A Hall. Enter a Servant leading in Serjeant FLOWER, *and Counsellors* TRAVERSE *and* TRUEMAN, *all booted.*

Servant.

THIS way, if you please, gentlemen! my master is at breakfast with the family at present, but I'll let him know, and he will wait on you immediately.

Flow. Mighty well, young man, mighty well.

Serv. Please to favour me with your names, gentlemen.

Flow. Let Mr. Sterling know, that Mr. Serjeant Flower, and two other gentlemen of the bar, are come to wait on him according to his appointment.

Serv. I will, sir.   [*Going.*

Flow. And hark'e, young man, [*Servant returns.*] desire my servant—Mr. Serjeant Flower's servant, to bring in my green and gold saddle-cloth and pistols, and lay them down here in the hall with my portmanteau.

Serv. I will, sir.   [*Exit.*

Flow. Well, gentlemen! the settling these marriage articles falls conveniently enough, almost just on the eve of the circuits.——Let me see—the Home, the Midland, and Western; ay, we can all cross the country well enough to our several destinations.—— Traverse, when do you begin at Hertford?

Trav. The day after to-morrow.

Flow. That is commission-day with us at Warwick **too**. But my clerk has retainers for every cause in **the** paper, so it will be time enough if I am there the next morning. Besides, I have about half a dozen cases that have lain by me ever since the spring assizes, and I must tack opinions to them before I see my country clients again ; so I will take the evening before 'me, and then *current calamo,* **as I say** —eh, Traverse !

Trav. True, Mr. Serjeant ; and the easiest **thing** in the world too ; **for** those country attornies are such ignorant **dogs,** that in case of the devise of an estate to **A, and his** heirs **for ever,** they'll make a query whether he takes in fee or in tail.

Flow. Do you expect to **have** much to do on the Home Circuit these assizes ?

Trav. Not much *nisi* **prius** business, but a good deal on the crown side, I believe. The gaols are brim-full, and some of the felons in good circumstances, and likely to be tolerable clients. Let me see ! I am engaged for three highway robberies, two murders, one **for**gery, and half a dozen larcenies, at Kingston.

Flow. A pretty decent gaol-delivery !—Do you expect to bring off Darkin, for the robbery on Putney-Common ? Can you make out your alibi ?

Trav. Oh ! no ! the crown witnesses are sure to prove our identity. We shall certainly be hanged : but that don't signify.——But, Mr. Serjeant, have

F

you much to do?——Any remarkable cause on the Midland this circuit?   .

Flow. Nothing very remarkable——except two rapes, and Rider and Western at Nottingham, for crim. con.——but, on the whole, I believe a good deal of business.——Our associate tells me, there are above thirty *venires* for Warwick.   .

Trav. Pray, Mr. Serjeant, are you concerned in Jones and Thomas at Lincoln?

Flow. I am——for the plaintiff.

Trav. And what do you think on't?

Flow. A nonsuit.

Trav. I thought so.

Flow. Oh, no matter of doubt on't——*luce clarius*—— we have no right in us——we have but one chance.

Trav. What's that?   ,

Flow. Why, my Lord Chief does not go the circuit this time, and my brother Puzzle being in the commission, the cause will come on before him.

True. Ay, that may do indeed, if you can but throw dust in the eyes of the defendants counsel.

Flow. True.——Mr. Trueman, I think you are concerned for Lord Ogleby in this affair?   [*To* True.

True. I am, sir——I have the honour to be related to his lordship, and hold some courts for him in Somersetshire——go the Western circuit——and attend the sessions at Exeter, merely because his lordship's interests and property lie in that part of the kingdom.

Flow. Ha !——and pray, Mr. Trueman, how long have you been called to the bar ?

True. About nine years and three quarters.

Flow. Ha !——I don't know that I ever had the pleasure of seeing you before.——I wish you success, young gentleman !

Enter STERLING.

Sterl. Oh, Mr. Serjeant Flower, I am glad to see you——Your servant, Mr. Serjeant ! gentlemen, your servant !——Well, are all matters concluded ? Has that snail-paced conveyancer, old Ferret, of Gray's-Inn, settled the articles at last ? Do you approve of what he has done ? Will his tackle hold, tight and strong ?——Eh, Master Serjeant !

Flow. My friend Ferret's slow and sure, sir—— But then, *serius aut citius*, as we say, sooner or later, Mr. Sterling, he is sure to put his business out of hand as he should do.——My clerk has brought the writing, and all other instruments along with him, and the settlement is, I believe, as good a settlement as any settlement on the face of the earth !

Sterl. But that damn'd mortgage of 60,000l.—— There don't appear to be any other incumbrances, I hope ?

Trav. I can answer for that, sir——and that will be cleared off immediately on the payment of the first part of Miss Sterling's proportion.——You agree, on your part, to come down with 80,000l.

Sterl. Down on the nail.——Ay, ay, my money is ready to-morrow if he pleases——he shall have it in India-bonds, or notes, or how he chooses.——Your lords and your dukes, and your people at the court end of the town stick at payments sometimes—— debts unpaid, no credit lost with them——but no fear of us substantial fellows——Eh, Mr. Serjeant !

Flow. Sir John having last term, according to agree-ment, levied a fine, and suffered a recovery, has hi-therto cut off the entail of the Ogleby estate for the better effecting the purposes of the present intended marriage; on which above-mentioned Ogleby estate, a jointure of 2000l. per annum is secured to your eldest daughter, now Elizabeth Sterling, spinster, and the whole estate, after the death of the aforesaid earl, descends to the heirs male of Sir John Melvil, on the body of the aforesaid Elizabeth Sterling lawfully to be forgotten.

Trav. Very true——and Sir John is to be put in immediate possession of as much of his lordship's Somersetshire estate, as lies in the manors of Hog-more and Cranford, amounting to between two and three thousand per annum, and at the death of Mr. Sterling, a further sum of seventy thousand——

Enter Sir JOHN MELVIL.

Sterl. Ah, Sir John ! Here we are——hard at it ——paving the road to matrimony——First the law-yers, then comes the doctor——Let us but dispatch

the long-robe, we shall soon get pudding sleeves to work, I warrant you.

Sir John. I am sorry to interrupt you, sir——but I hope that both you and these gentlemen will excuse me——Having something very particular for your private ear, I took the liberty of following you, and beg you will oblige me with an audience immediately.

Sterl. Ay, with all my heart!——Gentlemen, Mr. Serjeant, you'll excuse it——Business must be done, you know. The writings will keep cold till to-morrow morning.

Flow. I must be at Warwick, Mr. Sterling, the day after.

Sterl. Nay, nay, I sha'n't part with you to-night, gentlemen, I promise you.——My house is very full, but I have beds for you all, beds for your servants, and stabling for all your horses.——Will you take a turn in the garden, and view some of my improvements before dinner? Or will you amuse yourselves on the green, with a game of bowls and a cool tankard?——My servants shall attend you.——Do you choose any other refreshment?——Call for what you please; do as you please;——make yourselves quite at home, I beg of you.——Here, Thomas! Harry! William! wait on these gentlemen!——[*Follows the lawyers out, bawling and talking, and then returns to Sir John.*] And now, sir, I am entirely at your service. What are your commands with me, Sir John?

Sir John. After having carried the negociation between our families to so great a length; after having
assented so readily to all your proposals, as well as
received so many instances of your cheerful compliance with the demands made on our part, I am extremely concerned, Mr. Sterling, to be the involuntary cause of any uneasiness.

Sterl. Uneasiness! what uneasiness?——Where business is transacted as it ought to be, and the parties
understand one another, there can be no uneasiness.
You agree, on such and such conditions, to receive
my daughter for a wife; on the same conditions I
agree to receive you as a son-in-law; and as to all
the rest, it follows of course, you know, as regularly
as the payment of a bill after acceptance.

Sir John. Pardon me, sir, more uneasiness has
arisen than you are aware of. I am myself, at this
instant, in a state of inexpressible embarrassment;
Miss Sterling, I know, is extremely disconcerted too;
and unless you will oblige me with the assistance of
your friendship, I foresee the speedy progress of dis-
content and animosity through the whole family.

Sterl. What the deuce is all this? I don't understand a single syllable.

Sir John. In one word then——it will be absolutely
impossible for me to fulfil my engagements in regard
to Miss Sterling.

Sterl. How, Sir John! Do you mean to put an affront upon my family? What? refuse to——

Sir John. Be assured, sir, that I neither mean to

affront, nor forsake your family. My only fear is, that you should desert me; for the whole happiness of my life depends on my being connected with your family, by the nearest and tenderest ties in the world.

Sterl. Why, did not you tell me, but a moment ago, that it was absolutely impossible for you to marry my daughter?

Sir John. True.——But you have another daughter, sir——

Sterl. Well!

Sir John. Who has obtained the most absolute dominion over my heart. I have already declared my passion to her; nay, Miss Sterling herself is also apprised of it, and if you will but give a sanction to my present addresses, the uncommon merit of Miss Sterling will no doubt recommend her to a person of equal, if not superior rank to myself, and our families may still be allied by my union with Miss Fanny.

Sterl. Mighty fine, truly! Why, what the plague do you make of us, Sir John? Do you come to market for my daughter, like servants at a statute-fair? Do you think that I will suffer you, or any man in the world, to come into my house, like the Grand Signior, and throw the handkerchief first to one, and then to t'other, just as he pleases? Do you think I drive a kind of African slave-trade with them? and——

Sir John. A moment's patience, sir! Nothing but the excess of my passion for Miss Fanny should have

induced me to take any step that had the least appearance of disrespect to any part of your family;
and even now I am desirous to atone for my transgression, by making the most adequate compensation
that lies in my power.

Sterl. Compensation! what compensation can you
possibly make in such a case as this, Sir John?

Sir John. Come, come, Mr. Sterling; I know you
to be a man of sense, a man of business, a man of the
world.   I'll deal frankly with you; and you shall see
that I don't desire a change of measures for my own
gratification, without endeavouring to make it advantageous to you.

Sterl. What advantage can your inconstancy be to
me, Sir John?

Sir John. I'll tell you, sir.——You know that by
the articles at present subsisting between us, on the
day of my marriage with Miss Sterling, you agree to
pay down the gross sum of eighty thousand pounds.

Sterl. Well!

Sir John. **Now if** you will but consent to my waving that marriage——

Sterl. I agree to your waving that marriage! Impossible, Sir John!

Sir John. **I** hope not, sir; as **on my part, I** will
agree to wave my right to thirty thousand pounds of
the fortune I was to receive with her.

Sterl. Thirty thousand, d'ye say?

Sir John. Yes, sir; and accept of Miss Fanny, with
fifty thousand, instead of fourscore.

Sterl. Fifty thousand——— [*Pausing.*

Sir John. Instead of fourscore.

Sterl. Why—why—there may be something in that.——Let me see—Fanny with fifty thousand, instead of Betsy with fourscore.——But how can this be, Sir John? For you know I am to pay this money into the hands of my Lord Ogleby; who, I believe, between you and me, Sir John, is not overstocked with ready money at present; and threescore thousand of it, you know, is to go to pay off the present incumbrances on the estate, Sir John.

Sir John. That objection is easily obviated.——Ten of the twenty thousand, which would remain as a surplus of the fourscore, after paying off the mortgage, was intended by his lordship for my use, that we might set off with some little eclat on our marriage; and the other ten for his own.—Ten thousand pounds, therefore, I shall be able to pay you immediately; and for the remaining twenty thousand, you shall have a mortgage on that part of the estate which is to be made over to me, with whatever security you shall require for the regular payment of the interest, till the principal is duly discharged.

Sterl. Why—to do you justice, Sir John, there is something fair and open in your proposal; and since I find you do not mean to put an affront upon the family——

Sir John. Nothing was ever farther from my thoughts, Mr. Sterling.——And after all, the whole affair is nothing extraordinary—such things happen every day ; and as the world has only heard generally of a treaty between the families, when this marriage takes place, nobody will be the wiser, if we have but discretion enough to keep our own counsel.

Sterl. True, true ; and since you only transfer from one girl to the other, it is no more than transferring so much stock, you know.

Sir John. The very thing !

Sterl. Odso ! I had quite forgot.——We are reckoning without our host here.—there is another difficulty——

Sir John. You alarm me. What can that be ?

Sterl. I cann't stir a step in this business without consulting my sister Heidelberg.——The family has very great expectations from her, and we must not give her any offence.

Sir John. But if you come into this measure, surely she will be so kind as to consent——

Sterl. I don't know that—Betsy is her darling, and I cann't tell how far she may resent any slight that seems to be offered to her favourite niece. However, I'll do the best I can for you. You shall go and break the matter to her first, and by that time I may suppose that your rhetoric has prevailed on her to listen to reason, I will step in to reinforce your arguments.

Sir John. I'll fly to her immediately ; you promise me your assistance ?

Sterl. I do.

Sir John. Ten thousand thanks for it! and now
success attend me!   [*Going.*

Sterl. Hark'e, Sir John! [*Sir* John *returns.*] Not a
word of the thirty thousand to my sister, Sir John.

Sir John. Oh, I am dumb, I am dumb, sir. [*Going.*

Sterl. You'll remember it is thirty thousand.

Sir John. To be sure I do.

Sterl. But, Sir John!—one thing more. [*Sir* John
returns.] My lord must know nothing of this stroke
of friendship between us.

Sir John. Not for the world. Let me alone! let
me alone!   [*Offering to go.*

Sterl. [*Holding him.*] And when every thing is agreed,
we must give each other a bond to be held fast to
the bargain.

Sir John. To be sure. **A bond by** all means! a
bond, or whatever you please.   [*Exit hastily.*

Sterl. I should have thought of more conditions—
he's in a humour to give me **every** thing—Why, what
mere children are your fellows **of** quality; that cry
for a plaything one minute, and throw it by the next!
as changeable as the weather, and as uncertain as the
stocks. Special fellows to drive **a** bargain! and yet
they are to take care **of** the interest of the nation
truly! Here does this whirligig man of fashion offer
to give up thirty thousand pounds in hard money,
with as much indifference as if it was a china orange.
By this mortgage, I shall have a hold on his *terra
firma*; and if he wants more money, as he certainly

will,—let him have children by my daughter or no, I shall have his whole estate in a net, for the benefit of my family.——Well, thus it is, that the children of citizens, who have acquired fortunes, prove persons of fashion; and thus it is, that persons of fashion, who have ruined their fortunes, reduce the next generation to cits.   [*Exit.*

SCENE II.

Changes to another Apartment. Enter Mrs. HEIDELBERG, *and Miss* STERLING.

Miss Sterl. This is your gentle-looking, soft-speaking, sweet-smiling, affable Miss Fanny for you!

Mrs. Heidel. My Miss Fanny! I disclaim her. With all her arts she never could insinuate herself into my good graces; and yet she has a way with her, that deceives man, woman, and child, except you and me, niece.

Miss Sterl. O ay; she wants nothing but a crook in her hand, and a lamb under her arm, to be a perfect picture of innocence and simplicity.

Mrs. Heidel. Just as I was drawn at Amsterdam, when I went over to visit my husband's relations.

Miss Sterl. And then she's so mighty good to servants—' pray, John, do this,—pray, Tom, do that—thank you, Jenny;' and then so humble to her relations—' to be sure, papa!—as my aunt pleases—my sister knows best.'——But with all her demureness and humility, she has no objection to be Lady Melvil, it seems, nor to any wickedness that can make her so.

Mrs. Heidel. She Lady Melvil! Compose yourself, niece! I'll ladyship her indeed :—a little creppin, cantin—She sha'n't be the better for a farden of my money.   But tell me, child, how does this intriguing with Sir John correspond with her partiality to Lovewell? I don't see a concatunation here.

Miss Sterl. There I was deceived, madam.   I took all their whisperings and stealing into corners to be the mere attraction of vulgar minds; but, behold! their private meetings were not to contrive their own insipid happiness, but to conspire against mine.   But I know whence proceeds Mr. Lovewell's resentment to me.   I could not stoop to be familiar with my father's clerk, and so I have lost his interest.

Mrs. Heidel. My spirit to a T.—My dear child! [*Kisses her.*]—Mr. Heidelberg lost his election for member of Parliament, because I would not demean myself to be slobbered about by drunken shoemakers, beastly cheesemongers, and greasy butchers and tallow-chandlers.   However, niece, I cann't help diffuring a little in opinion from you in this matter. My experunce and sagucity makes me still suspect, that there is something more between her and that Lovewell, notwithstanding this affair of **Sir John.** I had my eye upon them the whole time of breakfast. Sir John, I observed, looked a little confounded, indeed, though I knew nothing of what had passed in-

G

the garden. You seemed to sit upon thorns too: But Fanny and Mr. Lovewell made quite another guess-sort of a figur; and were as perfect a pictur of two distrest lovers, as if it had been drawn by Raphael Angelo. As to Sir John and Fanny, I want a matter of fact.

Miss Sterl. Matter of fact, madam! Did not I come unexpectedly upon them? Was not Sir John kneeling at her feet, and kissing her hand? Did not he look all love, and she all confusion? Is not that matter of fact? and did not Sir John, the moment that papa was called out of the room to the lawyer-men, get up from breakfast, and follow him immediately? And I warrant you that by this time he has made proposals to him to marry my sister——Oh, that some other person, an earl, or a duke, would make his addresses to me, that I might be revenged on this monster!

Mrs. Heidel. Be cool, child! you shall be Lady Melvil, in spite of all their caballins, if it costs me ten thousand pounds to turn the scale. Sir John may apply to my brother indeed; but I'll make them all know who governs in this fammaly.

Miss Sterl. As I live, madam, yonder comes Sir John. A base man! I can't endure the sight of him. I'll leave the room this instant. [*Disordered.*

Mrs. Heidel. Poor thing! Well, retire to your own chamber, child; I'll give it him, I warrant you; and by and by I'll come and let you know all that has pass between us.

Miss Sterl. Pray do, madam.—[*Looking back.*]——
A vile wretch ! [*Exit in a rage.*

Enter *Sir* JOHN MELVIL.

Sir John. Your most obedient humble servant, madam. [*Bowing very respectively.*

Mrs. Heidel. Your servant, Sir John.
[*Dropping a half curtsey, and pouting.*

Sir John. Miss Sterling's manner of quitting the
room on my approach, and the visible coolness of
your behaviour to me, madam, convince me that
she has acquainted you with what past this morning.

Mrs. Heidel. I am very sorry, Sir John, to be made
acquainted with any thing that should induce me to
change the opinion which I would always wish to entertain of a person of qualaty. [*Pouting.*

Sir John. It has always been my ambition to merit
the best opinion from Mrs. Heidelberg; and when
she comes to weigh all circumstances, I flatter myself——

Mrs. Heidel. You do flatter yourself, if you imagine
that I can approve of your behaviour to my niece, Sir
John.—And give me leave to tell you, Sir John, that
you have been drawn into an action much beneath
you, Sir John; and that I look upon every injury offered to Miss Betty Sterling, as an affront to myself,
Sir John. [*Warmly.*

Sir John. I would not offend you for the world,
madam ; but when I am influenced by a partiality for

G ij

another, however ill-founded, I hope your discernment and good sense will think it rather a point of honour to renounce engagements, which I could not fulfil so strictly as I ought; and that you will excuse the change in my inclinations, since the new object, as well as the first, has the honour of being your niece, madam.

Mrs. Heidel. I disclaim her as a niece, Sir John; Miss Sterling disclaims her as a sister, and the whole fammaly must disclaim her, for her monstrous baseness and treachery.

Sir John. Indeed she has been guilty of none, madam. Her hand and her heart are, I am sure, entirely at the disposal of yourself, and Mr. Sterling.

Enter STERLING *behind.*

And if you should not oppose my inclinations, I am sure of Mr. Sterling's consent, madam.

Mrs. Heidel. Indeed!

Sir John. Quite certain, madam.

Sterl. [*Behind.*] So! they seem to be coming to terms already. I may venture to make my appearance.

Mrs. Heidel. To marry Fanny?

[Sterling *advances by degrees.*

Sir John. Yes, madam.

Mrs. Heidel. My brother has given his consent, you say?

Sir John. In the most ample manner, with no other restriction than the failure of your concurrence, madam. [*Sees* Sterling.]—Oh, here's Mr. Sterling, who will confirm what I have told you.

Mrs. Heidel. What! have you consented to give up your own daughter in this manner, brother?

Sterl. Give her up! no, not give her up, sister; only in case that you——Zounds, I am afraid you have said too much, Sir John.   [*Apart to Sir John.*

Mrs. Heidel. Yes, yes.   I see now that it is true enough what my niece told me.   You are all plottin and caballin against her.   Pray, does Lord Ogleby know of this affair?

Sir John. I have not yet made him acquainted with it, madam.

Mrs. Heidel. No, I warrant you.   I thought so.— And so his lordship and myself, truly, are not to be consulted 'till the last.

Sterl. What! did not you consult my lord? Oh, fie for shame, Sir John!

Sir John. Nay, but Mr. Sterling——

Mrs. Heidel. We, who are the persons of most con-sequence and experunce in the two fammalies, are to know nothing of the matter, 'till the whole is as good as concluded upon.   But his lordship, I am sure, will have more generosaty than to countenance such a perceding.   And I could not have expected such be-haviour from a person of your qualaty, Sir John.— And as for you, brother——

Sterl. Nay, nay, but hear me, sister.

Mrs. Heidel. I am perfectly ashamed of you.——

Have you no spurrit? no more concern for the honour
of our fammaly than to consent——

Sterl. Consent! I consent! As I hope for mercy,
I never gave my consent.——Did I consent, Sir
John?

Sir John. Not absolutely, without Mrs. Heidelberg's concurrence. But in case of her approbation——

Sterl. Ay, I grant you, if my sister approved——
But that's quite another thing, you know——

[To Mrs. Heidel.

Mrs. Heidel. Your sister approve, indeed!——I
thought you knew her better, brother Sterling!——
What! approve of having your eldest daughter returned upon your hands, and exchanged for the
younger?——I am surprised how you could listen to
such a scandalous proposal.

Sterl. I tell you, I never did listen to it.—Did not
I say, that I would be entirely governed by my sister,
Sir John?——And unless she agreed to your marry-
ing Fanny——

Mrs. Heidel. I agree to his marrying Fanny!——
abominable!——The man is absolutely out of his
senses.——Cann't that wise head of yours forsee the
consequence of all this, brother Sterling? Will Sir
John take Fanny without a fortune?---No!——After
you have settled the largest part of your property on
your youngest daughter, can there be an equal por-
tion left for the eldest?---No!——Does not this over-

turn the whole systum of the fammaly?---Yes, yes, yes!——You know I was always for my niece Betsey's marrying a person of the very first qualaty. That was my maxum:——and, therefore, much the largest settlement was, of course, to be made upon her. As for Fanny, if she could, with a fortune of twenty or thirty thousand pounds, get a knight, or a member of parliament, or a rich common council-man for a husband, I thought it might do very well.

Sir John. But if a better match should offer itself, why should it not be accepted, madam?

Mrs. Heidel. What, at the expence of her elder sister! O fie, Sir John! How could you bear to hear such an indignaty, brother Sterling?

Sterl. I! Nay, I sha'n't hear of it, I promise you.——I cann't hear of it, indeed, Sir John.

Mrs. Heidel. But you have heard of it, brother Sterling.——You know you have; and sent Sir John to propose it to me. But if you can give up your daughter, I sha'n't forsake my niece, I assure you. Ah! if my poor dear Mr. Heidelberg and our sweet babes had been alive, he would not have behaved so.

Sterl. Did I, Sir John?——Nay, speak!—Bring me off, or we are ruined. [*Apart to Sir* John.

Sir John. Why, to be sure, to speak the truth——

Mrs Heidel. To speak the truth, I'm ashamed of you both. But have a care what you are about brother! have a care, I say. The counsellors are in the house, I hear; and if every thing is not settled to

my liking, I'll have nothing more to say to you, if I
live these hundred years.——I'll go over to Holland,
and settle with Mr. Vanderspracken, my poor husband's first cousin, and my own fammaly shall never
be the better for a farden of my money, I promise
you.   [*Exit.*

Sterl. I thought so. I knew she never would agree
to it.

Sir John. 'Sdeath, how unfortunate! What can we
do, Mr. Sterling?

Sterl. Nothing.

Sir John. What, must our agreement break off the
moment it is made, then?

Sterl. It cann't be helped, Sir John. The family,
as I told you before, have great expectations from my
sister; and if this matter proceeds, you hear yourself
that she threatens to leave us.—My brother Heidelberg was a warm man—a very warm man; and died
worth a plumb at least; a plumb! ay, I warrant you,
he died worth a plumb and a half.

Sir John. Well; but if I——

Sterl. And then, my sister has three or four very
good mortgages, a deal of money in the three per
cents, and old South Sea annuities, besides large con-
cerns in the Dutch and French funds. The greatest
part of all this she means to leave to our family.

Sir John. I can only say, sir——

Sterl. Why, your offer of the difference of thirty
thousand was very fair and handsome, to be sure, Sir
John.

Sir John. Nay, but I am even willing to——

Sterl. Ay, but if I was to accept it against her will, I might lose above a hundred thousand; so you see the balance is against you, Sir John.

Sir John. But is there no way, do you think, of prevailing **on** Mrs. Heidelberg to grant her consent?

Sterl. I am afraid not.——However, when her **pas**sion is a little abated—for she's very passionate—**you** may try what can be done: but you must not **use** my name any more, Sir John.

Sir John. Suppose I was to prevail on Lord Ogleby to apply **to her**, do you think that would have any influence over her?

Sterl. I think he would be more likely to persuade her to it than any other person in the family. She has a great respect for **Lord** Ogleby. She loves a lord.

Sir John. I'll apply to him this very day.—And if he should prevail on Mrs. Heidelberg, I may depend on your friendship, Mr. Sterling?

Sterl. Ay, ay, I shall be glad **to** oblige you, when it is in my power; but **as** the account stands now, you see it is not upon the figures. **And** so your servant, Sir John. [*Exit.*

Sir John. What a situation am I in!—Breaking off with her whom I was bound by treaty to marry; rejected by the object of my affections; and embroiled with this turbulent woman, who governs the whole

family.—And yet opposition, instead of smothering,
increases my inclination. I must have her. I'll apply immediately to Lord Ogleby; and if he can but
bring over the aunt to our party, her influence will
overcome the scruples and delicacy of my dear Fanny,
and I shall be the happiest of mankind.   [*Exit.*

ACT IV. SCENE I.

A Room.   Enter **Mr.** STERLING, *Mrs.* HEIDELBERG,
and Miss STERLING.

Sterling.

WHAT! will you send Fanny to town, sister?

Mrs. Heidel. To-morrow morning. I've given orders about it already.

Ster. Indeed!

Mrs. Heidel. Posatively.

Sterl. But consider, sister, at such a time as this,
what an **odd** appearance it will have.

Mrs. Heidel. Not half so odd as her behaviour,
brother.—This time was intended for happiness, and
I'll keep no incendiaries here to destroy it. I insist
on her going off to-morrow morning.

Sterl. I'm afraid this is all your doing, Betsey.

Miss Sterl. No, indeed, papa. My aunt knows that
it is not.—For all Fanny's baseness to me, I am sure
I would not do or say any thing to hurt her with you
or my aunt for the world.

Mrs. Heidel. Hold your tongue, Betsey; I will have my way.—When she is packed off, every thing will go on as it should do.——Since they are at their intrigues, I'll let them see that we can act with vigur on our part; and the sending her out of the way, shall be the purluminary step to all the rest of my perceedings.

Sterl. Well, but sister——

Mrs. Heidel. It does not signify talking, brother Sterling, for I'm resolved to be rid of her, and I will. —Come along, child. [*To Miss* Sterling.]—The post-shay shall be at the door by six o'clock in the morning; and if Miss Fanny does not get into it, why, I will—and so there's an end of the matter. [*Bounces out with Miss* Sterling; *then returns.*] One word more, brother Sterling.—I expect that **you** will take your eldest daughter in your hand, and make a formal complaint to Lord Ogleby, of Sir John Melvil's behaviour.—Do this, brother;—shew a proper regard for the honour of your fammaly yourself, and I shall throw in my mite to the raising of it. If not——but now you know my mind. So act as you please, and take the consequences.   [*Exit.*

Sterl. The devil's in the women for tyranny!—— Mothers, wives, mistresses, or sisters, they always will govern us.——As to my sister Heidelberg, she knows the strength of her purse, and domineers upon the credit of it.——' I will do this,' and ' you shall do that,' and ' you shall do t'other,—or else the fammaly sha'n't have a farden of'—[*Mimicking.*]——So abso-

lute with her money!—But, to say the truth, nothing
but money can make us absolute, and so we must e'en
make the best of her.   [*Exit.*

SCENE II.

Changes to the Garden.   Enter Lord OGLEBY, *and*
CANTON.

Lord Og. What! Mademoiselle Fanny to be sent
away!—Why?—Wherefore?—What's the meaning
of all this?

Can. Je ne sçais pas —I know nothing of it.

Lord Og. It cann't be—it sha'n't be:—I protest
against the measure. She's a fine girl, and I had
much rather that the rest of the family were annihilated, than that she should leave us.——Her vulgar
father, that's the very abstract of 'Change-alley—the
aunt, that's always endeavouring to be a fine ady—
and the pert sister, for ever shewing that she is one,
are horrid company indeed, and without her, would
be intolerable. Ah, la petite Farchon! she's the
thing: Isn't she, Canton?

Can. Dere is very good sympatie entre vous, and
dat young lady, mi lor.

Lord Og. I'll not be left among these Goths and
Vandals, your Sterlings, your Heidelbergs, and Devil-
bergs——if she goes, I'll positively go too.

Can. In de same post-chay, my lor? You have
no objection to dat, I believe, nor mademoiselle neither too—ha, ha, ha!

Lord Og. Pr'ythee hold thy foolish tongue, Cant. Does thy Swiss stupidity imagine that I can see and talk with a fine girl without desires !———My eyes are involuntarily attracted by **beautiful** objects———I fly as naturally to a fine girl————

Can. As de fine girl to you, my lor, ha, ha, ha! you alway fly togedre like un pair de pigeons————

Lord Og. Like un pair de pigeons—[*Mocks him.*]— Vous etes un sot, Mons. Canton———Thou art always dreaming of my intrigues, and never seest me badiner but you suspect mischief, you old fool, you.

Can. I am fool, I confess, but not always fool in dat, my lor, he, he, he!

Lord Og. He, he, he!———Thou art incorrigible, but thy absurdities amuse one. Thou art like my rappee here, [*Takes out his box.*] a most ridiculous superfluity, but a pinch of thee now and then is a more delicious treat.

Can. **You** do me great honeur, mi lor.

Lord Og. 'Tis fact, upon my soul. Thou art properly my cephalic snuff, and art no bad medicine against megrims, vertigoes, and profound thinking— ha, ha, ha!

Can. **Your flatterie, my** lor, **vil make** me **too** prode.

Lord Og. The girl has some little partiality for me, to be sure : but pr'ythee, Cant. is not that Miss Fanny yonder ?

Can. [*Looking with a glass.*] En verité, 'tis ske,

my lor——'tis one of de pigeons——de pigeons d'amour.

Lord Og. Don't be ridiculous, you old monkey.

[*Smiling.*

Can. I am monkee, I am ole, but I have eye, I have ear, and a little understand, now and den.

Lord Og. Taisez vous bête !

Can. Elle vous attend, my lor.——She vil make a love to you.

Lord Og. Will she ? Have at her then ! A fine girl cann't oblige me more——Egad, I find myself a little enjoué——Come along, Cant. I she is but in the next walk——but there is such a deal of this damned crinkum-crankum, as Sterling calls it, that one sees people for half an hour before one can get to them ——Allons, Mons. Canton, allons, donc !

[*Exeunt, singing in French.*

Another Part of the Garden. LOVEWELL *and* FANNY.

Lov. My dear Fanny, I cannot bear your distress ! it overcomes all my resolutions, and I am prepared for the discovery.

Fan. But how can it be effected before my departure ?

Lov. I'll tell you.——Lord Ogleby seems to entertain a visible partiality for you ; and, notwithstanding the peculiarities of his behaviour, I am sure that he is humane at the bottom. He is vain to an excess ; but withal extremely good-natured, and would do any thing to recommend himself to a lady.——Do you open the whole affair of our marriage to him immediately. It will come with more irresistible persuasion from you than from myself; and I doubt not but you'll gain his friendship and protection at once. His influence and authority will put an end to Sir John's solicitations, remove your aunt's and sister's unkindness and suspicions, and, I hope, reconcile your father and the whole family to our marriage.

Fanny. Heaven grant it! Where is my lord?

Lov. I have heard him and Canton, since dinner, singing French songs under the great walnut-tree by the parlour-door. If you meet with him in the garden, you may disclose the whole immediately.

Fanny. Dreadful as the task is, I'll do it.——Any thing is better than this continual anxiety.

Lov. By that time the discovery is made, I will appear to second you.——Ha! here comes my lord. ——Now, my dear Fanny, summon up all your spirits, plead our cause powerfully, and be sure of success.——— [*Going.*

Fanny. Ah, don't leave me!

Lov. Nay, you must let me.

Fanny. Well, since it must be so, I'll obey you, if I have the power. Oh, Lovewell!

Lov. Consider, our situation is very critical. To-morrow morning is fixed for your departure, and if we lose this opportunity, we may wish in vain for another.——He approaches——I must retire.—— Speak, my dear Fanny, speak, and make us happy! [*Exit.*

Fanny. Good Heaven! what a situation am I in! what shall I do? What shall I say to him? I am all confusion.

Enter Lord OGLEBY, *and* CANTON.

Lord Og. To see so much beauty so solitary, madam, is a satire upon mankind, and 'tis fortunate that one man has broke in upon your reverie for the credit of our sex. I say one, madam; for poor Canton here, from age and infirmities, stands for nothing.

Can. Noting at all, indeed.

Fanny. Your lordship does me great honour.——I had a favour to request, my lord!

Lord Og. A favour, madam!——To be honoured with your commands, is an inexpressible favour done to me, madam.

Fanny. If your lordship could indulge me with the honour of a moment's——What is the matter with me?   [*Aside.*

Lord Og. The girl's confused——He!——here's something in the wind, faith—I'll have a tete-à-tete with her——Allez vous en!   [*To* Canton.

Can. I go——Ah, pauvre Mademoiselle! my lor, have pitié upon the poor pigeone!

Lord Og. I'll knock you down, Cant. if you're impertinent.   [*Smiling.*

Can. Den I mus away.—[*Shuffles along.*]——You are mosh please, for all dat.   [*Aside, and exit.*

Fanny. I shall sink with apprehension.   [*Aside.*

Lord Og. What a sweet girl——she's a civilized being, and atones for the barbarism of the rest of the family.

Fanny. **My** lord! I——   [*She curtsies, and blushes.*

Lord Og. [*Addressing her.*] I look upon it, madam, to be one of the luckiest circumstances of my life, that I have this moment the honour of receiving your commands, and the satisfaction of confirming with my tongue, what my eyes perhaps have but too weakly expressed—that I am literally—the humblest of your servants.

Fanny. I think myself greatly honoured by your lordship's partiality to me ; but it distresses me, that I am obliged in my present situation to apply to it for protection.

Lord Og. I am happy in your distress, madam, because it gives me an opportunity to shew my zeal.—— Beauty to me **is a** religion in which I was born and bred a bigot, and would die a martyr.——I'm in tolerable spirits, faith !   [*Aside.*

Fanny. There is not, perhaps, at this moment, a more distressed creature than myself. Affection, duty, hope, despair, and a thousand different sentiments, are struggling in my bosom ; and even the presence of your lordship, to whom I have flown for protection, adds to my perplexity.

Lord Og. Does it, madam——Venus forbid !—— My old fault ; the devil's in me, I think, for perplexing young women. [*Aside, and smiling.*] Take courage, madam ! dear Miss Fanny, explain.——You have a powerful advocate in my breast, I assure you ——— My heart, madam———I am attached to you by all the laws of sympathy and delicacy.———By my honour, I am.

Fanny. Then I will venture to unburthen my mind ———Sir John Melvil, my lord, by the most misplaced and mistimed declaration of affection for me, has made me the unhappiest of women.

Lord Og. How, madam! Has Sir John made his addresses to you?

Fanny. He has, **my lord,** in the strongest terms. But I hope it is needless to say, that my duty to my father, love to my sister, and regard to the whole family, as well as the great respect I entertain for your lordship, [*Curtseying.*] made me shudder at his addresses.

Lord Og. Charming girl!—Proceed, my dear Miss Fanny, proceed!

Fanny. In a moment———give me leave, my lord! ———But if what I have to disclose should be received with anger or displeasure———

Lord Og. Impossible, by all the tender powers!— Speak, I beseech you, or I shall divine the cause before you utter it.

Fanny. Then, my lord, Sir John's addresses are not only shocking to me in themselves, but are more particularly disagreeable to me at this time—as—as—
[*Hesitating.*

Lord Og. As what, madam?

Fanny. As—pardon my confusion—I am entirely devoted **to another.**

Lord Og. If this is not plain, the devil's in it——
[*Aside.*] But tell me, my dear Miss Fanny, for I
must know; tell me the how, the when, and the
where——Tell me——

Enter CANTON *hastily.*

Can. My lor, my lor, my lor!

Lord Og. Damn your Swiss impertinence! how
durst you interrupt me in the most critical melting
moment that ever love and beauty honoured me with?

Can. I demande pardonne, my lor! Sir John Melvil, my lor, sent me to beg you do him de honeur to
speak a little to your lordship.

Lord Og. I'm not at leisure—I am busy—Get away,
you stupid old dog, you Swiss rascal, or I'll——

Can. Fort bien, my lor.   [*Canton goes out on tiptoe.*

Lord Og. By the laws of gallantry, madam, this
interruption should be death; but as no punishment
ought to disturb the triumph of the softer passions,
the criminal is pardoned and dismissed. Let us return, madam, to the highest luxury of exalted minds
—a declaration of love from the lips of beauty.

Fanny. The enterance of a third person has a little
relieved me, but I cannot go through with it; and
yet I must open my heart with a discovery, or it will
break with its burthen.

Lord Og. What passion in her eyes! I am alarmed
to agitation. [*Aside.*] I presume, madam, (and as you
have flattered me, by making me a party concerned,
I hope you'll excuse the presumption) that——

Fanny. Do you excuse my making you a party concerned, my lord, and let me interest your heart in my behalf, as my future happiness or misery in a great measure depend———

Lord Og. Upon me, madam?

Fanny. Upon you, my lord. [*Sighs.*

Lord Og. There's no standing this: I have caught the infection—her tenderness dissolves me. [*Sighs.*

Fanny. And should you too severely judge of a rash action which passion prompted, and modesty has long concealed———

Lord Og. [*Taking her hand.*] Thou amiable creature, command my heart for it is vanquished. Speak but thy virtuous wishes, and enjoy them.

Fanny. I cannot, my lord; indeed, I cannot. Mr. Lovewell must tell you my distresses; and when you know them, pity and protect me. [*Exit in tears.*

Lord Og. How the devil could I bring her to this? It is too much—too much—I cann't bear it—I must give way to this amiable weakness. [*Wipes his eyes.*] My heart overflows with sympathy, and I feel every tenderness I have inspired. [*Stifles a tear.*] How blind have I been to the desolation I have made! How could I possibly imagine that a little partial attention and tender civilities to this young creature should have gathered to this burst of passion! Can I be a man and withstand it? No—I'll sacrifice the whole sex to her. But here comes the father, quite apropos. I'll open the matter immediately, settle the business with him, and take the sweet girl down to Ogleby House to-morrow morning. But what the devil! Miss Sterling too! What mischief's in the wind now?

Enter **Mr.** STERLING, *and Miss* STERLING.

Sterl. My lord, your servant! I am attending my daughter here upon rather a disagreeable affair. Speak to his lordship, Betsey.

Lord Og. Your eyes, Miss Sterling; for I always read the eyes of a young lady, betray some little **emotion.** What are your commands, madam?

Miss Sterl. I have but too much cause for my emotion, my lord!

Lord Og. I cannot commend my kinsman's behaviour, madam. He has behaved like a false knight, I must confess. I have heard of his apostacy. Miss Fanny has informed me of it.

Miss Sterl. Miss Fanny's baseness has been **the** cause of Sir John's inconstancy.

Lord Og. Nay, now, my dear Miss Sterling, your passion transports you too far. Sir John may have entertained a passion for Miss Fanny, but believe me, my dear Miss Sterling, believe me, Miss Fanny has no passion for Sir John. She has a passion, indeed, a most tender passion. She has opened her whole soul to me, and I know where her affections are placed.   [*Conceitedly.*

Miss Sterl. Not upon Mr. Lovewell, my lord; for I have great reason to think that her seeming at-

tachment to him, is by his consent, made use of as
a **blind** to cover her designs upon Sir John.

Lord Og. Lovewell! **No,** poor **lad!** She does not
think **of** him.   [*Smiling.*

Miss Sterl. Have **a** care, my lord, that both the
families are not made the dupes of Sir John's artifice
and my sister's dissimulation! You don't know her;
indeed, my lord, you don't know her; a base, insinu-
ating, perfidious!—It is too much—She has been
beforehand with me, I perceive. Such unnatural behaviour to me! But since I see I can have no redress,
I am resolved that some way or other I will have revenge.   [*Exit.*

Sterl. This is foolish work, my lord!

, *Lord Og.* I have too much sensibility to bear the
tears of beauty.

Sterl. It is touching, indeed, my lord; and very
moving for a father.

Lord Og. To be sure, sir! You must be distressed
beyond measure! Wherefore, to divert your too exquisite feeling, suppose we change the subject, and
proceed to business.

Sterl. With all my heart, my lord!

Lord Og. You see, Mr. Sterling, we can make no
union in our families by the proposed marriage.

Sterl. And I am very sorry to see it, my lord.

Lord Og. Have **you set** your heart upon being allied **to our** house, **Mr. Sterling**?

Sterl. 'Tis my only **wish** at present, my omnium,
as I may call it.

Lord Og. Your wishes shall be fulfilled.

Sterl. Shall they, my lord! but how—how?

Lord Og. I'll marry in your family.

Sterl. What! my sister Heidelberg?

Lord Og. You throw me into a cold sweat, Mr. Sterling. No, not your sister; but your daughter.

Sterl. My daughter!

Lord Og. Fanny! now the murder's out!

Sterl. What you my lord!

Lord Og. Yes; I, I, Mr. Sterling!

Sterl. No, no, my lord; that's too much. [*Smiling.*

Lord Og. Too much! I don't comprehend you.

Sterl. What, you, my lord, marry my Fanny! Bless me, what will the folks say?

Lord Og. Why, what will they say?

Sterl. That you're a bold man, my lord; that's all.

Lord Og. Mr. Sterling, this may be city wit for aught I know. Do you court my alliance?

Sterl. To be sure, my lord.

Lord Og. Then I'll explain—My nephew won't marry your eldest daughter; nor I neither.——Your youngest daughter won't marry him; I will marry your youngest daughter.

Sterl. What! with a youngest daughter's fortune, my lord?

Lord Og. With any fortune, or no fortune at all, sir. Love is the idol of my heart, and the dæmon interest sinks before him. So, sir, as I said before, I will marry your youngest daughter; your youngest daughter will marry me.

Sterl. Who told you so, my lord?

Lord Og. Her own sweet self, sir.

Sterl. Indeed?

Lord Og. Yes, sir; our affection is mutual; your advantage double and treble; your daughter will be a countess directly—I shall be the happiest of beings; and you'll be father to an earl instead of a baronet.

Sterl. But what will my sister say? and my daughter?

Lord Og. I'll manage that matter; nay, if they won't consent, I'll run away with your daughter in spite of you.

Sterl. Well said, my lord! your spirit's good; I wish you had my constitution; but if you'll venture, I have no objection, if my sister has none.

Lord Og. I'll answer for your sister, sir. Apropos! the lawyers are in the house. I'll have articles drawn, and the whole affair concluded to-morrow morning.

Sterl. Very well! and I'll dispatch Lovewell to London immediately for some fresh papers I shall want, and I shall leave you to manage matters with my sister. You must excuse me, my lord, but I cann't help laughing at the match.—He, he, he! what will the folks say?   [*Exit.*

Lord Og. What a fellow am I going to make a father of? He has no more feeling than the post in his warehouse—But Fanny's virtues tune me to rapture again, and I won't think of the rest of the family.

Enter LOVEWELL, *hastily.*

Lov I beg your lordship's pardon, my lord; are you alone, my lord?

Lord Og. No, my lord, I am not alone; I am in company, the best company.

Lov. My lord!

Lord Og. I never was in such exquisite enchanting company since my heart first conceived, or my senses tasted pleasure.

Lov. Where are they, my lord?   [*Looking about.*

Lord Og. In my mind, sir.

Lov. What company have you there, my lord?

[*Smiling.*

Lord Og. My own ideas, sir, which so crowd upon my imagination, and kindle in it such a delirium of ecstacy, that wit, wine, music, poetry, all combined, and each perfection, are but mere mortal shadows of my felicity.

Lov. I see that your lordship is happy, and I rejoice at it.

Lord Og. You shall rejoice at it, sir; my felicity shall not selfishly be confined, but shall spread its influence to the whole circle of my friends. I need not say, Lovewell, that you shall have your share of it.

Lov. Shall I, my lord?—then I understand you; you have heard; Miss Fanny has informed you——

Lord Og. She has; I have heard, and she shall happy; 'tis determin'd.

I

Lov. Then I have reached the summit of **my** wishes. And will your lordship pardon the folly?

Lord Og. O yes, poor creature, how could she help it? 'Twas unavoidable—Fate and necessity.

Lov. It was indeed, my lord. Your kindness distracts me.

Lord Og. And so it did the poor girl, faith.

Lov. She trembled to disclose the secret, and declare her affections?

Lord Og. The world, I believe, will not think her affections ill placed.

Lov. [*Bowing.*] **You** are too good, my lord.—— And do you really excuse the rashness of the action?

Lord Og. From my very soul, Lovewell.

Lov. Your generosity overpowers me. [*Bowing.*] I was afraid of her meeting with a cold reception.

Lord Og. More fool you then.

Who pleads her cause with never-failing beauty,
Here finds a full redress.   [*Strikes his breast.*
She's a fine girl, Lovewell.

Lov. Her beauty, my lord, is her least merit. She has an understanding——

Lord Og. Her choice convinces me of that.

Lov. [*Bowing.*] That's your lordship's goodness. Her choice was a disinterested one.

Lord Og. No, no; not altogether; it began with interest, and ended in passion.

Lov. Indeed, my lord, if you were acquainted with her goodness of heart, and generosity of mind, as well as you are with the inferior beauties of her face and person————

Lord Og. I am so perfectly convinced of their existence, and so totally of your mind, touching every amiable particular of that sweet girl, that were it not for the cold unfeeling impediments of the law, I would marry her to-morrow morning.

Lov. My lord!

Lord Og. I would, by all that's honourable in man, and amiable in woman.

Lov. Marry her!——What do you mean, my lord?

Lord Og. Miss Fanny Sterling that is; the Countess of Ogleby that shall be.

Lov. I am astonished!

Lord Og. Why, could you expect less from me?

Lov. I did not expect this, my lord.

Lord Og. Trade and accounts have destroyed your feeling.

Lov. No, indeed, my lord. [*Sighs.*

Lord Og. The moment that love and pity entered my breast, I was resolved to plunge into matrimony, and shorten the girl's tortures—I never do any thing by halves; do I, Lovewell?

Lov. No, indeed, my lord. [*Sighs.*] What an accident!

Lord Og. What's the matter, Lovewell? thou seem'st to have lost thy faculties. Why don't you wish me joy, man?

Lov. O, I do, my lord. [*Sighs.*

Lord Og. She said that you would explain what she

had not power to utter; but I wanted no interpreter for the language of love.

Lov. But has your lordship considered the consequences of your resolution?

Lord Og. No, sir, I am above consideration, when my desires are kindled.

Lov. But consider the consequences, my lord, to your nephew, Sir John.

Lord Og. Sir John has considered no consequences himself, Mr. Lovewell.

Lov. Mr. Sterling, my lord, will certainly refuse his daughter to Sir John.

Lord Og. Sir John has already refused Mr. Sterling's daughter.

Lov. But what will become of Miss Sterling, my lord?

Lord Og. What's that to you?——You may have her if you will. I depend upon Mr. Sterling's city-philosophy, to be reconciled to Lord Ogleby's being his son-in law, instead of Sir John Melvil, baronet. Don't you think that your master may be brought that, without having recourse to his calculations! Eh, Lovewell!

Lov. But, my lord, that is not the question.

Lord Og. Whatever is the question, I'll tell you my answer.——I am in love with a fine girl, whom I resolve to marry.

Enter *Sir* JOHN MELVIL.

What news with you, Sir John?—You look all hurry and impatience—like a messenger after a battle.

Sir John. After a battle, indeed, my lord. I have this day had a severe engagement, and wanting your lordship as an auxiliary, I have at last mustered up resolution to declare what my duty to you and to myself have demanded from me some time.

Lord Og. To the business then, and be as concise as possible, for I am upon the wing—eh, Lovewell ? .

      [*He smiles, and* Lovewell *bows.*

Sir John. I find 'tis in vain, my lord, to struggle against the force of inclination.

Lord Og. Very true, nephew ; I am your witness, and will second the motion——sha'n't I, Lovewell ?

      [*Smiles, and* Lovewell *bows.*

Sir John. Your lordship's generosity encourages me to tell you, that I cannot marry Miss Sterling.

Lord Og. I am not at all surprised at it—she's a bitter potion, that's the truth of it; but as you were to swallow it, and not I, it was your business, and not mine——Any thing more ?

Sir John. But this, my lord; that I may be permitted to make my addresses to the other sister.

Lord Og. O yes; by all means——have you any hopes there, nephew ?—Do you think he'll succeed, Lovewell ?   [*Smiles, and winks at* Lovewell.

Lov. I think not, my lord.   [*Gravely.*

Lord Og. I think so too; but let the fool try.

Sir John. Will your lordship favour me with your good offices to remove the chief obstacle to the match, the repugnance of Mrs. Heidelberg ?

Lord Og. Mrs. Heidelberg ?—Had not you better

begin with the young lady first? It will save you a great deal of trouble: won't it, Lovewell? [*Smiles.*] But do what you please, it will be the same thing to me: won't it, Lovewell? [*Conceitedly.*] Why don't you laugh at him?

Lov. I do, my lord.   [*Forces a smile.*

Sir John. And your lordship will endeavour to prevail on Mrs. Heidelberg to consent to my marriage with Miss Fanny?

Lord Og. I'll speak to Mrs. Heidelberg about the adorable Fanny as soon as possible.

Sir John. Your generosity transports me.

Lord Og. Poor fellow, what a dupe! he little thinks who's in possession of the town.   [*Aside.*

Sir John. And your lordship is not in the least offended at this seeming inconstancy?

Lord Og. Not in the least. Miss Fanny's charms will even excuse infidelity. I look upon women as the *seræ naturæ*—lawful game—and every man who is qualified, has a natural right to pursue them;—Lovewell as well as you, and I as well as either of you.—Every man shall do his best, without offence to any —what say you, kinsmen?

Sir John. You have made me happy, my lord.

Lov. And me, I assure you, my lord.

Lord Og. And I am superlatively so—*allons donc!* to horse and away, boys!—you to your affairs, and to mine——*suivons l'amour.*   [*Sings.*

[*Exeunt severally.*

ACT V. SCENE I.

FANNY's *Apartment.* *Enter* LOVEWELL *and* FANNY,
followed by BETTY.

Fanny.

WHY did you come so soon Mr. Lovewell? the family is not yet in bed, and Betty certainly heard
somebody listening near the chamber-door.

Betty. My mistress is right, Sir! evil spirits are
abroad; and I am **sure** you are both too good, not to
expeƈt mischief from them.

Lov. But who can be so curious, or so wicked?

Betty. I think we have wickedness and curiosity
enough in this family, sir, to expeƈt the worst.

Fanny. I do expeƈt the worst.——Pr'ythee, Betty,
return to the outward door, and listen if you hear any
body in the gallery; and let us know direƈtly.

Betty. I warrant you, madam—the lord bless you
both!   [*Exit.*

Fanny. What did my father want with you this
evening?

Lov He gave me the key of his closet, with orders
to bring from London some papers relating to Lord
Ogleby.

Fanny. And why did you not obey him?

Lov. Because I am certain that his lordship has
opened his heart to him about you, and those papers
are wanted merely on that account——but as we shall

discover all to-morrow, there will be no occasion for them, and it would be idle in me to go.

Fanny. Hark!—hark! bless me, how I tremble!——I feel the terrors of guilt——indeed, Mr. Lovewell, this is too much for me.

Lov. And for me too, my sweet Fanny. Your apprehensions make a coward of me.——But what can alarm you? your aunt and sister are in their chambers, and you have nothing to fear from the rest of the family.

Fanny. I fear every body, and every thing, and every moment——My mind is in continual agitation and dread; indeed, Mr. Lovewell, this situation may have very unhappy consequences.   [*Weeps.*

Lov. But it sha'n't——I would rather tell our story this moment to all the house, and run the risque of maintaining you by the hardest labour, than suffer you to remain in this dangerous perplexity.—What! shall I sacrifice all my best hopes and affections, in your dear health and safety, for the mean, and in such case, the meanest consideration—of our fortune!—Were we to be abandoned by all our relations, we have that in our hearts and minds will weigh against the most affluent circumstances. I should not have proposed the secrecy of our marriage, but for your sake; and with hopes that the most generous sacrifice you have made to love and me, might be less injurious to you, by waiting a lucky moment of reconciliation.

Fanny. Hush! hush! for Heaven's sake, my dear

Lovewell, don't be so warm! your generosity gets
the better of your prudence; you will be heard, and
we shall be discovered.——I am satisfied—indeed I
am———Excuse this weakness, this delicacy, this
what you will.——My mind's at peace—indeed it is
—think no more of it, if you love me!

Lov. That one word has charmed me, as it always
does, to the most implicit obedience: it would be the
worst of ingratitude in me to distress you a moment.

[*Kisses* **her.**

Re-enter BETTY.

Betty. [*In a low voice.*] I'm sorry to disturb you.

Fanny. Ha! what's the matter?

Lov. Have you heard any body?

Betty. Yes, yes, I have; and they have heard you
too, or I'm mistaken—if they had seen you too, we
should have been in a fine quandary!

Fanny. Pr'ythee, don't prate now, Betty!

Lov. What did you hear?

Betty. I was preparing myself, as usual, to take me
a little nap——

Lov. A nap!

Betty. Yes, sir, a nap; for I watch much better
so than wide awake; and when I had wrapped this
handkerchief round my head, for fear of the ear-ach
from the key-hole, I thought I heard a kind of a sort
of a buzzing, which I first took for a gnat, and shook
my head two or three times, and went so with my
hand.

Fanny. Well—well—and so———

Betty. And so, madam, when I heard Mr. Lovewell a little loud, I heard the buzzing louder too——and pulling off my handkerchief softly, I could hear this sort of noise———

[*Makes an indistinct sort of noise like speaking.*

Fanny. Well, and what did they say?

Betty. O! I could not understand a word of what was said.

Lov. The outward door is lock'd?

Betty. **Yes;** and I bolted it too, for fear of the worst.

Fanny. Why did you? they must have heard you, if they were near.

Betty. And I did it on purpose, madam, and cough'd a little too, that they might not hear Mr. Lovewell's voice—when I was silent, they were silent, and so I came to tell you.

Fanny. What shall we do?

Lov. Fear nothing; we know the worst; it will only bring on our catastrophe a little too soon—but Betty might fancy this noise—she's in the conspiracy, and can make a man a mouse at any time.

Betty. I can distinguish a man from a mouse as well as my betters——I'm sorry you think so ill of me, sir.

Fanny. He compliments you, don't be a fool!——Now you have set her tongue a running, she'll mutter for an hour. [*To Lovewell.*] I'll go and hearken myself.   [*Exit.*

Betty. I'll turn my back upon no girl for sincerity and service. [*Half aside and muttering.*

Lov. Thou art the first in the world for both; and I will reward you soon, Betty, for one and the other.

Betty. I am not mercenary neither—I can live on a little, with a good carreter.

Re-enter FANNY.

Fanny. All seems quiet—suppose, my dear, you go to your own room—I shall be much easier then—and to-morrow we will be prepared for the discovery.

Betty. You may discover, if you please ; but for my part, I shall still be secret.

[*Half aside and muttering.*

Lov. Should I leave you now, if they still are upon the watch, we shall lose the advantage of our delay. Besides, we should consult upon to-morrow's business. Let Betty go to her own room, and lock the outward door after her; we can fasten this; and when she thinks all safe, she may return and let me out as usual.

Betty. Shall I, madam ?

Fanny. Do! let me have my way to-night, and you shall command me ever after. I would not have you surprised here for the world. Pray leave me ! I shall be quite myself again, if you will oblige me.

Lov. I live only to oblige you, my sweet Fanny I I'll be gone this moment. [*Going.*

Fanny. Let us listen first at the door, that you may

not be intercepted. Betty shall go first, and if they
lay hold of her——

Betty. They'll have the wrong sow by the ear, I
can tell them that.   [*Going hastily.*

Fanny. Softly—softly—Betty! don't venture out,
if you hear a noise. Softly, I beg of you! See, Mr.
Lovewell, the effects of indiscretion!

Lov. But love, Fanny, makes amends for all.
                              [*Exeunt all softly.*

SCENE II.

*Changes to a Gallery, which leads to several Bed-cham-
    bers. Enter Miss* STERLING, *leading Mrs.* HEIDEL-
    BERG *in a Night-cap.*

Miss Sterl. This way, dear madam, and then I'll
tell you all.

Mrs. Heidel. Nay, but niece—consid era little——
don't drag me out this figure; let me put on my fly-
cap!—if any of my lord's fammaly, or the counsellors
at law, should be stirring, I should be perdigus disconcerted.

Miss Sterl. But, my dear madam, a moment is an
age, in my situation. I am sure my sister has been
plotting my disgrace and ruin in that chamber——O!
she's all craft and wickedness.

Mrs. Heidel. Well, but softly, Betsey!—you are all
in emotion—your mind is too much flustrated—you
can neither eat, nor drink, nor take your natural rest——

compose yourself, child; for if we are not as warysome as they are wicked, we shall disgrace ourselves and the whole fammaly.

Miss Sterl. We are disgraced already, madam.   Sir John Melvil has forsaken me; my lord cares for nobody but himself; or if any body, it is my sister; my father, for the sake of a better bargain, would marry me to a 'Change broker; so that if you, madam, don't continue my friend—if you forsake me—if I am to lose my best hopes and consolation—in your tenderness—and affections—I had better—at once—give up the matter—and let my sister enjoy—the fruits of her treachery—trample with scorn upon the rights of her elder sister, the will of the best of aunts, and the weakness of a too interested father.

[*She pretends to be bursting into tears all this speech.*

Mrs. Heidel. Don't, Betsey—keep up your spurrit —I hate whimpering—I am your friend—depend upon me in every particular—but be composed, and tell me what new mischief you have discovered?

Miss Sterl. I had no desire to sleep, and would not undress myself, knowing that my Machiavel sister would not rest till she had broke my heart:—I was so uneasy that I could not stay in my room, but when I thought that all the house was quiet, I sent my maid to discover what was going forward; she immediately came back and told me that they were in high consultation; that she had heard only, for it was in the dark, my sister's maid conduct Sir John Melvil to her mistress, and then lock the door.

K

Mrs. Heidel. And how did you conduct yourself in this dalimma?

Miss Sterl. I returned with her, and could hear a man's voice, though nothing that they said distinctly; and you may depend upon it, that Sir John is now in that room, that they have settled the matter, and will run away together before morning, if we don't prevent them.

Mrs. Heidel. Why, the brazen slut! she has got her sister's husband (that is to be) lock'd up in her chamber! at night too!—I tremble at the thoughts!

Miss Sterl. Hush, madam! I hear something.

Mrs. Heidel. You frighten me—let me put on my fly-cap—— I would not be seen in this figur for the world.

Miss Sterl. 'Tis dark, madam; you cann't be seen.

Mrs. Heidel. I protest there's a candle coming, and a man too!

Miss Sterl. Nothing but servants; let us retire a moment!　　　　　　　　　　　　　　　[*They retire.*

Enter BRUSH, *half drunk, laying hold of the* Chambermaid, *who has a Candle in her Hand.*

Cham. Be quiet, Mr. Brush; I shall drop down with terror!

Brush. But my sweet, and most amiable chambermaid, if you have no love, you may hearken to a little reason! that cannot possibly do your virtue any harm.

Cham. But you may do me harm, Mr. Brush, and

a great deal of harm too; pray let me go; I am ruined if they hear you; I tremble like an asp.

Brush. But they sha'n't hear us; and if you have a mind to be ruined, it shall be the making of your fortune, you little slut, you! therefore I say it again, if you have no love, hear a little reason!

Cham. I wonder at your impurence, Mr. Brush, to use me in this manner; this is not the way to keep me company, I assure you. You are a town-rake, I see, and now you are a little in liquor, you fear nothing.

Brush. Nothing, by Heavens, but your frowns, most amiable chamber-maid; I am a little electrified, that's the truth on't; I am not used to drink Port, and your master's is so heady, that a pint of it oversets a claret-drinker.

Cham. Don't be rude! bless me!—I shall be ruined —what will become of me?

Brush. I'll take care of you, by all that's honourable.

Cham. You are a base man to use me so—I'll cry out, if you don't let me go. That is Miss Sterling's chamber, that Miss Fanny's, and that Madam Heidelberg's.

Brush. And that my Lord Ogleby's, and that my Lady What-d'ye-call-'em: I don't mind such folks when I'm sober, much less when I am whimsical— rather above that too.

Cham. More shame for you, Mr. Brush!—you terrify me—you have no modesty.

Brush. O, but I have, my sweet spider-brusher!—for instance; I reverence Miss Fanny—she's a most delicious morsel, and fit for a prince.——With all my horrors of matrimony, I could marry her myself—but for her sister——

Miss Sterl. There, there, madam, all in a story!

Cham. Bless me, Mr. Brush!—I heard something!

Brush. Rats, I suppose, that are gnawing the old timbers of this execrable old dungeon—If it was mine, I would pull it down, and fill your fine canal up with the rubbish; and then I should get rid of two damn'd things at once.

Cham. Law! law! how you blaspheme!—we shall have the house upon our heads for it.

Brush. No, no, it will last our time—but as I was saying, the eldest sister ———Miss Jezebel———

Cham. Is a fine young lady, for all your evil tongue.

Brush. No——we have smoaked her already; and unless she marries our old Swiss, she can have none of us——no, no, she won't do—we are a little too nice.

Cham. You're a monstrous rake, Mr. Brush, and don't care what you say.

Brush. Why, for that matter, my dear, I am a little inclined to mischief; and if you don't have pity upon me, I will break open that door, and ravish Mrs. Heidelberg.

Mrs. Heidel. [*Coming forward.*] There's no bearing this—you profligate monster!

Cham. Ha! I am undone!

Brush. Zounds! here she is, by all that's monstrous.   [*Runs off.*

Miss Sterl. A fine discourse you have had with that
fellow!

Mrs. Heidel. And a fine time of night it is to be
here with that drunken monster!

Miss Sterl. What have you to say for yourself?

Cham. I can say nothing.—I'm so frightened, and
so ashamed—but indeed I am vartuous—I am vartuous, indeed.

Mrs. Heidel. Well, well—don't tremble so; but,
tell us what you know of this horrable plot here.

Miss Sterl. We'll forgive you, if you'll discover all.

Cham. Why, madam—don't let me betray my fellow servants—I sha'n't sleep in my bed, if I do.

Mrs. Heidel. Then you shall sleep somewhere else
to-morrow night.

Cham. O dear! what shall I do!

Mrs. Heidel. Tell us this moment, or I'll turn you
out of doors directly.

Cham. Why, our butler has been treating us below
in his pantry—Mr. Brush forced us to make a kind
of a holiday night **of it.**

Miss Sterl. Holiday! for what?

Cham. Nay, I only made one.

Miss Sterl. Well, well; but upon what account?

Cham. Because, as how, madam, there was a change
in the family, they said——that his honour, Sir John,
was to marry Miss Fanny instead of your ladyship.

Miss Sterl. And so you make a holiday for that—Very fine!

Cham. I did not make it, ma'am.

Mrs. Heidel. But do you know nothing of Sir John's being to run away with Miss Fanny to night?

Cham. No, indeed, ma'am!

Miss Sterl. Nor of his being now locked up in my sister's chamber?

Cham. No, as I hope for marcy, ma'am.

Mrs. Heidel. Well, I'll put an end to all this directly——do you run to my brother Sterling——

Cham. Now, ma'am!——'Tis so very late, ma'am—

Mrs. Heidel. I don't care how late it is. Tell him there are thieves in the house—that the house is on fire—tell him to come here immediately—go, I say.

Cham. I will, I will, though I'm frighten'd out of my wits.   [*Exit.*

Mrs. Heidel. Do you watch here, my dear; and I'll put myself in order, to face them. We'll plot 'em, and counter-plot 'em too.   [*Exit into her chamber.*

Miss Sterl. I have as much pleasure in this revenge, as in being made a countess.——Ha! they are unlocking the door.——Now for it!   [*Retires.*

FANNY's *Door is unlock'd, and* BETTY *comes out with a Candle. Miss* STERLING *approaches her.*

Betty. [*Calling within.*] Sir! sir!—now's your time—all's clear. [*Seeing Miss* Sterl.] Stay, stay—not yet—we are watch'd.

Miss Sterl. And so you are, Madam Betty. [*Miss
    Sterl. lays hold of her, while* Betty *locks the
    door, and puts the key into her pocket.*]

Betty. [*Turning round.*] What's the matter, madam?

Miss Sterl. Nay, that you shall tell my father and
aunt, madam.

Betty. I am no tell-tale, madam, and no thief;
they'll get nothing from me.

Miss Sterl. You have a great deal of courage, Betty;
and considering the secrets you have to keep, you
have occasion for it.

Betty. My mistress shall never repent her good
opinion of me, ma'am.

Enter Mr. STERLING.

Sterl. What's all this? What's the matter? Why
am I disturb'd in this manner?

Miss Sterl. This creature, and my distresses, sir, will
explain the matter.

Re-enter Mrs. HEIDELBERG, *with another Head-dress.*

Mrs. Heidel. Now I'm prepar'd for the rancounter.
——Well, brother, have you heard of this scene of
wickedness?

Sterl. Not I—but what is it? speak.——I was got
into **my** little closet, all the lawyers were in bed, and
I had almost lost my senses in the confusion of Lord
Ogleby's mortgages, when I was alarmed with a foolish girl, who could hardly speak; and whether it's
fire, or thieves, or murder, or a rape, I'm quite in the
dark.

Mrs. Heidel. No, no, there's no rape, brother!—
all parties are willing, I believe.

Miss Sterl. Who's in that chamber?

[*Detaining* Betty, *who seemed to be stealing away.*

Betty. My mistress.

Miss Sterl. And who's with your mistress?

Betty. Why, who should there be?

Miss Sterl. Open the door then, and let us see.

Betty. The door is open, madam, [*Miss* Sterl. *goes to the door.*] I'll sooner die than peach. [*Exit hastily.*

Miss Sterl. The door is lock'd; and she has got the key in her pocket.

Mrs. Heidel. There's impudence, brother! piping hot from your daughter Fanny's school!

Sterl. But, zounds! what is all this about? You tell me of a sum total, and you don't produce the particulars.

Mrs. Heidel. Sir John Melvil is locked up in your daughter's bed-chamber——There is the particular.

Sterl. The devil he is!——That's bad.

Miss Sterl. And he has been there some time too.

Sterl. Ditto!

Mrs. Heidel. Ditto! worse and worse, I say. I'll raise the house, and expose him to my lord, and the whole fammaly.

Sterl. By no means! we shall expose ourselves, sister!—the best way is to insure privately—let me alone! I'll make him marry her to-morrow morning.

Miss Sterl. Make him marry her! this is beyond all patience!—You have thrown away all your affection; and I shall do as much by my obedience; unnatural fathers make unnatural children. My revenge is in my own power, and I'll indulge it.——Had they made their escape, I should have been exposed to the derision of the world: but the deriders shall be derided; and so——help! help, there! thieves! thieves!

Mrs. Heidel. Tit-for-tat, Betsey! you are right, my girl.

Sterl. Zounds! you'll spoil all—you'll raise the whole family——the devil's in the girl.

Mrs. Heidel. No, no; the devil's in you, brother; I am ashamed of your principles.——What! would you connive at your daughter's being locked up with her sister's husband? Help! thieves! thieves, I say.

[*Cries out.*

Sterl. Sister, I beg you!——daughter, I command you!—If you have no regard for me, consider yourselves!——we shall lose this opportunity of ennobling our blood, and getting above twenty *per cent.* for our money.

Miss Sterl. What, by my disgrace and my sister's triumph! I have a spirit above such mean considerations; and to shew you that it is not a low-bred, vulgar 'Change-alley spirit——help! help! thieves! thieves! thieves! I say!

Sterl. Ay, ay, you may save your lungs—the house is in an uproar; women at best have no discretion; but in a passion they'll fire a house, or burn themselves in it, rather than not be revenged.

Enter CANTON, *in a Night-gown and Slippers,*

Can. Eh, diable! vat is de raison of dis great noise, dis tantamarre?

Sterl. Ask those ladies, sir; 'tis of their making.

Lord Og. [*Calls within.*] Brush! Brush!—Canton! where are you?—What's the matter? [*Rings a bell.*] Where are you?

Sterl. 'Tis my lord calls, Mr. Canton.

Can. I com, mi lor!————   [*Exit* Canton.

    [*Lord* Ogleby *still rings.*

Serj. Flow. [*Calls within.*] A light! a light here!— where are the servants? Bring a light for me and my brothers.

Sterl. Lights here! lights for the gentlemen!

    [*Exit* Sterling.

Mrs. Heidel. My brother feels, I see—your sister's turn will come next.

Miss Sterl. Ay, ay, let it go round, madam, it is the only comfort I have left.

Re-enter STERLING, *with lights, before Serjeant* FLOWER, *with one boot and a slipper, and* TRAVERSE.

Sterl. This way, sir! this way, gentlemen!

Flow. Well; but Mr. Sterling, no danger I hope. Have they made a burglarious entry? Are you prepared to repulse them? I am very much alarmed about thieves at circuit-time. They would be particularly severe with us gentlemen of the bar.

Trav. No danger, **Mr.** Sterling,—no trespass, **I** hope ?

Sterl. None, gentlemen, but of those ladies making.

Mrs. Heidel. You'll be ashamed to know, gentlemen, that all your labours and studies about this young lady are thrown away—Sir John Melvil is at this moment locked up with this lady's younger sister.

Flow. The thing is a little extraordinary, to be sure ; but, why were we to be frighten'd out of our beds for this ? Could not we have tried this cause to-morrow morning ?

Miss Sterl. But, sir, by to-morrow morning, perhaps, even your assistance would not have been of any service—the birds now in that cage would have flown away.

Enter Lord OGLEBY, *in his robe-de-chambre, night-cap, &c. leaning on* CANTON.

Lord Og. I had rather lose a limb than my night's rest.   What's the matter with you all ?

Sterl. Ay, ay, 'tis all over !—Here's my lord too.

Lord Og. What's all this shrieking and screaming ? Where's my angelic Fanny ? She's safe, I hope ?

Mrs. Heidel. Your angelic Fanny, my lord, is lock'd up with your angelic nephew in that chamber.

Lord Og. My nephew ! then will I be excommunicated.

Mrs. Heidel. Your nephew, my lord, has been plotting to run away with the younger sister ; and the younger sister has been plotting to run away with your nephew : and if we had not watched them and call'd up the fammaly, they had been upon the scamper to Scotland by this time.

Lord Og. Look'e, ladies! I know that Sir John has conceived a violent passion for Miss Fanny; and I know too that Miss Fanny has conceived a violent passion for another person; and I am so well convinced of the rectitude of her affections, that I will support them with my fortune, my honour, and my life.——Eh, shan't I, Mr. Sterling? [*Smiling.*] what say you?

Sterl. [*Sulkily.*] **To be** sure, my lord.——These bawling women have been the ruin of every thing.

[*Aside.*

Lord. Og. But come, I'll end this business in a trice—if you, ladies, will compose yourselves, and Mr. Sterling will ensure Miss Fanny from violence, I will engage to draw her from her pillow with a whisper through the key-hole.

Mrs. Heidel. The horrid creatures!—I say, my lord, break the door open.

Lord Og. Let me beg of your delicacy not to be too precipitate! Now to our experiment!

[*Advancing towards the door.*

Miss Sterl. Now, what will they do?—my heart will beat through my bosom.

Enter BETTY *with the key.*

Betty. There's no occasion for breaking open doors, my lord; we have done nothing that we ought to be ashamed of, and my mistress shall face her enemies.

[*Going to unlock the door.*

Mrs. Heidel. There's impudence.

Lord Og. The mystery thickens. Lady of the bed-chamber, [*To* Betty.] open the door, and intreat Sir John Melvil (for the ladies will have it that he is there) to appear and answer to high crimes and mis-demeanors.—Call Sir John Melvil into the court!

Enter Sir JOHN MELVIL, *on the other side.*

Sir John. I am here, my lord.

Mrs. Heidel. Hey-day!

Miss Sterl. Astonishment!

Sir John. What's all this alarm and confusion? there is nothing but hurry in the house; what is the reason of it?

Lord Og. Because you have been in that chamber; have been! nay, you are there at this moment, as these ladies have protested, so don't deny it——— ;

Trav. This is the clearest alibi I ever knew, Mr. Serjeant.

— Flow. *Luce clarius.*

Lord Og. Upon my word, ladies, if you have often these frolicks, it would be really entertaining to pass a whole summer with you. But come [*To* Betty.] open the door, and intreat your amiable mistress to come forth, and dispel all our doubts with her smiles.

Betty. [*Opening the door.*] Madam, you are wanted in this room.   [*Pertly.*

Enter FANNY, *in great confusion.*

Miss Sterl. You see she's ready dressed—and what confusion she's in!

Mrs. Heidel. Ready to pack off, bag and baggage! her guilt confounds her!

Flow. Silence in the court, ladies!

Fanny. I am confounded, indeed, madam!

Lord Og. Don't droop, my beauteous lily! but with your own peculiar modesty declare your state of mind.—Pour conviction into their ears and raptures into mine.   [*Smiling.*

Fanny. I am at this moment the most unhappy—most distressed—the tumult is too much for my heart —and I want the power to reveal a secret, which to conceal has been the misfortune and misery of my—
                                    [*Faints away.*

Lord Og. She faints; help, help! for the fairest and best of women!

Betty. [*Running to her.*] O, my dear mistress!—help, help, there!——

Sir John. Ha! let me fly to her assistance.

LOVEWELL *rushes out of the Chamber.*

Lov. My Fanny in danger! I can contain no longer. —Prudence were now a crime; all other cares were lost in this!—speak, speak, speak to me, my dearest Fanny!—let me but hear thy voice, open your eyes, and bless me with the smallest sign of life!
                [*During this speech they are all in amazement.*

Miss Sterl. Lovewell!——I am easy.——

Mrs. Heidel. I am thunderstruck!

Lord Og. I am petrified!

Sir John. And I undone!

Fanny. [*Recovering.*] O, Lovewell!—even supported by thee, I dare not look my father nor his lordship in the face.

Sterl. What now! did not I send you to London, sir?

Lord Og. Eh!—What! How's this! by what right and title have you been half the night in that lady's bed chamber?

Lov. By that right which makes me the happiest of men; and by a title which I would not forgo, for any the best of kings could give.

Betty. I could cry my eyes out to hear his magnimity.

Lord Og. I am annihilated!

Sterl. I have been choked with rage and wonder; but now I can speak.—Zounds, what have you to say to me? Lovewell, you are a villain.——You have broke your word with me.

Fanny. Indeed, sir, he has not—you forbad him to think of me when it was out of his power to obey you; we have been married these four months.

Sterl. And he sha'n't stay in my house four hours. What baseness and treachery! As for you, you shall repent this step as long as you live, madam.

Fanny. Indeed, sir, it is impossible to conceive the tortures I have already endured in consequence of my disobedience. My heart has continually upbraided me for it; and though I was too weak to struggle with affection, I feel that I must be miserable for ever without your forgiveness.

Sterl. Lovewell, you shall leave my house directly; and you shall follow him, madam.

Lord Og. And if they do, I will receive them into mine. Look ye, Mr. Sterling, there have been some mistakes, which we had all better forget for our own sakes; and the best way to forget them is to forgive the cause of them; which I do from my soul.—Poor girl! I swore to support her affection with my life and fortune;—'tis a debt of honour, and must be paid—you swore as much too, Mr. Sterling; but your laws in the city will excuse you, I suppose; for you never strike a balance without errors excepted.

Sterl. I am a father, my lord; but for the sake of all other fathers, I think I ought not to forgive her, for fear of encouraging other silly girls like herself to throw themselves away without the consent of their parents.

Lov. I hope there will be no danger of that, sir. Young ladies, with minds like my Fanny's, would startle at the very shadow of vice; and when they know to what uneasiness only an indiscretion has exposed her, her example, instead of encouraging, will rather serve to deter them.

Mrs. Heidel. Indiscretion, quoth-a! a mighty pretty delicat word to express obedience!

Lord Og. For my part, I indulge my own passions too much to tyrannize over those of other people. Poor souls, I pity them. And you must forgive them too. Come, come, melt a little of your flint, Mr. Sterling!

Sterl. Why, why, as to that, my lord—to be sure he is a relation of yours, my lord——what say you, sister Heidelberg?

Mrs. Heidel. The girl's ruin'd, and I forgive her.

Sterl. Well—so do I then.—Nay, no thanks—[*To* Lovewell *and* Fanny, *who seem preparing to speak.*] there's an end of the matter.

Lord Og. But, Lovewell, what makes you dumb all this while?

Lov. Your kindness, my lord——I can scarce believe my own senses—they are all in a tumult of fear, joy, love, expectation, and gratitude; I ever was, and am now more bound in duty to your lordship. For you, Mr. Sterling, if every moment of my life, spent gratefully in your service, will in some measure compensate the want of fortune, you perhaps will not repent your goodness to me. And you, ladies, I flatter myself, will not for the future suspect me of artifice and intrigue—I shall be happy to oblige and serve you.——As for you, Sir John ——

Sir John. No apologies to me, Lovewell, I do not deserve any. All I have to offer in excuse for what has happened, is my total ignorance of your situation. Had you dealt a little more openly with me, you would have saved me, and yourself, and that lady, (who, I hope, will pardon my behaviour) a great deal of uneasiness. Give me leave, however, to assure you, that light and capricious as I may have appeared, now my infatuation is over, I have sensibility enough to be ashamed of the part I have acted, and honour enough to rejoice at your happiness.

Lov. And now, my dearest Fanny, though we are seemingly the happiest of beings, yet all our joys will be dampt, if his lordship's generosity, and Mr. Sterling's forgiveness, should not be succeeded by the indulgence, approbation, and consent of these our best benefactors. [*To the audience.*] [*Exeunt omnes.*]

EPILOGUE.

Written by Mr. GARRICK.

CHARACTERS OF THE EPILOGUE.

Lord Minum, - - - -	Mr. Dodd.
Colonel Trill, - - -	Mr. Vernon.
Sir Patrick Mahony, -	Mr. Moody.
Miss Crotchet, - - -	Mrs.————
Mrs. Quaver, - - -	Mrs. Lee.
First Lady. - - -	Mrs. Bradshaw.
Second Lady, - - -	Miss Mills.
Third Lady, - - -	Mrs. Dorman.

SCENE, an Assembly.

Several Persons at Cards, at different Tables; among the rest, Colonel TRILL, *Lord* MINUM, *Mrs.* QUAVER, *Sir* PA-TRICK MAHONY.

At the Quadrille Table.

Colonel Trill.

LADIES, with leave——

    2d Lady. Pass !

      3d Lady. Pass !

        Mr. Qu. You must do more.

Col. T. Indeed I cann't.

      Mrs. Qu. I play in Hearts.

        Col. T. Encore !

2d Lady. What luck!

         Col. T. To night at Drury-Lane is play'd

A Comedy, and *tout nouvelle*——a Spade!

Is not Miss Crotchet at the play?

               Mrs. Qu. My niece

Has made a party, sir, to damn the piece.

At the Whist Table.

Ld. Min. I hate a playhouse—Trump—It makes me sick,

1st Lady. We're two by Honours, ma'am.

            Ld. Min. And we th' odd trick.

Pray, do you know the author, Colonel Trill?

Col. T. I know no poets, Heaven be prais'd——Spadille——

1st Lady. I'll tell you who, my lord.   [*Whispers Ld. Min.*

         Ld. Min. What, he again!

‘ And dwell such daring souls in little men?’

Be whose it will, they down our throats will cram it.

Col. T. O, no—I have a Club—the best——We'll damn it.

Mrs. Qu. O, bravo, colonel!—Music is my flame.

Ld. Min. And mine, by Jupiter!—We've won the game.

Col. T. What, do you love all music?

           Mrs. Qu. No, not Handel's.

And nasty plays——

        Ld. Min. Are fit for Goths and Vandals.

          [*Rise from the table and pay*

From the Piquette Table.

Sir Pat. Well, faith and troth, that Shakspere was no fool!

Col. T. I'm glad you like him, sir——so ends the Pool.

         [*They pay, and rise from the table*

SONG, by the Colonel.

I hate all their nonsense,

    Their Shakspere's and Johnson's,

Their plays, and their playhouse, and bards:

'Tis singing, not saying ;
    A fig for all playing,
But playing, as we do, at cards;

    I love to see Jonas,
    Am pleas'd too with Comus ;
Each well the spectator rewards.
    So clever, so neat in
    Their tricks and their cheating !
Like them, we would fain deal our cards.

Sir Pat. King Lare is touching !—And how fine to see
    Ould Hamlet's Ghost !—' To be, or not to be.'——
    What are your Op'ras to Othello's roar ?
    Oh, he's an angel of a Blackamoor !
Ld. Min. What, when he choaks his wife !——
                            Col. T. And calls her whore ?
Sir Pat. King Richard calls his horse—And then Macbeth,
    Whene'er he murders—takes away the breath.
    My blood runs cold at every syllable,
    To see the dagger that's invisible.   [*All laugh.*
    Laugh if you please—a pretty play——
                            Ld. Min. Is pretty.
Sir Pat. And when there's wit in't——
                    Col. T. To be sure 'tis witty.
Sir Pat. I love the playhouse now—so light and gay,
    With all those candles—they have ta'en away !
                                    [*All laugh.*
    For all your game, what makes it so much brighter ?
Col. T. Put out the lights, and then——
                    Ld. Min. 'Tis so much lighter.
Sir Pat. Pray, do you mane, sirs, more than you express ?
Col. T. Just as it happens——
        Ld. Min. Either more or less.

Mrs. Qu. An't you asham'd, sir ?   [*To Sir* Pat.

    Sir Pat. Me !—I seldom blush :—

For little Shakspere, faith, I'd take a push.   [play.

Ld. Min. News, news !—Here comes Miss Crotchet from the

     Enter Miss CROTCHET.

Mrs. Qu. Well, Crotchet, what's the news ?

      Miss Cro. We've lost the day.

Col. T. Tell us, dear miss, all you have heard and seen.

Miss Cro. I'm tir'd—a chair—here, take my capuchin.

Ld. Min. And isn't it damn'd, miss ?

     Miss Cro. No, my lord, not quite.

But we shall damn it.

    Col. T. When ?

     Miss Cro. To-morrow night.

There is a party of us, all of fashion,

Resolv'd to exterminate this vulgar passion :

A playhouse ! what a place !—I must forswear it ;

A little mischief only makes one bear it.

Such crowds of city folks !—so rude and pressing !

And their horse laughs, so hideously distressing !

Whene'er we hiss'd, they frown'd, and fell a swearing,

Like their own Guildhall giants—fierce and staring !

Col. T. What said the folks of fashion ; were they cross ?

Ld. Min. The rest have no more judgment than my horse.

Miss Cro. Lord Grimly said, 'twas execrable stuff.

Says one—Why so, my lord ?—My lord took snuff.

In the first act Lord George began to doze,

And criticis'd the author thro' his nose ;

So loud indeed, that as his lordship snor'd,

The pit turn'd round, and all the brutes encor'd.

Some lords, indeed, approv'd the author's jokes.

Ld. Min. We have among us, miss, some foolish **folks.**

Miss Cro. Says poor Lord Simper—Well, now to my mind,
　　　The piece is good ;—but he's both deaf and blind.
Sir Pat. Upon my soul, a very pretty story !
　　　And quality appears in all its glory.
　　　There was some merit in the piece, no doubt :
Miss Cro. O, to be sure !—if one could find it out.
Col. T. But tell us, miss, the subject of the play.
Miss Cro. Why, 'twas a marriage—yes—a marriage—stay——
　　　A lord, an aunt, two sisters, and a merchant——
　　　A baronet, ten lawyers, a fat serjeant,
　　　Are all produc'd—to talk with one another ;
　　　And about something make a mighty pother !
　　　They all go in and out, and to and fro ;
　　　And talk and quarrel—as they come and go——
　　　Then go to bed—and then get up—and then—
　　　Scream, faint, scold, kiss—and go to bed again.——
　　　　　　　　　　　　　　　　[All Laugh.

　　　Such is the play—Your judgment—never sham it :——
Col. T. Oh, damn it !
　　　Mrs. Qu. Damn it!
　　　　　1st Lady. Damn it !
　　　　　　　Miss Cro. Damn it !
　　　　　　　　　Ld. Min. Damn it !
Sir Pat. Well, faith, you speak your minds, and I'll be free—
　　　Good night—this company's **too** good for me. *[Going.*
Col. T. Your judgment, dear Sir Patrick, makes us proud.
　　　　　　　　　　　　　　　　[All laugh.
Sir Pat. Laugh, if you please, but, pray, don't laugh so loud.
　　　　　　　　　　　　　　　　[Exit.

RECITATIVE.

Col. T. 　Now the barbarian's gone, miss, tune your tongue ;
　　　And let us raise our spirits high with song.

RECITATIVE.

Miss Cro. Colonel, *de tout mon cœur*—I've one in *petto*,
　　　Which you shall join, and make it a *duetto*.

RECITATIVE.

Ld. Min. Bella Signora, et amico mio,
　　　I too will join, and then we'll make a *trio*.
Col. T. Come all and join the full-mouth'd chorus ;
　　　And drive all tragedy and comedy before us.

All the Company rise, and advance to the front of the Stage.

AIR.

Col. T. Would you ever go to see a tragedy ?
　　　　　　　　　Miss Cro. Never, never
Col. T. A comedy ?
　　　Ld. Min. Never, never.
　　　　　Live for ever !
　　　　　　　'Tweedle-dum, and tweedle-dee.
Col. T. Ld. Min. and Miss Cro. Live for ever.
　　　　　　　Tweedle-dum, and tweedle-dee

CHORUS.

Would you ever go to see, &c.

THE END.